family handyman

BEST
TIPS
& PROJECTS

family handyman

BEST
TIPS
& PROJECTS

by The Editors of *Family Handyman* magazine

FAMILY HANDYMAN BEST TIPS & PROJECTS 2021
(See page 288 for complete staff listing.)
Editor-in-Chief: Gary Wentz
Project Editor: Mary Flanagan
Contributing Designer: Andrea Sorensen
Contributing Copy Editors: Donna Bierbach, Peggy Parker
Indexing: Lisa Himes

Vice President, Integrated Sales: John Dyckman

Trusted Media Brands, Inc.
President & Chief Executive Officer: Bonnie Kintzer

Warning: All do-it-yourself activities involve a degree of risk. Skills, materials, tools, and site conditions vary widely. Although the editors have made every effort to ensure accuracy, the reader remains responsible for the selection and use of tools, materials, and methods. Always obey local codes and laws, follow manufacturers' operating instructions, and observe safety precautions.

ISBN 978-1-62145-542-4 (dated), 978-1-62145-543-1 (undated)

Address any comments about *Family Handyman Best Tips & Projects 2021* to:
Editor, Best Tips & Projects
2915 Commers Drive, Suite 700
Eagan, MN 55121

To order additional copies of *Family Handyman Best Tips & Projects 2021*, call 1-800-344-2560.

For more Trusted Media Brands products and information, visit our Web site at tmbi.com.
For more about Family Handyman magazine, visit familyhandyman.com.

Printed in the United States of America.
1 3 5 7 9 10 8 6 4 2

SAFETY FIRST–ALWAYS!

Tackling home improvement projects and repairs can be endlessly rewarding. But as most of us know, with the rewards come risks. DIYers use chain saws, climb ladders and tear into walls that can contain big and hazardous surprises.

The good news is, armed with the right knowledge, tools and procedures, homeowners can minimize risk. As you go about your projects and repairs, stay alert for these hazards:

Aluminum wiring

Aluminum wiring, installed in about 7 million homes between 1965 and 1973, requires special techniques and materials to make safe connections. This wiring is dull gray, not the dull orange characteristic of copper. Hire a licensed electrician certified to work with it. For more information go to cpsc.gov and search for "aluminum wiring."

Spontaneous combustion

Rags saturated with oil finishes like Danish oil and linseed oil, and oil-based paints and stains can spontaneously combust if left bunched up. Always dry them outdoors, spread out loosely. When the oil has thoroughly dried, you can safely throw them in the trash.

Vision and hearing protection

Safety glasses or goggles should be worn whenever you're working on DIY projects that involve chemicals, dust and anything that could shatter or chip off and hit your eye. Sounds louder than 80 decibels (dB) are considered potentially dangerous. Sound levels from a lawn mower can be 90 dB, and shop tools and chain saws can be 90 to 100 dB.

Lead paint

If your home was built before 1979, it may contain lead paint, which is a serious health hazard, especially for children six and under. Take precautions when you scrape or remove it. Contact your public health department for detailed safety information or call (800) 424-LEAD (5323) to receive an information pamphlet. Or visit epa.gov/lead.

Buried utilities

A few days before you dig in your yard, have your underground water, gas and electrical lines marked. Just call 811 or go to call811.com.

Smoke and carbon monoxide (CO) alarms

The risk of dying in reported home structure fires is cut in half in homes with working smoke alarms. Test your smoke alarms every month, replace batteries as necessary and replace units that are more than 10 years old. As you make your home more energy-efficient and airtight, existing ducts and chimneys can't always successfully vent combustion gases, including potentially deadly carbon monoxide (CO). Install a UL-listed CO detector, and test your CO and smoke alarms at the same time.

Five-gallon buckets and window covering cords

Anywhere from 10 to 40 children a year drown in 5-gallon buckets, according to the U.S. Consumer Products Safety Commission. Always store them upside down and store ones containing liquid with the covers securely snapped.

According to Parents for Window Blind Safety, hundreds of children in the United States are injured every year after becoming entangled in looped window treatment cords. For more information, visit pfwbs.org or cpsc.gov.

Working up high

If you have to get up on your roof to do a repair or installation, always install roof brackets and wear a roof harness.

Asbestos

Texture sprayed on ceilings before 1978, adhesives and tiles for vinyl and asphalt floors before 1980, and vermiculite insulation (with gray granules) all may contain asbestos. Other building materials, made between 1940 and 1980, could also contain asbestos. If you suspect that materials you're removing or working around contain asbestos, contact your health department or visit epa.gov/asbestos for information.

For additional information about home safety, visit homesafetycouncil.org. This site offers helpful information about dozens of home safety issues.

Contents

5. EXTERIOR REPAIRS & IMPROVEMENTS

6. OUTDOOR STRUCTURES, LANDSCAPING & GARDENING

7. USING DIY TOOLS & MATERIALS

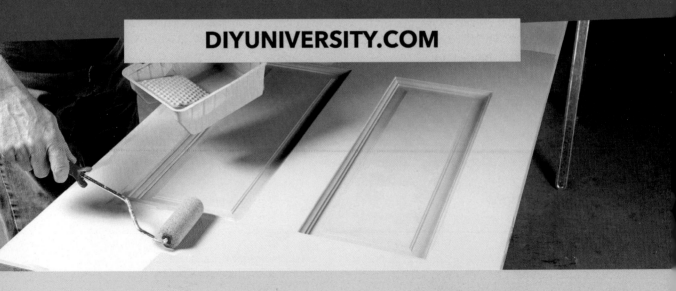

1 Interior Projects, Repairs & Remodeling

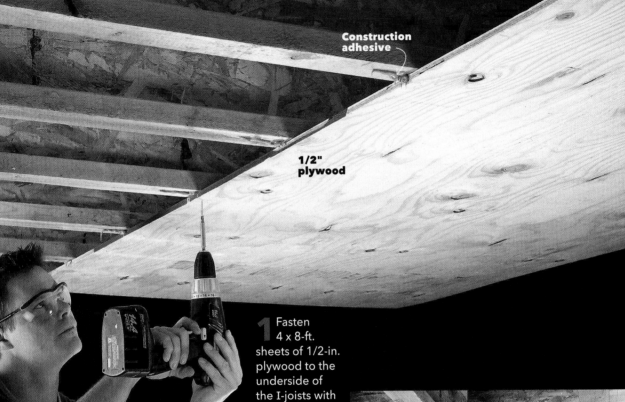

Construction adhesive

1/2" plywood

1 Fasten 4 x 8-ft. sheets of 1/2-in. plywood to the underside of the I-joists with 1-1/2-in. screws.

I-joist

Bridging

2 Toenail a line of I-joist blocks between the joists across the full length of the room.

Two Solutions for a Bouncy Floor

If your floor has engineered I-joists and feels a bit "springy" when you walk on it, the fix is relatively easy if you have access to the underside of the joists. You can install either bridging or a layer of plywood. Try bridging first. Just nail short I-joist sections between your existing joists (**Photo 2**). To prevent squeaks, apply construction adhesive to the top side of the bridging where it contacts your floor. If the joist span is shorter than 14 ft.,

install one row of bridging at the midpoint. If the span is longer than 14 ft., install two rows of bridging, dividing the span into thirds.

If the floor is still bouncy, glue and screw 1/2-in. plywood to the bottom of the joists (**Photo 1**). Start the first row at a corner, then stagger subsequent rows so the seams

don't fall on the same joists. The drawback to this method is that you have to leave ceiling access to plumbing and gas valves, electrical boxes and other fixtures. Of course, the surest method is to install a beam and posts near the mid-span, but they'll be obstacles in the room below.

Add Soft-Close to Cabinets

You don't have to buy new cabinets to get soft, quiet-closing doors and drawers. Soft-close doors and drawers not only keep the kitchen quiet but also help reduce wear and tear on your cabinetry.

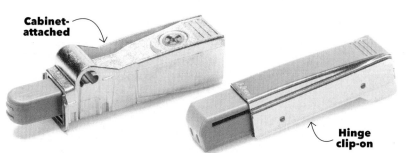

Cabinet-attached

Hinge clip-on

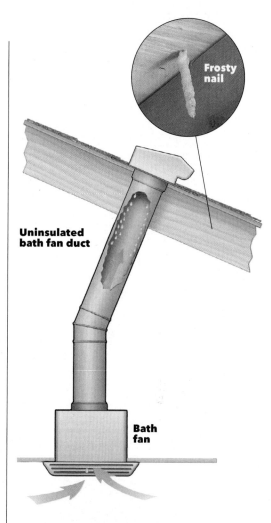

Frosty nail

Uninsulated bath fan duct

Bath fan

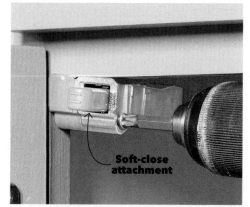

Soft-close attachment

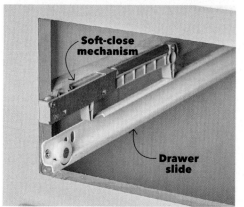

Soft-close mechanism

Drawer slide

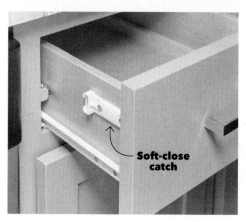

Soft-close catch

FOR THE DOORS

One thing you never need to hear again is a kitchen cabinet door slamming shut. Luckily, soft-close attachments are an easy add-on for doors with any type of hinge. Many hinge manufacturers offer soft-close hinges, but clip-on varieties are also available for retrofitting Euro-style hinges. There are many options for traditional face frame cabinetry with barrel hinges too. You'll also find a wide variety of soft-close adapters for doors. They're typically less than $5 each from specialty hardware stores or online.

FOR THE DRAWERS

Drawers can also be updated with soft-close mechanisms. Often the best solution is to swap out the existing drawer slides with soft-close slides. However, there are a few situations that allow for aftermarket soft-close add-ons. The Soft-Close Device from Rockler, designed for epoxy-coated "roller" slides, costs about $6 each.

PHANTOM ROOF LEAKS

As a roofing contractor for 35 years in the Denver area, I often got calls about leaky roofs after a big snowfall and low temperatures. In fact, all of those "leaks" were due to condensation.

The problem starts with warm, moist air that migrates into a cold, poorly vented attic. As trapped water vapor condenses, it freezes, most visibly on metal surfaces. When this ice eventually melts, the water finds a way to "leak" into the house. The problem is more common in a low-humidity area like Denver, where whole-house humidifiers introduce large amounts of moisture into the home.

Something similar happens around bath fans. Here the likely culprit is an uninsulated metal exhaust duct near a cold roof. As moist air passes through the duct, the moisture condenses and freezes. When warmer weather melts the ice, "leaks" appear, usually as a ceiling stain near the fan.

GUY SHINGLETON

Reinforce a sagging drawer bottom

You don't have to replace a sagging drawer bottom. A typical drawer has a cavity beneath it that's just deep enough to allow you to strengthen the bottom with a piece of plywood. First make sure the drawer box is square by using a large framing square or taking diagonal corner-to-corner measurements (equal diagonal measurements means the box is square). If the box isn't square, square it up, clamp it and drive brad nails through the bottom (**Photo 1**). Two brads placed near the middle of each side usually provide enough strength to hold the box square.

The back of the drawer shown here was bulging, so we used the clamps to draw it in while we drove in the brads. Stiffen the old drawer bottom with any 1/4-in. plywood. A full 4 x 8-ft. sheet costs about $20. Many home centers also sell half or quarter sheets. Measure between the drawer sides, front and back, and cut the plywood 1/4 in. smaller than the opening (1/8 in. less on each side).

Glue the plywood panel to the underside of the drawer bottom and place weights, such as a stack of books, on it until the glue sets (**Photo 2**). If the underside is unfinished, use wood glue. If it has a finish, you can sand it or use construction adhesive. Wood glue forms a strong bond in about 15 minutes. If you use construction adhesive, leave the weights in place overnight.

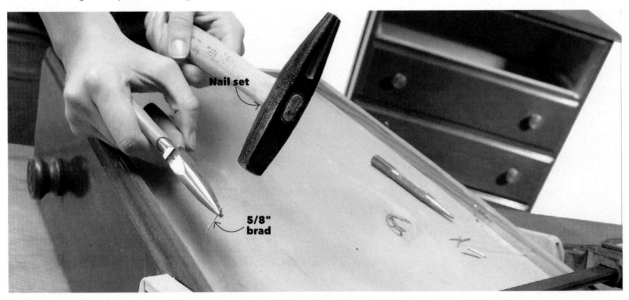

Nail set

5/8"
brad

1 Square the drawer box and drive 5/8-in. brad nails at an angle through the drawer bottom and into the drawer sides.

1/4"
plywood

2 Glue a plywood panel to the underside of the drawer bottom and place weights on it until the glue sets.

Can I ignore a foundation crack?

If you notice a crack, see if it changes over time. If there's little or no change over a year, you're probably safe to ignore it. If there's significant change over a year (or less), consult with a foundation repair specialist. If the crack is letting in groundwater, take care of drainage problems on the exterior, then patch the crack. It may be helpful to patch any crack so you can more easily track any changes.

MEET THE EXPERT
Reuben Saltzman has been a home inspector since 1997 and is the president of Structure Tech, a home inspection company.

Fan-safe junction boxes

Avoid a ceiling fan disaster

Years ago, a spinning ceiling fan crashed to the floor, missing my 2-year-old daughter by inches. It could have been catastrophic, but fortunately it was just a stern reminder to take ceiling fan installation seriously. It's a common mistake to think that any round junction box is fine for a ceiling fan. That's not the case, however. Boxes intended for light fixtures aren't meant to support the weight and vibration of a ceiling fan, and a falling ceiling fan is no joke.

So, when you're installing a ceiling fan, know how much it weighs and install a junction box rated for a ceiling fan of that weight. These boxes are marked by the manufacturer as approved for fans and typically support a fan weighing up to 70 lbs. Several varieties are available for both new construction and retrofits. They cost $3 to $15 at home centers.

BRAD HOLDEN, SENIOR EDITOR

MORE THAN A
HEADBOARD

Designer style—
plus lighting, charging
and a secret space

BY JASON INGOLFSLAND

At the end of the day, your nightstand can become a default charging station. Unfortunately, a cluttered bedside table creates a poor sleep environment, and your devices can disturb a prime REM cycle. It's not a great setup.

This smart headboard is designed to get the clutter off your nightstand and upgrade your bedroom lighting at the same time. It includes a USB charging station installed on a recessed shelf and a smart light strip to create a unique ambiance.

On top of that, it has a secret shelf to hide valuables and nice, cushy upholstery to recline against to read or watch a show. Best of all, while headboards like this might run about $1,000, you can build ours in a day for about $400. Here's how.

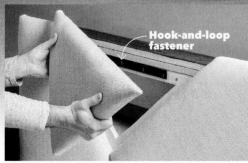

Hook-and-loop fastener

LED strip light

USB

SECRET COMPARTMENT You can store a few of your valuables in this hidden space.

POWER UP! Light up the room and power your devices with an LED strip light and a USB outlet.

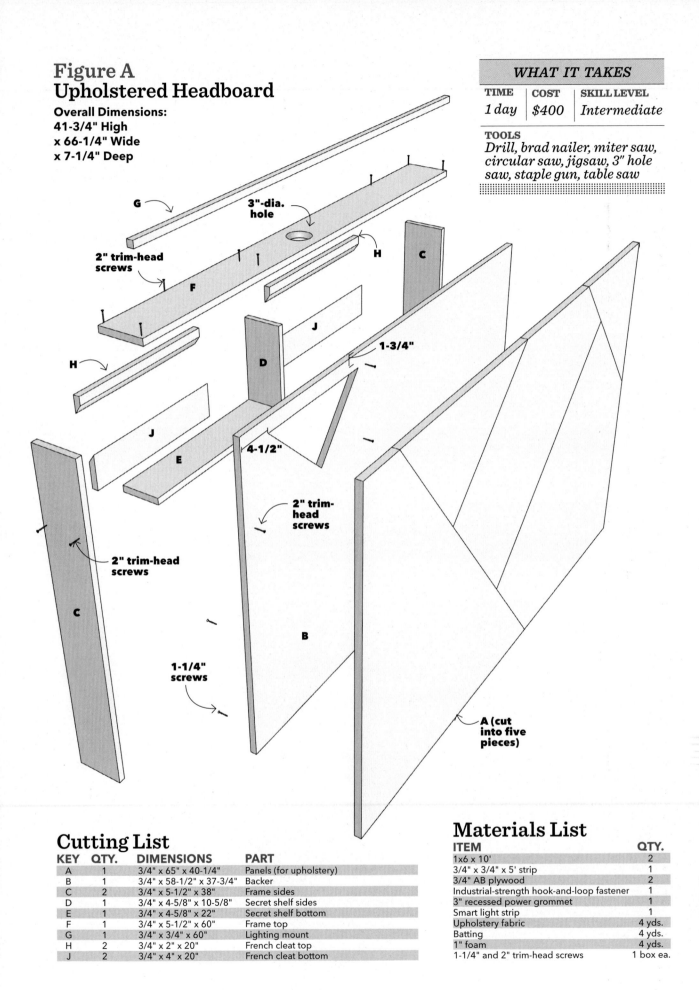

Figure A
Upholstered Headboard

Overall Dimensions:
41-3/4" High
x 66-1/4" Wide
x 7-1/4" Deep

G

3"-dia. hole

2" trim-head screws

F

H

C

H

D

J

1-3/4"

J

E

4-1/2"

2" trim-head screws

2" trim-head screws

C

B

1-1/4" screws

A (cut into five pieces)

WHAT IT TAKES

TIME	COST	SKILL LEVEL
1 day	*$400*	*Intermediate*

TOOLS
Drill, brad nailer, miter saw, circular saw, jigsaw, 3" hole saw, staple gun, table saw

Cutting List

KEY	QTY.	DIMENSIONS	PART
A	1	3/4" x 65" x 40-1/4"	Panels (for upholstery)
B	1	3/4" x 58-1/2" x 37-3/4"	Backer
C	2	3/4" x 5-1/2" x 38"	Frame sides
D	1	3/4" x 4-5/8" x 10-5/8"	Secret shelf sides
E	1	3/4" x 4-5/8" x 22"	Secret shelf bottom
F	1	3/4" x 5-1/2" x 60"	Frame top
G	1	3/4" x 3/4" x 60"	Lighting mount
H	2	3/4" x 2" x 20"	French cleat top
J	2	3/4" x 4" x 20"	French cleat bottom

Materials List

ITEM	QTY.
1x6 x 10'	2
3/4" x 3/4" x 5' strip	1
3/4" AB plywood	2
Industrial-strength hook-and-loop fastener	1
3" recessed power grommet	1
Smart light strip	1
Upholstery fabric	4 yds.
Batting	4 yds.
1" foam	4 yds.
1-1/4" and 2" trim-head screws	1 box ea.

BED FRAME

We built a simple, modern queen-size floating bed frame to match our headboard, but this headboard goes with virtually any bed frame. FYI, if you want to build ours, the design and classes are offered at **mydiyuniversity.com**.

1 ASSEMBLE THE FRAME
Screw the frame top to one of the sides. Then glue and nail them to the backer before adding the other side. Nail the lighting mount to the top of the frame.

2 INSTALL THE SECRET SHELF
Join the side and bottom of the shelf, then place it against the frame and around the triangle cutout (see **Figure B**). Trace the location of the shelf, then remove the shelf and drill pilot holes. Put the shelf back into place and fasten it with nails. Flip the assembly over and screw through the pilot holes to secure the shelf.

3 CUT THE PANELS
Cut plywood to 40-1/4 x 65 in. and mark the panels as shown in **Figure C**. Then lay the plywood on a sheet of foam insulation and cut the panels. Be as accurate as you can, but don't sweat it if your cuts are off a bit.

Frame

Backer

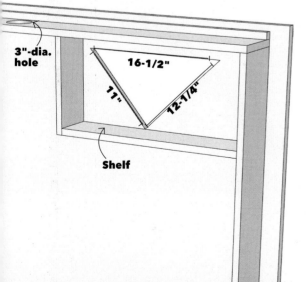

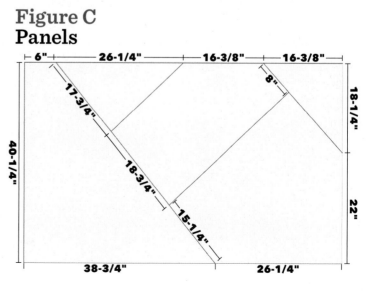

Figure B
Secret Shelf

3"-dia. hole

16-1/2"

11"

12-1/4"

Shelf

Figure C
Panels

6" 26-1/4" 16-3/8" 16-3/8"

8"

17-3/4"

18-1/4"

40-1/4"

18-3/4"

15-1/4"

22"

38-3/4" 26-1/4"

Foam

Batting

4 CUT THE FOAM, BATTING AND FABRIC

Cut the foam using the panels as templates. Adhere the foam to the panels with spray adhesive. Cut the fabric and batting roughly 3 in. larger than the panels. You'll trim off the excess once the staples are in place.

5 UPHOLSTER THE PANELS

Once all the materials are cut to size, pull the fabric and batting tight over the panel, starting at the middle of each side, and secure them with two staples. Then work toward the corners. Drive staples close to each other and frequently flip the panel over to check your results. If you're not satisfied, don't be afraid to pull out staples and start again. When you reach the corners, fold the fabric neatly over them and staple it in place. For more upholstery tips, search for "reupholster a chair" at **familyhandyman.com**.

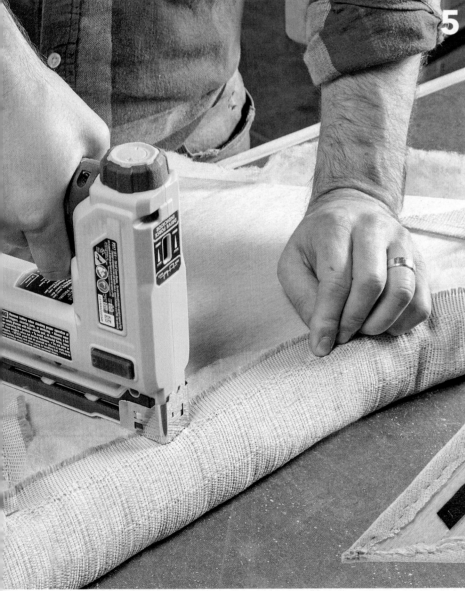

4

5

FASTEN THE HATCH

To attach the hidden shelf hatch, I used an industrial-strength hook-and-loop fastener. The adhesive doesn't stick well to wood, so add staples.

Hook-and-loop fastener

Hatch →

6

6 ATTACH THE UPHOLSTERED PANELS

Set the frame on sawhorses and position the upholstered panels. The top panels should protrude about 1-1/4 in. above the lighting mount. Clamp the panels in place and make sure they overhang the sides of the frame assembly equally. Then attach each panel (except the hatch) from below with 1-1/4-in. screws.

7 APPLY THE LED STRIP

Cut an LED light strip to length, pull the paper backing off the adhesive, and apply the light strip to the lighting mount. I used a Philips Hue smart light strip, but other options are available at home centers and online.

8 INSERT THE CHARGING STATION

Cut a 3-in.-diameter hole in the frame top, then insert the USB power grommet. Power grommets are available online for $20 to $35.

9 HANG THE HEADBOARD

Rip French cleats on a table saw tilted to 45 degrees. I screwed the cleats to studs 48 in. from the floor. Recruit a helper when you hang the headboard—it's heavy!

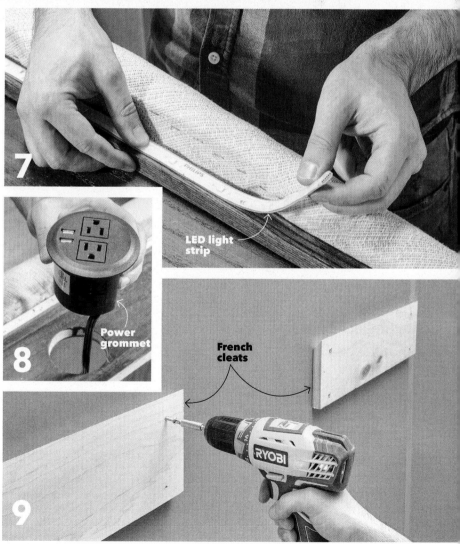

LED light strip

Power grommet

French cleats

7 TIPS FOR A *better* BATHROOM

Save time, money *and* energy with these simple tips

BY MIKE BERNER

Shower door treatment

If you're diligent about cleaning your glass shower door, you probably don't have problems with soap scum, mildew or mineral stains from hard water. But if you'd like to skip all that cleaning, apply Aquapel Glass Treatment on your door so it can shed the water completely and prevent the buildup. One treatment lasts for months, meaning no more grime for the same amount of time. A package of three treatments costs $15 online.

Easy aerator cleaning

Using a sink aerator is a really great way to reduce the amount of water going straight down the drain, but aerators can get clogged and disrupt the flow from a faucet. To clear the clog easily, try tossing the aerator into a small jar filled with vinegar. Let it soak for several hours, then rinse with water while scrubbing with a small brush. If that doesn't do the trick, you may have to take it apart. Watch out: Putting one piece in the wrong way will interfere with the flow.

Aerator

Vinegar

Moisture & motion-detecting vent fan

I recently installed a Panasonic WhisperChoice Auto vent fan in my bathroom—what an upgrade that was! My previous bathroom vent fan was only three years old, but it was loud. On top of that, I would forget to turn it on or off, letting the humidity build up or the fan run longer than it needed to.

With the Panasonic, I haven't had to flip a switch. It's equipped with a motion detector and a humidity sensor. Either one will turn the fan on when triggered. The fan is so quiet that I had to look to see if it was actually spinning. The Pick-A-Flow feature lets you choose an airflow of either 80 or 110 cubic feet per minute (cfm). Find this fan at Home Depot or online for $185.

Water-saving toilet upgrade

When your toilet flapper fails, water leaks into the bowl and then triggers the fill valve to refill the tank. It's annoying and it wastes water. Instead of just putting up with the rhythmic sound of running water, fix it with Fluidmaster's Toilet Fill Valve and Flapper Repair Kit ($14). It's a great kit for repairing common problems that can be solved with a new flapper, and while you're at it, upgrading to a quicker, quieter fill valve.

If you want to take it one step further, Fluidmaster also sells an easy retrofit flush valve kit called the DuoFlush System Toilet Converter ($25). It will turn your toilet into a dual flusher, letting you flush only half a tank, lowering your water bill and reducing water waste. You can find both products at home centers and online.

HALF / FULL

Fill valve

DuoFlush flush valve

Wash your shower curtain

Toss your grimy shower curtain or liner in the washing machine instead of the garbage and save a trip to the store and a few bucks. Add about a quarter cup of vinegar to a warm-water wash cycle and your shower curtain will come out fresh and clean. The vinegar also helps to kill mold and mildew.

Super scrubber

Whenever I do a fast clean of my bathroom, I reach for a Magic Eraser sponge. With just this one sponge, I can quickly make my bathroom shine without spraying a single cleaning product. I get it wet and start wiping away the soap scum and hard water marks. The bonus is that Magic Erasers are pretty cheap. You can find them at grocery stores, drugstores and online for $1.50 or less.

VERN JOHNSON
ASSOCIATE CREATIVE DIRECTOR

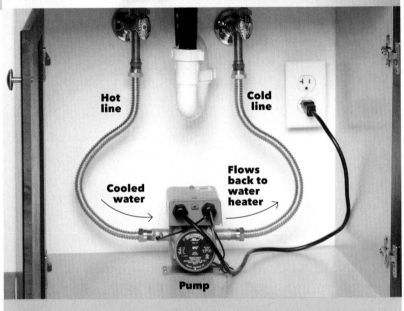

Hot line

Cold line

Cooled water

Flows back to water heater

Pump

Cost-cutting hot water pump

How long do you wait for the water in your shower to warm up? Three minutes? Seven minutes? To save time and stop wasting all that cool water down the drain, get instant hot water with a hot water recirculating pump.

The TacoGenie is a recirculating pump that is installed under a sink and ensures there is hot water at every faucet in your house, all the time. It gets installed between the hot- and cold-water supplies at the farthest faucet in your house, with no need to cut pipes or replumb. A built-in sensor detects when hot water has reached the pump and automatically shuts it off. With an optional motion detector or wireless button, you can choose how often you want the pump to operate. You can find the TacoGenie at plumbing supply stores and online. Shown is the model 006-CT-USK, which costs about $460.

HEATED FLOOR
THE EASY WAY

Heat film has big advantages over other options

BY JAY CORK

Who wouldn't want to step onto a toasty warm kitchen floor when they fetch their morning coffee? I recently found out how easy in-floor heat can be. With a film-type heating system, you don't have to deal with thin-set or glue. You basically just unroll the mats, run the wiring and install your floor. I was able to install it under my floating floor in a weekend. Here's what you need to know.

MEET THE EXPERT
Jay Cork has been a carpenter, cabinetmaker and craftsman for more than 20 years.

PHOTO: REDPIXEL.PL/SHUTTERSTOCK

Junction box for thermostat and power supply

Junction box for lead wires

Lead wires

Temperature sensors

Flooring

Heating elements

Underlayment

Subfloor

Floor heat simplified

To install a film-type system, you first lay down foam underlayment, securing it with duct tape. Then you tape down the plastic film, which contains the electric heating elements. The power supply to the film is controlled by a thermostat connected to temp sensors in the floor. When the wiring is done, you're ready to install the flooring.

Selecting a system

■ Film is a super-easy DIY option; but it's not cheap. The total cost for most systems is about $8 to $10 per square foot. Mine cost about $9 per square foot.

■ I chose a QuietWarmth system, but several brands of film-type systems are available. To find more, search online for "in-floor heat film."

■ Systems like this are intended to keep your feet comfy. They'll add a little heat to the room, but they're no substitute for the HVAC system in your home. Just as the seat warmer in your car won't heat the whole cabin, this system won't heat an entire room.

■ Most film-type heating elements can be cut to length to perfectly suit the dimensions of the room. Others come in various lengths. If they don't match your room perfectly, you'll have unheated areas along the edges of the floors, but that's usually not a serious problem.

■ To learn more about your floor-heating options, search for "floor heat" at familyhandyman.com.

COST OF OPERATION
The typical electricity cost is about 30 cents a day. QuietWarmth provides a handy energy cost calculator at mpglobalproducts.com.

What floor is it good for?

Most film-type systems are suitable for flooring that's not nailed or glued to the subfloor. That includes carpet and wood, vinyl and laminate floating floors. You can even install the system on top of a concrete slab. But be sure to check the manufacturer's fine print for restrictions. The system I used, for example, isn't recommended for bathrooms.

Powering the system

Wiring the system isn't complicated, but getting power from your main panel to the room might be. For help with that, go to familyhandyman.com and search for "fishing wire."

The system I used requires a dedicated 20-amp circuit. Since the actual dimension for the heated area is 120 sq. ft., it'll work with a 120-volt circuit. Floors larger than 200 sq. ft. will need 240-volt service.

A dedicated thermostat is required

This system must be controlled by its own thermostat. Connecting it to your whole-house thermostat won't work and may damage the heating elements as well as the floor. There are many thermostat choices for this purpose, but I wanted one I could control with an app on my phone. The programmable Wi-Fi thermostat from QuietWarmth was a great choice. It doesn't talk to Alexa or Google Assistant yet, but it will in the near future.

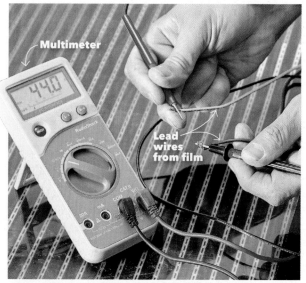

You'll need a multimeter

It would be a disaster to finish installing brand new heating elements, only to find that one was damaged in the process. That's why it's very important to confirm the impedance reading for each roll of film with a multimeter set to "Ohms" and to double-check that reading every step of the way. QuietWarmth provided a handy spec sheet that helps me keep track of these readings. A good multimeter costs about $30 at a hardware store or home center.

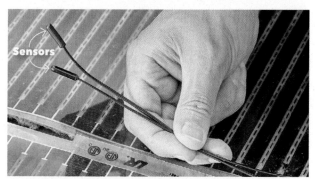

Install a backup sensor

If you're installing one temperature sensor, you might as well take the time to install a second one as a backup. It'll cost an extra $25, but it's a small price to pay for peace of mind. If the primary sensor fails, it's so much easier to swap two wires in the thermostat than to pull up your flooring to replace the bad sensor! Don't count on an extra sensor being included; you must specify that you want an extra one when you place your order.

Best Pro Tips

Expert advice from the job site. By Gary Wentz

Smooth walls with beginner skills

9 LESSONS FROM VETERAN DRYWALL TAPERS

Non-tapered (cut) edge against wall

Joint over stud

Butt edge, no taper

Tapered edge

Added 2x2

STAND 'EM UP!
Hang drywall vertically on walls to eliminate butt joints. Nail 2x2s to studs that don't align with the edges of the sheets.

❶ Eliminate as many hard-to-hide butt joints as you can

To hide "butt joints" (where two non-tapered ends of drywall meet), you have to build up a hump of joint compound that's very thin and wide. This is time consuming and difficult to do well. So if you're a novice drywall finisher, you'd be smart to avoid butt joints.

The best way to avoid butt joints is to use sheets of drywall that are long enough to run the entire length of walls and ceilings. As a result, you'll have only tapered joints to finish. Drywall sheets are commonly available in 8- and 12-ft. lengths, and specialty drywall suppliers carry longer sheets (up to 20 ft.!).

If your ceiling is longer than your sheets, you can't avoid butt joints. But you can still avoid butt joints on a long wall. Simply hang the sheets vertically rather than horizontally. That way, you'll have several tapered joints to cover, but no butt joints. Hanging drywall vertically is slower than hanging it horizontally because you have to make sure the tapered edges fall at the centers of studs. Cut the first sheet to width so the tapered edge lands on the center of a stud. After that, the edges of each sheet should fall perfectly on studs. If you run into misplaced studs, nail 2x2s to them. If you have 9-ft. ceilings, call a drywall supplier to find 10-ft. sheets.

❷ Use mesh tape, not paper

Paper tape is the strongest choice for joints. But in less-skilled hands, it can ripple, slip or trap air bubbles. If you push too hard as you embed it, you'll squeeze out all the joint compound behind it and the tape will peel off later.

Adhesive-backed mesh tape eliminates those glitches. Just stick it in place and it stays put. And since it doesn't require an underlying layer of compound, mesh allows for a thinner buildup over butt joints and repairs. You can use it anywhere except on inside corners.

Since mesh tape isn't as strong as paper, some pros insist on using setting-type joint compound because it's stronger than premixed types. Whichever compound you choose, apply mesh tape no more than a few hours before covering it. Left uncovered, it will eventually fall off.

❸ Fill joints faster with setting-type compound

Mixing setting compound is a messy nuisance, but it's sometimes worth it. Setting compound has three advantages over premixed types: It's stronger, it hardens faster and it shrinks much less. Quick hardening and low shrinkage make setting compound perfect for deep filling. A thick layer of premixed compound takes days to dry and it shrinks. You'll need several coats to fill the depression, and the more layers you add, the harder it is to get smooth results.

For small repair jobs, you can mix setting compound with a paint paddle. For larger jobs, use a corded drill with a mixer attachment. The key to a smooth, chunk-free mix is to let it stand for about five minutes after the initial mixing. That lets the chunks absorb water before final mixing.

The hardening time for setting compounds ranges from 5 to 210 minutes. The 45- or 90-minute versions are best for most jobs. Use a "lightweight" setting compound; other versions become so hard that sanding away mistakes is nearly impossible. Even lightweight versions are harder to sand than premixed compound, so it's best to use setting compound for the first coat and premixed for later coats. Clean up tools before the setting compound hardens.

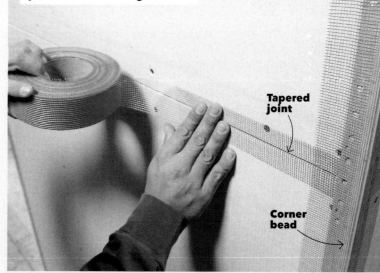

FIRST TAPE, THEN MUD
Paper tape and joint compound are applied together. Mesh lets you focus on one thing at a time.

Tapered joint

Corner bead

Setting compound

Corner bead

Ridge

MAKE INSIDE CORNERS EASY
Smooth both sides of inside corners at once with an inside corner knife. Scrape off the ridges with a taping knife.

❹ Coat inside corners faster and smoother with a corner knife

It takes a steady hand to embed tape in inside corners with a standard drywall knife. One little slip of the knife and you'll gouge one side while you're smoothing the other. An inside corner knife ($10) not only eliminates that problem but does the job faster. Outside corner knives are also available, but we don't recommend them, since corner bead makes smoothing outside corners almost foolproof.

Apply compound and place the tape as usual. Load some mud onto the corner knife to lubricate the knife and then spread a thin coat of compound over the paper. Start at the top of the corner and drag the knife down to about 16 in. from the floor. Then start at the floor and drag upward. Ease off when you reach the area that's already smooth. You may have to repeat this process two or three times to fully embed the tape and create a smooth, straight corner. A corner knife doesn't ensure straight corners, so reinforced corner tape is a good idea (see p. 29). Use a corner knife for the first coat only; after that, coat one side at a time, allowing the first side to harden before you coat the other.

WET PAPER WORKS BETTER
Tear paper tape to length and wet it. Pull the tape between your fingers to squeegee off the excess water.

Paper tape

❺ Dunk paper tape to avoid bubbles and bulges

Paper tape can ripple, slip, bulge and bubble. But if you choose to use it, minimize these problems by dropping it into a bucket of water. Wet paper tape is more pliable, so fewer air bubbles get trapped behind it. Water also makes the paper slick; your knife slides over the tape without creating ripples or creases. Wetting doesn't eliminate the squeeze-out problem, so you still have to be careful to leave a thin layer of mud between the tape and the drywall. Don't let the tape soak—that will soften the paper and make it more susceptible to scuffs and tears.

Metal strip

❻ Keep corners straight with reinforced tape

Inside corners are tough to keep neat and straight. Unless you have a very steady hand, your knife can wander as you embed the tape. And if you create a wavy corner with the first coat of mud, straightening the corner with subsequent coats is almost impossible. The solution is to use tape that's backed with metal or plastic strips ($12 for 100 ft. at home centers). This tape is especially helpful on odd-angled corners, which are very hard to keep straight. It's still possible to create a wavy corner if you push too hard, so apply light, even pressure as you smooth the joint compound. The strips reduce ripples and bubbles too, so there's no need to wet the tape. Don't overlap the tape where inside corners meet the ceiling. Instead, cut the tape short to avoid a triple-thick buildup of tape.

❼ To lessen sanding, flatten bumps between coats

Everyone hates the dust cloud raised by sanding drywall. And the best way to minimize sanding later is to knock down high spots between coats. Left alone, high spots will grow higher and wider (and harder to fix) with each coat. Don't worry about low spots; subsequent coats will fill them.

If you used setting-type compound, inspect the joints before the compound has hardened completely. Run a 12-in.-wide knife over every joint. The blade will scrape off small ridges and nubs. More important, it will act as a straightedge, revealing larger bumps and bulges. When the compound is about the consistency of a bar of soap, you can easily shave down bulges without gouging. You can sand and scrape it after it's completely hard, but that's more work.

With standard joint compound, however, let each coat dry completely before inspecting, scraping and sanding. If you don't, the surface may be firm while the underlying material remains soft and easy to gouge.

SCRAPE BETWEEN COATS
Shave off high spots in setting-type compound before they harden. Allow standard joint compound to dry completely before you scrape and sand.

Partially hardened setting compound

Knockdown knife

Rubber blade

⑧ Create a smooth surface with a knockdown knife

Feathering out a butt joint or skim-coating a whole wall is difficult. Your knife leaves ridges on the broad surface—and touching them up often creates even more ridges. The solution is a "knockdown" knife. With its soft rubber blade, this squeegee-like tool floats over the surface, flattening ridges without creating new ones.

A knockdown knife won't scrape down big bulges or fill wide depressions, so make the surface as flat as you can with a 12- or 14-in. metal knife first. Then drag the knockdown knife gently over the surface in one continuous pass. Apply light, even pressure and don't stop or hesitate. On a butt joint, you'll have to make two or three passes to smooth the whole surface. You can make more passes, but stop before the compound starts to harden. The blade is soft, but it can still make a mess of partially hardened compound.

Knockdown knives are available in 18- and 22-in. widths at drywall suppliers and some home centers and hardware stores. A 22-in. is best for butt joints.

⑨ Keep crumbs out of your mud to prevent scars

You can't create a smooth surface using joint compound that has crumbs of hardened compound in it. One tiny chunk clinging to your knife will leave a scar across the whole joint.

Cleanliness is the key to keeping your mud free of chunks. Scrape down the inside of the bucket every time you scoop out mud. Then wipe the sides clean with a wet rag. At the end of the day, cover the compound with a thin layer of water. The water will remain on top of the compound, so you can pour it off before you use the remaining mud. Never dump leftover compound from your mud pan back into the bucket; just throw it away.

To keep the pan and tools clean between uses, scour them with an abrasive sponge or immerse them in water. Setting-type compound will continue to harden even under water, so wash tools as soon as you're done. Never send large amounts of setting compound down the drain—it can plug pipes.

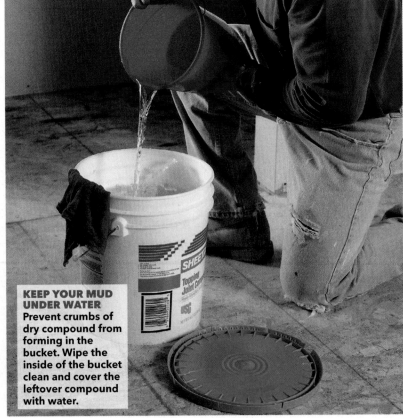

SET TILE
WITHOUT TROUBLE

BY JAY CORK

Expert tools and techniques for rock-solid results

Installing tile in a kitchen or bathroom is hard work. And for lasting results, the installation needs to be done right. I sat down with Josh Risberg, our resident tile expert, to talk about his favorite tools and his approach to setting tile. Josh, our lead carpenter, has more than 16 years of tiling experience. This collection of tips will help you avoid the most common mistakes.

MEET THE EXPERT
Aside from being a master carpenter, Josh Risberg is a skilled tile setter, certified with the Ceramic Tile Education Foundation.

Back-butter with the flat side of the trowel

BACK-BUTTER FOR A BETTER BOND
Because larger tiles (12 x 12 in. or bigger) have more surface area, it's critical that you "back-butter" the tile to ensure a strong bond. It takes only a few extra seconds for each tile. Before setting it, trowel a thin layer of thin-set on the back of the tile by placing the flat edge of the loaded trowel near the center and spreading a thin layer out to the edge. Rotate the tile a quarter turn and repeat until the back is evenly covered. Then when you set the tile, it will create a strong connection with the thin-set you've troweled onto the floor or wall.

Josh's tool kit

Josh has spent years trying out tile tools. Here are a few of his favorites.

LASER-WELDED CORING BIT

Josh uses laser-welded diamond coring bits ($70 and up) to drill holes in tile. A laser-welded diamond coating is more durable than a coating made from braze-welded diamonds and can cut wet or dry.

KNEEPADS

These kneepads from SuperiorBilt allow Josh to work all day on his knees without fatigue. You can find a pair for about $50 online.

SILICONE FLOATS

Josh prefers soft silicone grout floats to hard ones. They conform to rough surfaces without having to be pressed down as much. You can get them for about $10 at a home center.

LEVELING WEDGES AND SHIMS

These wedges and shims help you set tiles evenly and avoid uneven tile edges, called "lippage." They're available at most home centers and all tile stores.

TROWELS WITH ROUNDED NOTCHES

Rounded ridges in thin-set collapse more uniformly for better coverage and fewer air pockets. That makes for a better bond.

CHINA PENCIL

Josh uses china pencils to mark tile cuts. The marks are easy to see, and they won't rinse off if you're using a wet saw.

GRINDING STONE
A grinding stone is used to ease the edge of cut tile. Josh really likes to use one when he's working with natural stone. It helps him dress the cut edge to make it appear more like a natural break.

VARIABLE-SPEED GRINDER
Josh only uses a grinder that has variable speed when he works with tile. Slowing down allows him to work safely, handle details and avoid overheating his diamond blades. Variable-speed grinders cost about $150.

FLUSH-CUTTING DIAMOND BLADE
Most blades for angle grinders don't cut flush. These do. Josh uses these when he has to cut close to a tub or cut under a tile that needs to come up in one piece. They're available for about $25 each online.

MARGIN TROWEL
Most trowels are triangular, but a rectangular shape is better for mixing, scraping and scooping from a bucket. Josh prefers a long margin trowel, which costs about $10.

SUCTION CUPS
Suction cups (about $7 at home centers) help you move large tile around or pull it back up after laying it. Be careful with textured tiles; the uneven surface may not hold suction well.

DOUBLE BOX MIXING PADDLE
This style mixing paddle minimizes air buildup in the thin-set, and costs about $16 at home centers.

TILE NIPPERS
Nippers can make the small detail cuts that a tile cutter just can't. They're available in the tile section of your home center for about $15.

SCRUBBER SPONGES
Start grout cleanup with the plain side of the sponge. When the joints are nicely shaped, switch to the scrubber side. The scrubber side can be used to clean tools, too.

Josh's tips for a flawless tile job

Remember to add spacers during layout

PLAN YOUR LAYOUT

The last thing you want when you're tiling is to reach the end of the course and have a sliver of a space to fill. To avoid this, measure and mock up a row of tile to determine your layout. Doing this bit of layout planning will make setting the tile the easy part. Remember to add spacers between the tiles if you'll be using them to create grout lines. Use this mock-up to determine whether you should shift the layout to get a wider tile in the corner or along a wall.

Ledger board

START OUT LEVEL ON A WALL

Laying your first course of tile on baseboard or a tub surround will lead to trouble. That first course of tile will likely be unlevel, which will force you to adjust the following courses, and as the tiles get stacked higher, your grout lines will get farther off. Use a ledger instead. Screw a straight board to the level line and stack your tile on the board. When you've completed tiling above the board and the tiles are held firmly, remove it and cut the first row of tile to fit.

Aim for the consistency of peanut butter

LET THE THIN-SET SLAKE

After the thin-set is initially mixed, it's important to let it sit long enough to absorb all the water. This is called slaking. Remix the thin-set after letting it slake for about 10 minutes, adding a little water if needed until it's the consistency of peanut butter. Play the same waiting game when you're mixing the grout later.

SNAP CUTTERS ARE STILL GREAT

Affordable tile saws are available at any home center, making it easy to overlook the primitive, old-fashioned tile snap cutter. But don't. It's inexpensive, and it doesn't make a dusty mess, throw water all over the place or need power. While you could spend hundreds on one, you don't have to; basic models cost less than $40.

Mark right on the tile

MARK, DON'T MEASURE

Using a china pencil to mark the cutting lines on your tile is not only faster but also more accurate. By eliminating the step of using a measuring tape or ruler and then transferring your lines, marking directly on the tile will save you time and avoid miscuts.

CLEAN SQUEEZE-OUT NOW, NOT LATER

When you're done setting the tile, inspect all the joints for thin-set that has squeezed out between tiles, and clean it out before it hardens. Also look for smudges of thin-set on the face of the tile. If a smudge has hardened and won't wipe off easily, wet it and scrub with a synthetic abrasive pad. But don't rub too hard! It's possible to dull polished stone or glazed tile.

Long, straight trowel lines

TROWEL THIN-SET IN STRAIGHT LINES

It seems so natural to spread thin-set by sweeping your trowel back and forth, but that's absolutely wrong. The problem with a swirly bed of thin-set is it will trap air, which will prevent a strong bond. This is especially true for large tiles. It's important to trowel in long, straight lines in the direction of the long edge of the tile. This allows the ridges to collapse properly and let all the air escape.

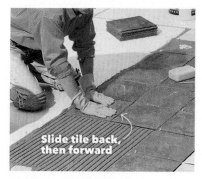

Slide tile back, then forward

SLIDE THE TILE INTO PLACE

If there are air pockets or voids under the tile, it's likely to crack or loosen eventually. In the tip above, we talked about the importance of troweling in straight lines. Here's where it matters. When you set tile, slide it forward then back about the width of your trowel notch. This motion needs to be perpendicular to the trowel lines; it collapses the ridges and eliminates the air channels, creating a strong, uniform bond.

Self-leveling rotary laser

KEEP THINGS LEVEL WITH A LASER

A laser level is a great tool for helping you place ledger boards on the wall or guide boards on the floor. When you're using it for laying tile, it's better than chalk lines because the lines won't get covered by the thin-set. You'll find laser levels at home centers and online starting at about $70.

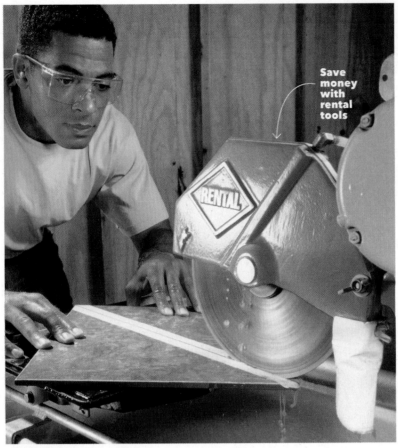

Save money with rental tools

RENT, DON'T BUY

A large wet saw will set you back at least $300, probably more. So, if you're setting large tiles in your home, just rent one. Renting will cost about $70 a day, plus you won't have to explain another new tool in the garage!

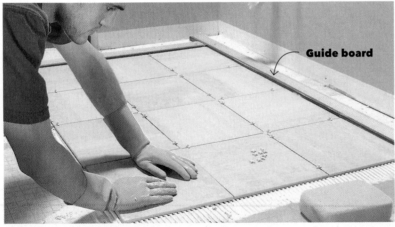

Guide board

GUIDE BOARDS BEAT CHALK LINES

The usual way to position the first row of tile is to snap chalk lines. But there are two problems with that method: First, chalk lines are hard to see if you've slopped thin-set over them. Second, the first row of tile can move as you set the next row. Guide boards solve both problems. Position the boards the same way you would position layout lines and screw them to the floor. Choose perfectly straight boards or strips of plywood, and wrap the edge of the guide with duct tape so the thin-set won't stick to it.

ELIMINATE LIPPAGE ON LARGE TILE

Uneven tile edges, called "lippage," are hard to avoid with large tile. Leveling clips and wedges will help you lay the tile flat. Just slip the clip under the tile and push in the wedge until the two edges are even with each other. After the thin-set hardens, break off the exposed clip. LASH brand clips are available at tile stores and some home centers.

Tile wedges eliminate lippage

DON'T TRUST THIS LABEL!

Your thin-set probably has a chart like this on the label. Don't rely on it. The recommendations are a good starting point, but they don't guarantee you'll have enough for the job. Buy a little more than you think you'll need. It's better to have some leftover thin-set than not enough!

AVERAGE COVERAGE / COBERTURA PROMEDIO

TILE SIZE TAMAÑO DE AZUELOS Y BALDOSAS	TROWEL SIZE TAMAÑO DE LLANA	PER 25 L POR BO DE 11
		45 - 50
	1/4" x 1/4" x 1/4" Square-Notch	4.2 - 4
	6 x 6 x 6 mm Dentada Cuadrada	32 - 3
Up to 8" Hasta 20 cm	1/4" x 3/8" x 1/4" Square-Notch	2.9 -
	6 x 9 x 6 mm Dentada Cuadrada	23 -
8" to 12" 20 a 30 cm	1/2" x 1/2" x 1/2" Square-Notch	2.1
12" or larger 30 cm o más	13 x 13 x 13 mm Dentada Cuadrada	

Handy Hints®

Clever solutions from our readers

Hose to shop vacuum

Less-Mess Tile Cutting

If you're cutting tile using a grinder, build yourself a vacuum bucket. Drill a hole the same size as your vacuum's hose into the side of the bucket, near the bottom. As you're cutting tile over the bucket, the vacuum will capture most of the dust.

MIKE HALLORAN

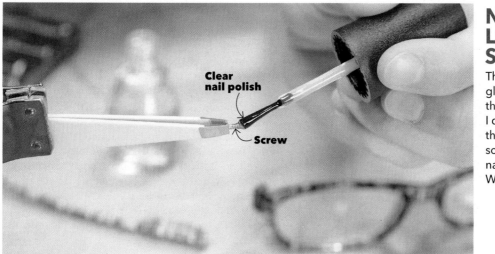

Clear nail polish

Screw

NO MORE LOOSE SCREWS

The tiny screws in my glasses used to back themselves out over time. I didn't have a thread-locking product, so I decided to try clear nail polish instead. Worked like a charm!

SARAH HYSER

INSULATION SUPPORT

Installing ceiling insulation by yourself is tricky. Make it easier by tightening a bar clamp across the rafter bay you're working on to hold up the insulation in the middle. This allows you to work down each side without holding on to the roll.

CRAIG BINGMAN

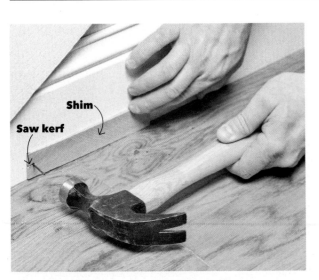

Dent Preventer

Prevent dings in finished surfaces by cutting a kerf into a shim and then slipping the shim around the nail as you hammer it in. The shim shields the surface against errant hammer blows.

JEFF WINZELER

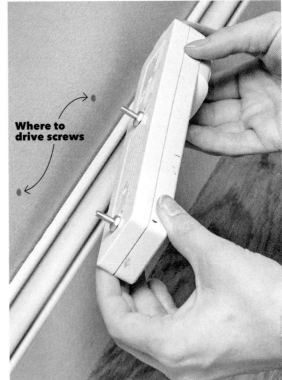

NO-MEASURE MOUNTING

Here's a foolproof method to perfectly position the mounting screws for your power strip—no measuring necessary. Slide pan-head machine screws head first into the keyholes and over to their locked positions. Thread a nut on each one, just finger tight, to hold it in place. Set the power strip against the wall right where you want it, and push on it so the machine screws make slight indents in the wall. Drive screws (or anchors) into those spots and you're set!

BRAD HOLDEN

Great Goofs®

Laughs and lessons from our readers

A SNAG IN THE SHAG

A few years ago, I was installing bypass closet doors in a customer's newly finished basement, which had beautiful, expensive new carpet. Everything was going fine until it was time to screw the door guides to the concrete floor. I got out my hammer drill to drill the pilot holes for the concrete screws.

In a split second, the drill bit grabbed a carpet fiber and ripped a perfectly straight snag right down the middle of the $30 a yard woven carpet. I had to recruit my friend the carpet expert to fix the problem—he said it happens to carpenters all the time. I just wish I had cut a little slit in the carpeting before drilling. Then I wouldn't have lost money on that job.

PETE BOUMAN

SHORT-CIRCUIT SHORTCUT

Mike, a carpenter buddy of mine, shared one of his cool remodeling tricks with me. When he encounters a hump in a wall caused by a badly bowed stud, he cuts right through the drywall and into the stud with a long reciprocating saw blade. The cut relieves the stress and the stud straightens itself. Just a little patching to fix the saw kerf and you're done. Brilliant! I had that exact problem in my downstairs bedroom—a hump that had always driven me nuts.

I stuck the saw blade into the drywall and started cutting. All of a sudden, the room went black and the saw went dead. The bad stud happened to be the one with electrical cable stapled to the side to feed the overhead light. I had cut through the cable and blown the circuit breaker. Needless to say, there was a lot of electrical work, drywall patching and painting ahead of me. But at least the wall was flat—mission accomplished!

MILO AMUNDSEN

NOT A BIG-FAN FAN

When the ceiling fan in our kitchen started making a loud noise, we decided to replace it. We bought a new one with larger blades for more air circulation. My husband and I worked on the installation together (that's usually a challenge in itself!). We turned the fan on, then stood back and admired how quiet it was.

A couple days later, I was working in the kitchen with the fan on and opened an upper cupboard door. I felt and heard a loud collision, which scared the daylights out of me. You guessed it—the longer fan blades whacked the edge of the door. Now we keep a small rubber band on the handle for that cupboard to remind us not to open it when the fan is on.

PAM MARTIN

Bathroom Storage
PLUGGED IN!

Your gear is always ready to go!

BY MIKE BERNER

We step into our bathrooms every morning to get ready for the day. We pull out hair dryers, curling irons and trimmers, untangle their cords and fumble around for the outlet to plug them in. Then we unplug them and stuff them in a drawer, just to untangle them all again the next morning. What a waste of time! But this cabinet rollout has built-in outlets to eliminate those hassles and get you on your way.

Built-in power strip

Cord storage area

1 START WITH TWO RIP CUTS
Set the table saw fence to 19 in. to cut the width of the drawer front and back pieces. Then make another rip at 14 in. for the drawer sides and shelf parts. This approach keeps similar parts the exact same length and helps keep the drawer square and easy to assemble. Crosscut the front, back and tall side at 20 in., then crosscut the remaining parts.

2 CUT THE FRONT AND BACK
You can cut the front and back of the L-shaped drawer with a jigsaw or circular saw. But here's how to make straighter cuts using a table saw: Mark the cutouts on both sides of the front and back. Set the fence to 6 in. to make the first cut for the depth of the shelf. When you're 3 in. from the end of the cut, stop, turn the saw off and wait for the blade to stop. Do the same with the second part, then flip both parts, set your fence to 5-3/4 in. and make the second cut the same way. Finish the cuts with a handsaw or jigsaw.

3 SIZE THE BOTTOM
Cut the grooves as shown in **Figure A**. Glue and nail the front and one side together. Slide the bottom into the grooves and mark 5/16 in. inside the front of the drawer and 3/16 in. beyond the side. Then adjust the fence to the marks and cut the bottom to size. Glue and nail the sides, front, and back together, leaving the bottom panel floating in the grooves.

4 FIT THE POWER STRIP
Find a spot where there will be enough room for the drawer to close once the power strip is installed. Trace the power strip on your drawer, then drill a 1/4-in.-diameter hole in each corner. Fit a jigsaw blade into one of the holes and connect the holes. Insert the power strip and secure it with two screws.

WHAT IT TAKES

TIME	COST	SKILL LEVEL
1 day	$120	Intermediate

TOOLS
Table saw, handsaw, jigsaw, drill, 18-gauge brad nailer

1 — 14"

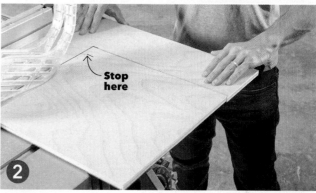

2 — Stop here

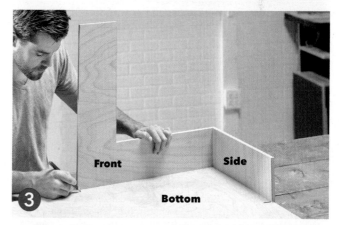

3 — Front / Side / Bottom

4 — Power strip

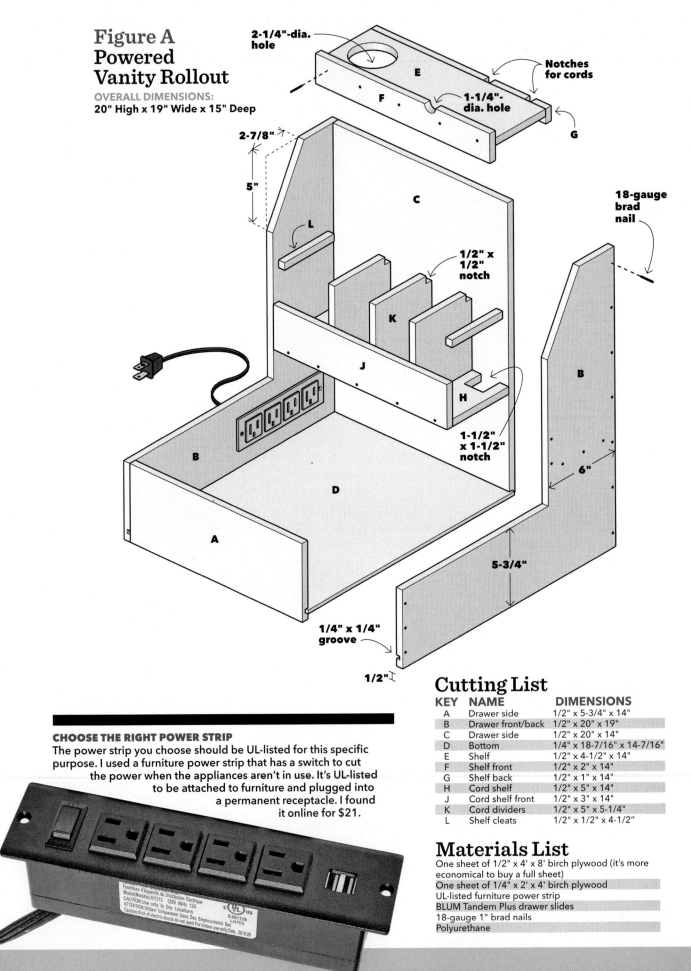

Figure A
Powered Vanity Rollout

OVERALL DIMENSIONS:
20" High x 19" Wide x 15" Deep

2-1/4"-dia. hole

Notches for cords

1-1/4"-dia. hole

E

F

G

2-7/8"

5"

C

L

18-gauge brad nail

1/2" x 1/2" notch

K

J

H

B

1-1/2" x 1-1/2" notch

B

D

6"

5-3/4"

A

1/4" x 1/4" groove

5-3/4"

1/2"

CHOOSE THE RIGHT POWER STRIP
The power strip you choose should be UL-listed for this specific purpose. I used a furniture power strip that has a switch to cut the power when the appliances aren't in use. It's UL-listed to be attached to furniture and plugged into a permanent receptacle. I found it online for $21.

Cutting List

KEY	NAME	DIMENSIONS
A	Drawer side	1/2" x 5-3/4" x 14"
B	Drawer front/back	1/2" x 20" x 19"
C	Drawer side	1/2" x 20" x 14"
D	Bottom	1/4" x 18-7/16" x 14-7/16"
E	Shelf	1/2" x 4-1/2" x 14"
F	Shelf front	1/2" x 2" x 14"
G	Shelf back	1/2" x 1" x 14"
H	Cord shelf	1/2" x 5" x 14"
J	Cord shelf front	1/2" x 3" x 14"
K	Cord dividers	1/2" x 5" x 5-1/4"
L	Shelf cleats	1/2" x 1/2" x 4-1/2"

Materials List

One sheet of 1/2" x 4' x 8' birch plywood (it's more economical to buy a full sheet)
One sheet of 1/4" x 2' x 4' birch plywood
UL-listed furniture power strip
BLUM Tandem Plus drawer slides
18-gauge 1" brad nails
Polyurethane

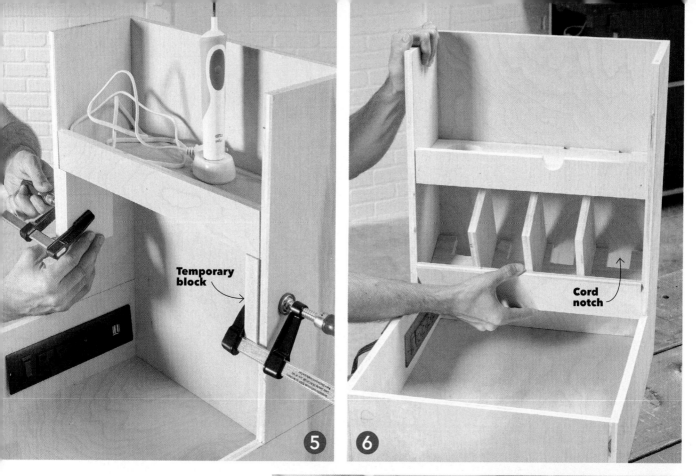

Temporary block

Cord notch

5　**6**

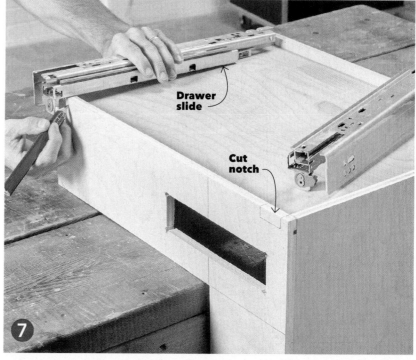

Drawer slide

Cut notch

7

5 CUSTOMIZE THE SHELF

Determine the height of the shelf by placing the tallest appliance on it and adjusting it up and down to fit. Clamp blocks against the drawer to hold it in place, then mark its position and glue and nail the shelf cleats into place. Use the appliances to map out where and how they will be held. I used a 2-1/4-in. hole saw to make a hair dryer holster and a 1-1/4-in. Forstner bit to cut a half-moon shape for my beard trimmer. I made notches for the charging cords with a pull saw and a chisel.

6 BUILD STORAGE FOR YOUR CORDS

The cord storage shelf separates each set of cords so they don't get tangled. The dividers are spaced between the appliances and fastened with glue and 18-gauge brad nails. I cut 1-1/2-in. square notches for the plugs with a jigsaw to provide a path for the plugs to get to the power strip. The removable appliance shelf allows easy access to the cords when needed, and the opening in front lets you shove cords in when they're not in use.

7 CUT NOTCHES FOR THE SLIDES

Flip the drawer over, hook the slides over the side lip on the bottom and mark where each slide meets the back. Use a handsaw, coping saw or jigsaw to cut the notches to fit the slides. The notches should be 1/2 in. deep and flush with the inside edge of the drawer.

DON'T FEAR FANCY DRAWER SLIDES

I used Blum Tandem Plus drawer slides ($32 online), which can be mounted to the side or bottom of a cabinet. They're completely hidden when the drawer is open, which gives it a high-end look. They're much easier to install than they look. You'll need to build the drawer to match the length of the slides, which require a 1/2-in. recess underneath the drawer. I chose the 15-in. slides to fit into the 18-in.-deep vanity and allow room for the inset door and the power strip.

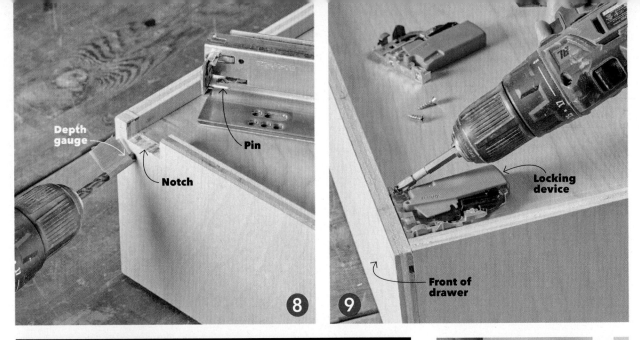

Depth gauge

Pin

Notch

Locking device

Front of drawer

8

9

ADDING AN OUTLET UNDER THE SINK

This project requires an outlet inside the vanity. If there's power above your sink that shares a stud bay inside your vanity, it's an easy job. First switch off the power to the circuit at the electrical panel. Remove the existing outlet and send a few feet of cable to a new single-gang box behind the vanity and make the connections to a new outlet. If there's a stud between the old outlet and the spot for the new one, the job becomes more complicated. To learn more, search for "add an outlet" at familyhandyman.com.

10

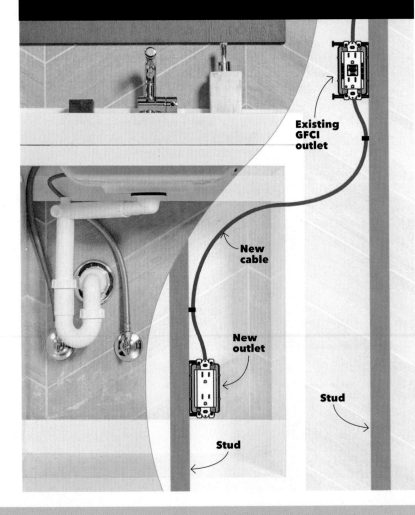

Existing GFCI outlet

New cable

New outlet

Stud

Stud

Stud

8 DRILL THE PIN HOLE

The pin that keeps the drawer slide in place requires a 1/4-in.-diameter hole. Put the slide in place and mark the back of the drawer where the pin hits. Drill a hole just deep enough to fit the pin without going through the back. Then apply your choice of finish to the drawer.

9 FASTEN THE LOCKING DEVICES

Fit the locking devices into the front corners on the underside of the drawer. Drill angled pilot holes for the screws and fasten the devices in place. The locking devices hold the drawer on the slides and allow you to easily remove the drawer.

10 ATTACH THE SLIDES

Screw the first slide to the side of the cabinet opposite the hinges, then measure the inside of the drawer and add 1-5/8 in. to determine the location of the second slide. Draw a parallel line and screw the slide to the bottom of the cabinet inside the line.

MORE BATHROOM STORAGE

Turn unused space into a hidden cabinet

BY BRAD HOLDEN

Got plans to hang a mirror or a large painting? Consider using the stud cavity behind it for handy, secret storage. I installed this mirror cabinet in the bathroom—like a giant medicine cabinet. The mirror glides on ball-bearing drawer slides to open and close the cabinet. When the mirror is in place, nobody knows the cabinet is even there!

Getting started

Including the frame, my mirror was 21-1/4 in. wide, so I needed about 23 in. of open wall space to the left of the mirror for it to slide left. You can mount the drawer slides to go either direction.

I bought a frameless beveled mirror for $125. I could have purchased a framed mirror to save some work, but I decided to build my own frame. The mirror is heavy, so I wanted the frame to be solid lumber for strength. I also needed it to be thick enough for 3/4-in. screws to attach the drawer slides.

I chose 1x4 poplar boards. Poplar is easy to find, inexpensive and lightweight. It also has good screw-holding capability and takes paint well. For the cabinet, I used precut melamine shelving from the home center. Its front edge is already banded, so if you plan your cuts, you won't need to edge-band your shelves.

WHAT IT TAKES

TIME	COST	SKILL LEVEL
2 days	$250	Intermediate

TOOLS
Table saw, dado set, router, rabbeting bit, miter saw, drill/driver, finish nailer

1 PEEK INSIDE THE WALL

Check for obstructions in the wall cavity. Cut a slot big enough for your phone, and take one photo up and one down. If there are pipes or electrical cables in your way, you can choose a different stud cavity, size the cabinet so it doesn't interfere, or reroute the pipes or wires. If you pick a different location, you can easily patch the small slot.

2 CUT THE OPENING

Starting from the slot, cut a hole large enough to reveal the exact stud locations. Draw the opening using a level and a framing square, and then cut on the line.

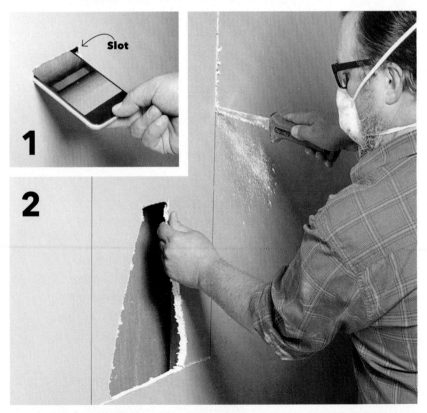

Slot

1

2

MEET THE BUILDER
Brad Holden, a senior editor, has been building cabinets and furniture for more than 30 years.

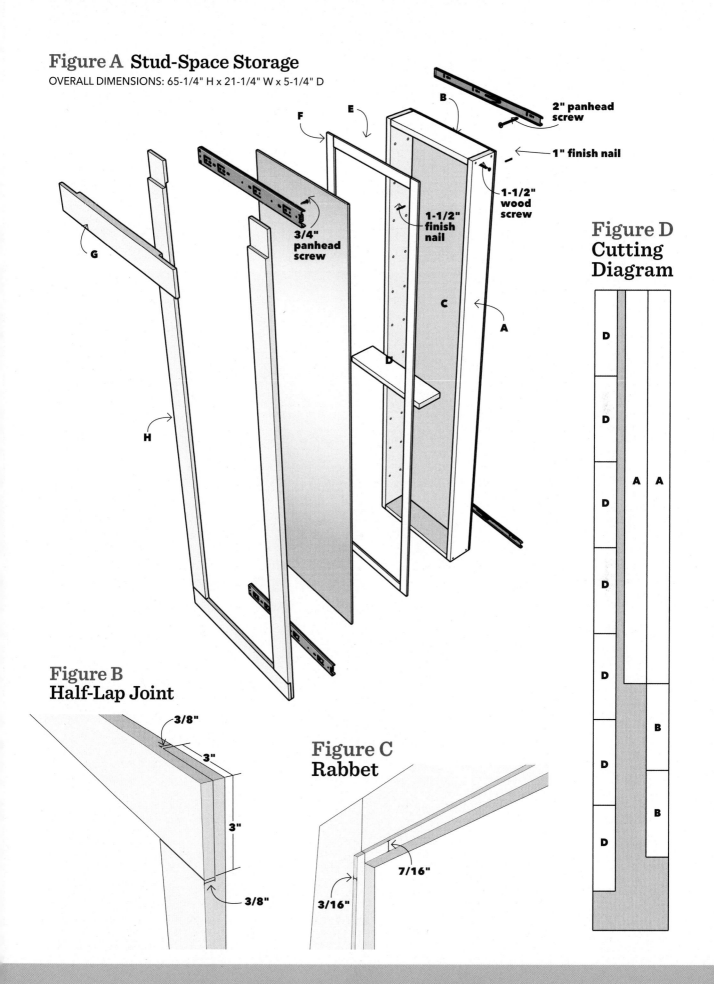

Figure A Stud-Space Storage

OVERALL DIMENSIONS: 65-1/4" H x 21-1/4" W x 5-1/4" D

2" panhead screw

1" finish nail

1-1/2" wood screw

3/4" panhead screw

1-1/2" finish nail

B

F

E

A

C

D

G

H

Figure D
Cutting Diagram

D

D

D

D

D

D

A   A

D

D

B

D

B

D

Figure B
Half-Lap Joint

3/8"

3"

3"

3/8"

Figure C
Rabbet

3/16"

7/16"

3 BUILD THE SHELVES

Cut a strip for the shelves (D) from the front edge of the melamine. Next, cut the sides (A), top and bottom (B) from the remaining piece (see **Figure D**). Assemble the parts using 1-1/2-in. wood screws. Cut the back (C) and paint it white. You may need to resize the cabinet slightly to fit your stud cavity.

4 DRILL FOR SHELF SUPPORTS

Make a jig to drill the holes by drilling evenly spaced holes in a length of hardwood. Hold the jig in place on the cabinet side and drill the first hole. Slip a drill bit of the same size into the hole you just drilled to keep the jig in place. When you get to the end of the jig, slip the drill bit into the last hole and continue. Use a depth stop on the bit to ensure you won't drill through the side. Nail on the back with 1-in. finish nails.

5 ADD THE TRIM

Glue and nail on the trim (E and F) to cover the edges of the cabinet as well as any gap between the cabinet and the wall opening. Choose trim that's 3/8 in. thick or less. Because standard drawer slides are 1/2 in. thick and the wall may not be dead flat, thicker trim could keep the mirror from sliding.

Depth stop • Drill bit • Drilling jig

Materials List

ITEM	QTY.
16" x 60" mirror	1
3/4" x 12" x 96" melamine shelf	1
1/4" x 48" x 96" plywood	1
1/4" x 1-1/2" mullion	15'
1x4 x 8' poplar boards	2
18" full-extension drawer slides (screws included)	2
Shelf supports	28
No. 6 x 2" panhead screws	8
No. 8 x 1-1/2" wood screws	8
1" finish nails	
3/4" panhead screws	8
Clear silicone	
Paint	1 qt.
Wood glue	
Glass safety film	

Cutting List

KEY	QTY.	DIMENSIONS	PART
A	2	3/4" x 3-3/4" x 59"	Cabinet sides
B	2	3/4" x 3-3/4" x 13"	Cabinet top and bottom
C	1	1/4" x 14-1/2" x 59"	Cabinet back
D	7	3/4" x 3-3/4" x 12-7/8"	Shelves
E	2	1/4" x 1-1/4" x 13"	Trim rails
F	2	1/4" x 1-1/4" x 60"	Trim stiles
G	2	3/4" x 3" x 21-1/4"	Frame rails
H	2	3/4" x 3" x 65-1/4"	Frame stiles

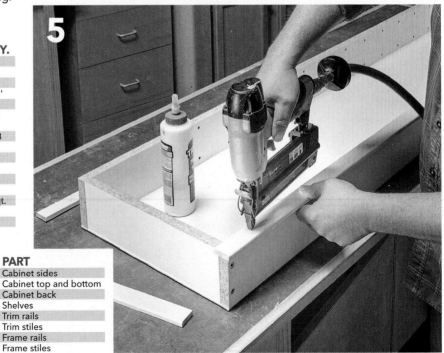

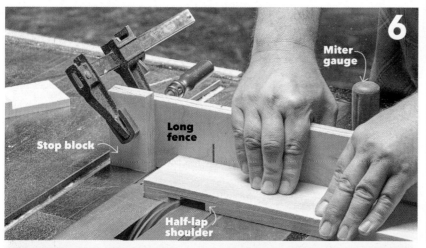

6

8

9

7

6 CUT HALF-LAP JOINTS

Cut the frame parts (G and H) to length, then make half-lap joints at their ends. I cut half-laps using a dado set on my table saw. I attach a long fence to the miter gauge, and then add a stop block to set the joint's shoulder. Start with two scrap pieces, making passes in both until you get the right depth.

7 CHAMFER THE JOINTS

Add a very slight chamfer to the shoulders of the joints on the side pieces, and on the entire inner edge of the top and bottom. This creates a shallow "V" where the joints come together. The groove is optional but adds some visual interest. I like to use a block plane for this, but a sanding block works fine.

8 ASSEMBLE THE FRAME

Glue the half-lap joints, and then clamp them until the glue dries. Set the frame on blocks or sawhorses to provide room for the clamp heads. Because of their ample gluing surface, these half-lap joints are super strong.

9 ROUT THE MIRROR RECESS

Rout a 7/16-in.-wide recess the depth of your mirror's thickness, using a rabbeting bit in your router. To avoid router tear-out, make the cut in two or three passes. Sand the mirror frame up to 150 grit and then apply paint.

10 ATTACH THE SLIDES

Separate the two components of the drawer slides. Fasten the wide tracks to the frame. If you mount the narrow tracks to the frame, the slides' release levers won't be accessible. Placement of the slides isn't critical; just center them side to side and be sure they're above and below the cabinet's trim.

11 INSTALL BLOCKING

The drawer slides don't carry weight the usual way, so they must be firmly attached to the wall. Instead of relying on drywall anchors, I installed blocking. Using the drawer slide placement on the frame to determine where the slides would attach to the wall, I cut 2x4s to fit between the studs and screwed them into place. Mark centerlines on the wall for the drawer slide locations.

12 INSTALL THE CABINET

Set the cabinet in the opening, plumb and level. Fasten it into place with 3-in. wood screws through the sides, into the studs.

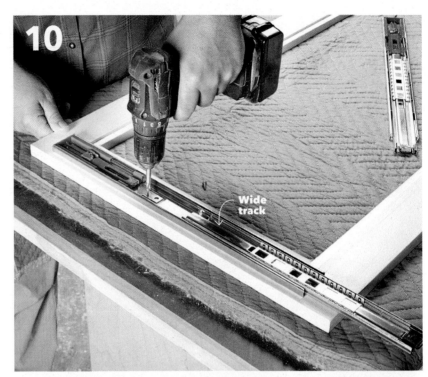

Wide track

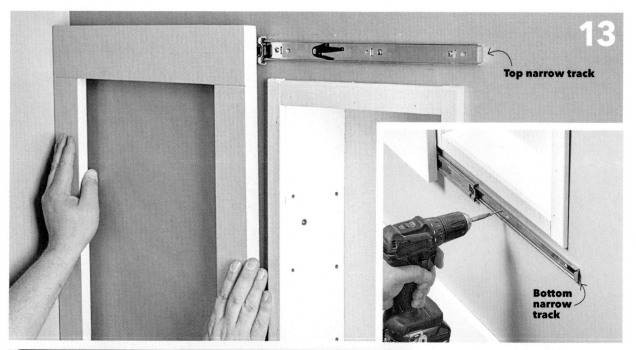

Top narrow track

Bottom narrow track

Safety film

13 HANG THE FRAME

Fasten the top narrow track on its centerline above the cabinet, centered side to side. Slip the other narrow track into its wide track at the bottom of the frame, making sure the narrow track is fully extended. Slide the frame onto the top narrow track. Plumb the frame, and then fasten the bottom narrow track to the wall.

14 APPLY SAFETY BACKER

This mirror will be in motion regularly, so I applied transparent window safety film ($15 for an 18-in. x 8-ft. roll online) on the back. In case of breakage, the glass shards won't crash to the floor. Just peel the backing and press the film onto the back of the mirror. Since this isn't a window, I wasn't picky about removing every last air bubble.

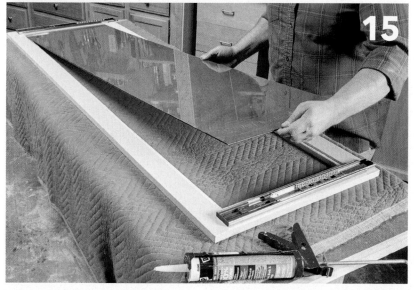

15 INSTALL THE MIRROR

It's easier to hang the frame by itself, without the added weight, so I installed the mirror last. Apply a bead of silicone in the rabbet, and then carefully place the mirror in the silicone. Let the silicone set for a day and then trim off any excess with a razor blade before hanging the mirror.

UNDER-SINK CLUTTER CONTROL

The space under a kitchen sink is often a black hole where cleaning supplies go to be forgotten. You want to keep this stuff close at hand, but drawers and shelving aren't usually an option because the sink, garbage disposal and plumbing are in the way. But the solution is simple: Insert a curtain tension rod across the cabinet box, and then hang spray bottles, rags and other cleaning supplies on the rod.

EMMA WONG

Extra shower storage

Need more space to hang storage bins in the shower? Next time you're at the home center, grab a shower curtain tension rod. Install it near the wall of your shower for 6 ft. of bin-hanging space!

IZZY OSMOND

Catch detergent drips

To keep detergent from dripping all over your laundry room floor, add a wire handle to the cup. Poke two holes in the cup, thread wire through the holes, and hang the cup from the spout to catch the drips.

CHRIS BOULE

Copper wire bail

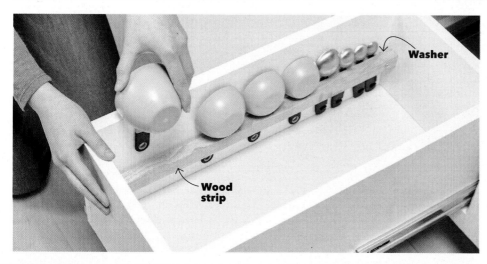

DRAWER ORGANIZER

Keep measuring cups and spoons from cluttering up a drawer. Just attach a strip of wood to the drawer's side. Install washers behind the wood strip to create a gap for the handles to slide into.

CHRIS GRIMAL

Washer

Wood strip

EASY DRILL HANGER

I use pegboard to hang tools in my shop. Instead of buying special large hooks to hang my drill, I just tighten a screw eye in the chuck. This way, I can hang it on a standard small hook or even a nail in the wall.

DOUG WIOSKY

Centered handle

Offset crank

Bucket-lid cord reel

Make this handy cord reel using extra bucket lids from drywall mud pails or other 5-gallon buckets. Cut a 5-in. length of 4x4 and then cut a groove in the side just wide enough to fit your cord. Fasten the lids to the 4x4 with 1/4 x 2-in. lag screws. Make handles from an old 1-1/8-in.-diameter broom handle and drill a 1/2-in. hole through the centers. Fasten the crank to the lid with bolts, nuts and washers, and apply Loctite sealant to the end nut. Fasten the handle to the 4x4 through the lid with a 6-1/2-in. lag screw. Then just insert your cord and reel it in.

DOUG KOENIG

Marbles

MAKE YOUR OWN LAZY SUSAN

I was shopping for a lazy Susan for my spices, but the ones I found were expensive and wouldn't fit in my cabinet anyway. I made my own with two matching pie tins and marbles. You just spread a single layer of marbles in the bottom tin and set the other tin on top. Spins just like the store-bought variety!

CAROL SCHULTZ

2 Electrical & High-Tech

Home Care

HEALTH | MAINTENANCE & REPAIR | STORAGE & ORGANIZATION

LED Lightbulb Brightness Test

We had two theories about LED lightbulbs: that some bulbs with the same lumen rating are brighter than others, and that some fade very quickly. So, we bought six 800-lumen bulbs online and put them to the test by measuring their brightness over one month of constant use.

Not all bulbs shine equally

As expected, some of the lightbulbs burned brighter than the others right out of the box, with the Philips ($12 for a four-pack) being brightest. But our second theory didn't pan out. None of the bulbs dimmed significantly—at least not in their first 750 hours of use. We'll continue to monitor them over the coming months.

BULB BRIGHTNESS
These readings were taken immediately after installing the bulbs. Later readings didn't vary significantly.

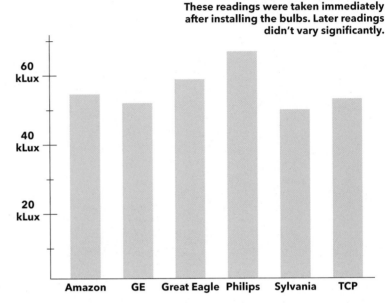

Amazon | GE | Great Eagle | Philips | Sylvania | TCP

HOW WE TESTED THEM
We inserted six 800-lumen LED lightbulbs into a light bar. We left them on all day and night and tested their brightness by placing the light meter against each bulb.

WHERE DO I NEED AFCI OUTLETS?

The basic answer is, pretty much everywhere. In fact, it's easier to list the places where AFCIs (arc-fault circuit interrupters) aren't required by the National Electrical Code: bathrooms, garages, unfinished basements and outdoors. Also, existing wiring doesn't require upgrading to AFCI protection unless you make changes to the branch circuit wiring.

AFCIs help prevent electrical fires caused by damaged or deteriorated wiring. The best method is to install an AFCI circuit breaker. If your breaker box doesn't accept new AFCI breakers, install a feed-through outlet branch circuit (OBC) receptacle next to the breaker box to protect the entire branch circuit. OBC receptacles are also used for AFCI protection where branch circuits are modified, replaced or extended. Locate the OBC AFCI receptacle at the first receptacle outlet of the existing branch circuit.

AFCI circuit breaker

AFCI outlet

Reviving Dead Outlets

When an outlet isn't working, the next step is usually to check the electrical service panel. But if no circuit breakers are tripped, the trouble could stem from a tripped GFCI outlet. That's because the same GFCI outlets that protect against shocks in kitchens, bathrooms and other wet or exposed areas are sometimes wired to shut off standard outlets downstream. These outlets might be in the same room as the GFCI or more distant, so you'll need to search carefully. New homes might have GFCI outlets installed in every room.

Typically, a green light indicates normal operation, while a red light shows the outlet has been tripped. If the outlet is tripped, first push the "Test" button and then "Reset." If there is no light and/or the outlet will not reset, the GFCI might not be receiving power or it might need replacing. If an outlet works but trips frequently, it's possible that a hot wire is loose and/or contacting bare metal. In that case, you'll need to fix the problem before you can reset the outlet and restore power to the downstream outlets. If you see or smell smoke around the outlet or discover singed areas, call an electrician and/or replace the GFCI outlet.

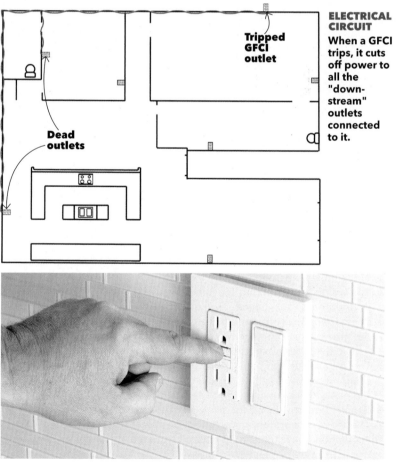

Tripped GFCI outlet

Dead outlets

ELECTRICAL CIRCUIT
When a GFCI trips, it cuts off power to all the "downstream" outlets connected to it.

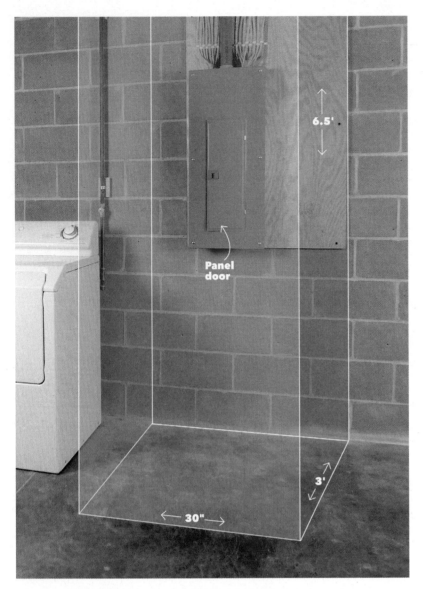

6.5'

Panel
door

3'

30"

Don't crowd
YOUR ELECTRICAL PANEL

When you're remodeling, it's tempting to gain some living space by building walls close to the electrical panel. But that might come back to haunt you during an inspection or when you sell your home. Here are the space requirements as outlined by the NEC (National Electrical Code):

1. There must be 3 ft. of working clearance in front of the panel.
2. The width of the working space needs to be at least 30 in. (the panel isn't required to be centered on the 30-in. width).
3. The panel door must open at least 90 degrees.
4. For new construction, the height of the working space needs to be at least 6.5 ft. (there is an exception for existing homes).
5. The area above and below the panel is reserved for other electrical equipment, which can't extend more than 6 in. beyond the front of the panel.
6. Illumination is required for all working spaces at electrical panels.
7. The required working space cannot be used for storage.

Think of it this way: You should have a clear area about the size of a refrigerator in front of the electrical panel.

AN ELECTRICAL PERMIT IS A BARGAIN!

When the topic of permits and inspections comes up, people often want to "avoid the red tape." Here are three excellent reasons to get an inspection:
1. In Minnesota, for as little as $35 (the minimum fee for a single inspection), you'll get a professional consultant on your project.
2. You'll be positive your work is done correctly. Most homeowners do a good job because of all the do-it-yourself resources available. It's rare for an inspector to recommend hiring a contractor to fix the project. Inspectors want to help people pass inspection!
3. If you're planning to sell your home, you can avoid selling problems. Real estate agents are wary of lawsuits, and home buyers are savvy, so it's easy—particularly with the help of a home inspector—to discover unpermitted work, which you may then be required to fix.

The National Electrical Code lays out all the requirements for protecting people and property from electrical hazards. But it's lengthy and at times hard to understand; it's best to contact your local, county or state inspector about projects you're planning.

Inspections are not only a bargain; they're required for the following projects:
- Wiring a new home
- Upgrading electrical services
- Room and porch additions
- Finishing basements
- Replacing light fixtures and ceiling fans
- Installing or replacing appliances, furnaces and air conditioners
- Installing wiring to detached garages and sheds
- Installing outdoor wiring and wiring for hot tubs and swimming pools

ELECTRICAL CODE CHANGES: WHAT DIYers NEED TO KNOW

The National Electrical Code is revised every three years, and the 2020 code includes the following revisions that may affect DIYers.

A. GFCI protection is required almost anywhere current is drawn outdoors, including receptacles and AC condensing units. The only exception is lighting outlets.

B. Outlets in bath and shower areas are not allowed within an imaginary 3 x 8-ft. zone around tubs and showers.

C. All garbage disposals must have GFCI protection. Also, islands and peninsulas must have a GFCI receptacle every 9 sq. ft. An island of 15 sq. ft., for example, requires two outlets.

D. One- and two-family dwelling units must have an emergency disconnect at a readily accessible outside location.

E. To protect the ever-growing collection of sensitive electronics, all new construction and panel board replacements must include surge protection.

F. All basement receptacles—in finished or unfinished basements—must have GFCI protection. Before, only 15- and 20-amp 125-volt receptacles were required to have it.

MEET THE EXPERT
John Williamson is a master electrician and an electrical inspector in Minnesota.

In-use covers are safer for you—and your walls

If you keep anything plugged into an outdoor outlet during wet weather—a pond pump, holiday lights, a low-voltage lighting transformer—the plug is bound to get wet and pose a potentially dangerous shock hazard. The solution is an in-use outlet cover, which keeps the outlet sheltered and dry even while a cord is plugged in. That reduces the risk of shocks and keeps GFCI outlets from getting wet and shutting off power. In-use covers help to protect your walls, too. When a standard outlet cover is held open by a cord, it can let water into your walls—not much water, but enough to encourage wood rot and peeling paint.

Home centers and hardware stores carry in-use covers to accommodate horizontal, vertical, rectangular and duplex outlets. A tough metal cover like the one shown here costs about $15. The gasket that comes with the cover forms a watertight seal over smooth surfaces, but seal around the cover with caulk if you have rough brick or stucco siding.

AVOID RISKY ELECTRICAL PRODUCTS

I recently inspected a new apartment building for which the builder had ordered hundreds of light fixtures online. None of the fixtures were certified by a testing organization recognized by code officials. The fixtures may have been perfectly safe, or they may have been a disaster waiting to happen. I just couldn't let the builder install them.

Here's the moral of the story: When you shop online, be sure any electrical products you buy—from desk lamps to furnaces—carry one of the common labels shown here. Those that don't are a dangerous gamble. For a full list of testing labs, go to osha.gov/dts/otpca/nrtl/nrtllist.html

MEET THE EXPERT
John Williamson is the chief electrical inspector for the state of Minnesota.

Great Goofs®

Laughs and lessons from our readers

NIGHT-LIGHT NIGHTMARE

I installed a motion sensor switch in our laundry room, and my wife loves it. Every time she walks in carrying a load of laundry, the light automatically comes on, and it turns off soon after she leaves. So, since the kids are always leaving the light on in their bedroom, I decided to put one there, too.

Big mistake. Sure, the light turned off when there wasn't anyone in the room. But it also turned on when we didn't want it to—like when the kids rolled over in their sleep or the cat entered the room on its nightly patrol and jumped up on their beds. The instant-on light woke up the kids, who in turn woke me up with their yelling. I swapped it with the old switch the next morning. Now if I can just keep out the cat, I'll be able to get a peaceful night's sleep.

DAVE AHRENDT

BLINDSIDED BY THE LIGHT

My friend had installed a kitchen backsplash and asked me to help him change the wall outlets to match the new décor. Since I didn't have my voltage sniffer with me, I needed something to plug into the outlet so I'd know when the power was off. I found a clothes iron and plugged it in, and my friend flipped the circuit breakers until the iron light went off.

I changed the first two outlets and started on the third. Plugged in the iron—yup, the light was off. When I touched the wire, there was a flash of sparks and my arm went numb. I was floored—how could I get a shock when the iron showed the power was off? I learned the hard way that the light goes off when the iron reaches the right temperature. I think I'll stick with my voltage sniffer from now on.

SHAWN TOMBOLINI

Clearing the Air on VOCs and Paint

We see them everywhere: home maintenance and building products labeled "low VOC" or "no VOC." But we had never seen a clear, basic explanation of what VOCs are or why they should concern us. So, we tracked down some experts for the straight scoop.

What are VOCs?

VOCs (volatile organic compounds) are natural or manufactured chemicals that easily turn into a gas at room temperature and enter the air we breathe. This process is called "off-gassing." VOCs are found everywhere: paints (to aid mixing and hardening), varnishes, caulks, adhesives, composite wood, carpet and upholstery. Even home and personal care products such as air fresheners, cleaners and perfume contain VOCs.

What is a safe level?

Many people assume that if you can smell a chemical, it must be hazardous. But some high-odor VOCs are relatively safe. Others are dangerous at levels you can't smell. And sometimes things that smell good contain high levels of VOCs. Most products contain more than one VOC, and there isn't much research on health effects of exposure to products with multiple VOCs. Each chemical has specific toxicity and health concerns.

What's the health risk?

The health risk of inhaling any chemical depends on the concentration and the duration of exposure. Common symptoms of short-term exposure (hours to days) to high levels of VOCs include eye, nose and throat irritation; headaches; nausea; and dizziness. For long-term exposure (years to a lifetime), health concerns include cancer, liver and kidney damage and central nervous system problems. If you have asthma or chemical sensitivities, you may show symptoms at lower levels than others.

How do I know how much is in the air?

Our noses are ineffective judges of safe levels of VOCs. The only way to determine the level is by testing the air, but that requires a professional, and it's expensive. The Occupational Safety and Health Administration (OSHA) sets permissible exposure limits for the workplace, but that's a different environment than the general public most often spends time in. There are no federal or state standards for VOC levels in settings other than the workplace.

MEET THE EXPERTS

SARAH PRILL is an industrial hygienist in the Indoor Air Unit with the Minnesota Department of Health.

KELLY SMELTZER is an indoor air quality specialist with the Minnesota Department of Health.

NICK SLAVIK has been a craftsman for more than 25 years. His company, Nick Slavik Painting & Restoration Co., has received many national awards.

Preventive measures

Public health professionals advise limiting exposure to products containing VOCs by following these guidelines:

- Use a low- or no-VOC product if you can.
- Maintain good ventilation.
- Let building materials like composite wood products off-gas outside.
- Buy only what you need. Stored paints, solvents and adhesives can leak VOCs into the air.
- Dispose of these products properly through your local hazardous waste collection.
- Control the humidity and temperature in your home. High temperatures and high humidity increase off-gassing.

A painter's perspective

All modern high-end paints are low-VOC and perform well. In paints, zero-VOC is scientifically impossible. Insignificant levels? Sure, but not zero. About 5 percent of my customers ask for zero-VOC paint, but what they're really after is no smell. Because of the unique finish and application properties of low- and zero-VOC paints, some clients choose traditional paints to get the look they're after.

To sum it up, low- and zero-VOC paints, because they don't contain glycol, are thicker, don't flow as well and dry faster, so the texture isn't quite as smooth. I never use them on trim or cabinets, only walls. When we use these paints, we change our work technique. Because of the fast drying time, we work in teams: one person doing the brush work, cutting in at the ceiling and trim, and another person rolling the large areas.

– Nick Slavik

ONE-COAT PAINT TEST

Few people want to mess around applying more than one coat of paint, but more often than not, you need to put on that second coat. Several paint brands, however, have high-end products that claim one-coat coverage. It seemed to us a little too good to be true, so we bought a gallon of Behr Marquee ($38), Sherwin-Williams Infinity ($44) and Benjamin Moore Aura ($72) to see how well they covered in one coat.

How we tested them

We painted the entire wall gray, but to see how the one-coat performs on darker and lighter paints, we also painted three white and black squares. We used a roller with a 3/8-in. nap for each paint.

Coat thickness makes a difference

How much paint you apply with your first roll makes a big difference. At first, we used a light amount of paint to test the one-coat claim and realized that for one-coat coverage, the coat needs to be a thick one. And it's also important to consider other factors, like color, shade, quality and the roller you use.

One-coat paint is pretty great

We were impressed by how well the one-coat paint in the color we chose covered the black and white squares. The paints differed subtly, but all three brands covered the white and black squares well. We liked Benjamin Moore Aura for its ease of application, but they all completely covered the underlying color in one coat.

Sherwin-Williams Infinity　　　**Benjamin Moore Aura**　　　**Behr Marquee**

MINERAL SPIRITS VS. PAINT THINNER

The terms "mineral spirits" and "paint thinner" are often used interchangeably. But the products aren't the same. Both are petroleum distillates and work well for cleaning oil-based paint from brushes and tools, but that's where the similarities end. Compared with paint thinner, mineral spirits and especially "odorless" mineral spirits are refined to a much higher grade. That's why you pay nearly twice as much for mineral spirits as for paint thinner. What this means for you is reduced toxic fumes.

Paint thinner, not being as refined, typically contains 5 percent VOCs such as benzene or toluene, which accounts for the strong odor. It also evaporates faster, and depending on your application, that can be important. If you're cleaning, faster evaporation is fine. If you're thinning a finish for spraying, however, choose mineral spirits.

PAINTING

IS URETHANE PAINT WORTH THE PRICE TAG?

Quality urethane paints cure to a harder, more durable finish than non-urethane paints. But they cost substantially more than non-urethane paints, ranging from $65 to $100 per gallon. Are they worth it? It depends on what you're painting. If you're painting walls and ceilings, surfaces that don't get hard use, acrylic latex paints are better. For trim, doors or cabinets, however, urethane paints might save you money over the long run, as they won't need to be repainted as often. Sherwin-Williams Emerald Urethane Trim Enamel, for example, was formulated specifically for durability, resistance to stains, scratches, abrasions, weathering and washing.

Urethane paints also have their place in exterior applications. Obviously, exterior doors benefit from a hard-wearing coating, but I wouldn't use urethane to paint my whole house. Because of its hardness, urethane

paint may not expand and contract with building materials as well as acrylic latex paints. But for small projects such as railings, light posts and mailboxes, urethane paint may be more durable than other exterior paints.

That said, there are a few caveats: (1) No paint performs well without good prep work. (2) You can buy inexpensive urethane paints. You get what you pay for. (3) Don't skimp on application tools. For the highest quality finish, I recommend a synthetic soft-woven roller cover such as Purdy's White Dove series, and a nylon/polyester brush.

MEET THE EXPERT
Rick Watson has been with Sherwin-Williams for 32 years and is the director of product information and technical services.

LEARN TO PAINT LIKE A PRO

Tools and tips for a flawless paint job

BY JAY CORK

Bryan Alft is a lifelong painter. It's in his blood; the Alft family has been in the business since 1948. Bryan learned the tricks of the trade working side by side with his grandfather, his father and his uncles. Collectively, they've seen all the trends, innovations and silly ideas come and go. Now a business owner himself, Bryan sat down with me and shared some of his best tips.

ALWAYS ROLL WITH AN EXTENSION HANDLE Even when you don't need the extra reach, using an extension on your roller will give you greater leverage and more control. Bryan prefers poles that are extendable; they can be easily adjusted for any situation.

MEET THE EXPERT
Bryan Alft, a pro painter since 1995, is the owner of Shipshape Interior Painting.

Bryan's tool kit

Bryan paints every day—he needs tools he can rely on. Here's what he brings to every jobsite:

SMALL LED FLASHLIGHT
It will help you find those little imperfections on the wall.

WIRE BRUSH
Great for cleaning dried paint off paintbrushes.

SCRAPER
This scraper will clean roller covers, open paint cans, spread spackling paste, remove old paint and more!

ROLLER SCREEN
Hang it in a 5-gallon bucket of paint for an instant roller tray.

ROLLER COVER CANISTER
Attach a hose to this canister and clean the roller cover the easy way.

PRESS'N SEAL
Wrap this around your roller covers or brushes to keep the paint fresh for later.

MINI ROLLER PAIL
This dual-purpose pail can be used as a handheld bucket for brushing.

SANDER/ MOP ATTACHMENT
A must-have tool! First use it to sand, then put the mophead on to clean the surface.

BRUSH AND ROLLER SPINNER
This tool dries your roller covers and brushes without damaging them.

PAIL HOOK
Be hands-free on the ladder! Clip this to the handle of a paint bucket, then hang it from a ladder rung.

SHERWIN-WILLIAMS MINI ROLLER
The mini roller is great for spot touch-ups, getting into tight spaces and painting cabinets.

PAINT REMOVER
Drips happen. If not caught right away, a little paint remover can save the day.

REPAIR PATCHES
Self-adhesive wall patches simplify and speed up repairs to damaged walls.

SHERWIN-WILLIAMS CAULK GUN
This caulk gun is both ergonomic and rugged.

PAINTING

Bryan's tips for a perfect finish

PAINT ALL THE TRIM FIRST

Bryan paints the trim first in most situations. This allows him to do it faster, but also makes it easier to sand the first coat without being concerned about hitting the walls. It also allows him to caulk the trim to the wall (see the next tip) to get a perfect line.

BETTER TAPE FOR BETTER PAINT LINES

Tapes like FrogTape and 3M Edge-Lock are formulated to seal the edge when it's exposed to the moisture in the paint. But occasionally a little paint still seeps in. After masking natural wood, Bryan pre-seals the tape with a clear water-based urethane. Even if the poly bleeds in a little, it will be invisible. The same goes for masking an area where two different colors meet: Use the paint color that's underneath the tape to pre-seal the edge, and you'll get a perfect paint line.

MASK AND CAULK TO HIDE GAPS

Often there are gaps between the top of the base molding and the wall. Bryan has a great trick for this situation. Tape the base molding, and then run a small bead of caulk along the top of the base and the wall. Using your finger, remove as much caulk as possible, leaving only what fills the gaps. Paint the wall and remove the masking tape as you normally would. No more gaps!

SAVE TIME BY MASKING THE BASE

Even if you're good at "cutting in" with a brush, painting along the baseboard takes more time than masking. Besides eliminating the need to cut in, 2-in.-wide tape shields against roller splatter.

COVER TOUGH STAINS

There are many stain blockers on the shelf, so I asked Bryan which he uses. He always has a quart of Zinsser BIN on the job, which in his experience does a great job and dries fast. He said that oil-based stain blockers do a better job of covering stains than water-based products, but they can also be harder to work with because of the fumes. Always work in a well-ventilated area when you use oil-based stain blockers.

PREP WITH SANDPAPER, NOT LIQUID

Liquid surface conditioners and deglossing products claim to "etch" the surface to improve bonding. They seem like a quick fix, but sandpaper does the job without nasty chemicals. For some hard-to-sand profiles or shapes, a liquid surface conditioner may be the best option, but use it with care; always do a small test to see how it affects the surface you're preparing.

MAKE TOUCH-UPS DISAPPEAR

Even if you use paint from the same can, touch-ups sometimes stand out from the surrounding paint. But for walls, here's a technique to help blend them in: Dab paint in the center of the patch and move it outward in a circular motion, feathering the paint into the surrounding color. Wait until the paint dries to see if you need to go over it again. You shouldn't expect an absolute perfect match, but it's easier than repainting the entire wall! To help blend the color, thin the paint with a little water before you paint the repair.

SPOT FLAWS WITH A LITTLE LIGHT

Raking light across any surface highlights little flaws, so in addition to his movable light stand, Bryan uses a small hand-held LED light. It can reveal small surface imperfections that a central light source might miss or even hide.

■ DO I HAVE TO USE PRIMER?

At times Bryan uses a full coat of primer, such as when he's working on new drywall or large repairs. For smaller areas, he'll use a trick called self-priming—that is, spot-priming with the top-coat paint instead of a dedicated primer. I also asked Bryan about the primer/paint-in-one formulations, and he said since they always apply at least two coats of paint, there is no need.

■ THINK TWICE BEFORE SPRAYING

Sprayers are an essential tool for Bryan. But unless you're painting a completely empty room in a remodel or new construction, spraying is often more work than painting by hand. You have to mask absolutely everything and wear protective gear. It's also likely you'll need to back-roll (run a roller over the sprayed finish) to achieve an even texture, eliminate runs and improve adhesion. After all that, you've still got to clean the equipment.

■ WATER VS. TSP

While trisodium phosphate (TSP) is a popular choice for cleaning walls before painting, it can leave a residue if not rinsed well. This can mess up your paint job. Bryan finds that a damp rag cleans well. For some situations, like behind a stovetop where there's a buildup of grease, you'll need to break out a degreaser, but water is a pretty amazing cleaner all by itself!

DRY PAINT FASTER WITH A FAN
Getting the air moving will help paint dry faster so you can apply the next coat sooner. Bryan has tried many different fans over the years, but Vornado fans are his favorite. They're quiet, and they move air very effectively. You can get one for about $130 online.

LED WORKLIGHT
Utilitech Worklights are versatile, rugged and, at $130, won't break the bank.

WIDE PAINT BUCKET
Wider rollers need wider buckets. Bryan installed some wheels on his bucket.

**1/8"
hole**

SAVE A PAINTBRUSH

If you've fossilized a paintbrush by forgetting to clean it, don't throw it out. Quality paintbrushes aren't cheap, so try to rescue it first.

Pick up a quart of brush cleaner ($7) at a paint or hardware store and pour some into a glass or metal container. Drill a 1/8-in. hole through the brush so you can suspend it by a stiff wire. The brush cleaner gives off nasty, flammable vapors, so cover the container with a plastic bag and set it in the garage or outside, out of reach of children and pets.

After the brush has soaked for a day or two, most of the paint will have come off. Now, pour fresh brush cleaner into another container and slosh the brush around to wash out the remaining paint. Let both containers sit overnight. The paint will settle to the bottom as sludge, so you can pour most of the brush cleaner back into the can, ready to rescue another brush. This method works on oil- or water-based finishes of any type.

**KENT
WASHINGTON**

**Stiff
wire**

NOT GOOD WITH COLORS?

You can no doubt do a better job than this...but if envisioning the perfect color palette for your house is outside your skill set, get expert help from a nearby Sherwin-Williams paint store. For $100, a consultant will come to your house, help you pick colors for the whole house and estimate quantities. Considering the huge impact that color choices have on a home, we think this is a great deal. If your local store isn't offering in-home consultations at this time, you can request a free virtual consultation at sherwin-williams.com/homeowners/color.

WET YOUR BRUSH FOR EASY CLEANUP

After a long painting session, paint builds up and dries on the bristles near the ferrule, and it's tough to clean off. To prevent this, wet the bristles with water before you paint and dab off the excess on a paper towel. For oil-based paints, use paint thinner.

KELLY YURICH

Quick roller tray liner

Put a layer of aluminum foil in your paint tray before you pour in the paint. This makes cleanup and color changes fast and easy.

ZOE WALKER

Paint Preservers

Save leftover paint in mason jars for future touch-ups. A well-sealed jar keeps the paint usable longer than the can does, and it's easier to store. Label the jar with the room the paint was used in.

BERIT THORKELSON

3 Plumbing, HVAC & Appliances

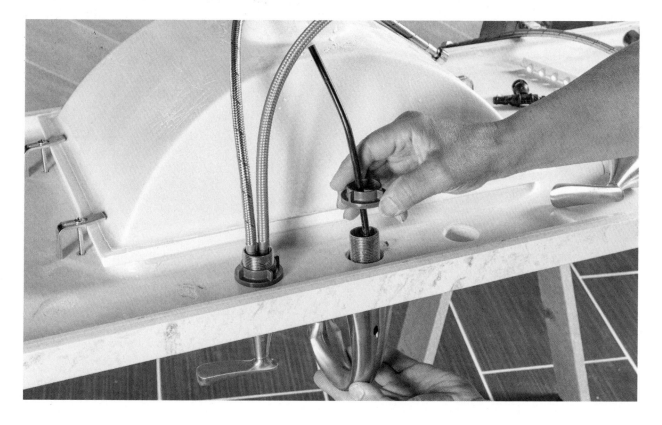

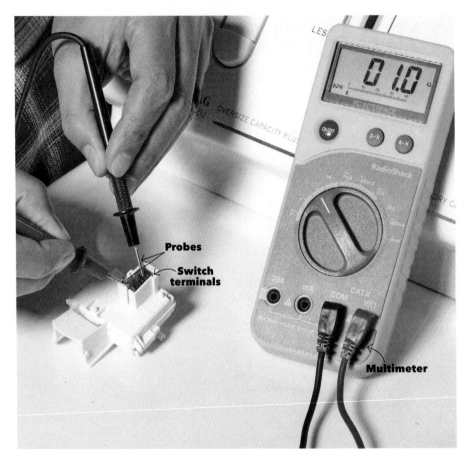

Probes

Switch terminals

Multimeter

Washing machine lid switch

If your washing machine fills but won't spin, check the lid switch. If the switch is bad, your machine won't spin. A new switch is less than $20 and takes minutes to install.

If your switch has a wiring harness, unplug it and test the side of the harness that connects to the switch. If there's no wiring harness, test directly on the switch's terminals.

To test, move your multimeter dial to the lowest ohms setting. Zero the meter, and then touch the probes to the "line" and "machine" terminals. The meter should read zero. Touch the probes to the "line" and "motor" terminals. The meter should again read zero. If it doesn't pass both tests, replace the switch.

QUICK FIX FOR A LEAKY PIPE

If you have a slight leak in a copper pipe joint, you might be able to fix it without disassembling and resoldering. First, shut off the water and drain the pipe. Start heating the joint, brush on some flux and continue applying heat until the solder melts and fills the gap. Let the joint cool, and then turn on the water to test the joint. If it still leaks, you'll have to disassemble and resolder, but you won't have lost much time trying this first. And if it does work, you'll have saved some time!

De-stink your fridge

When your power goes out and the food in your fridge and freezer goes bad, you've got a really stinky mess on your hands. Obviously the first two steps are to remove the food and wipe the interior down with a disinfecting cleaning spray. Then you have to follow that with a thorough cleaning.

The most common mistake DIYers make here is not cleaning all the nooks and crannies inside. Most often overlooked are the shelf supports. Remove them and clean behind them with detergent and disinfectant to get rid of any blood or crud. If they're permanently attached, soak them with cleaning spray. Next, forget about those expensive charcoal odor removers or coffee (which is even more expensive). Just use newspaper and charcoal briquettes. Finally (and this is the most important part), replace the old newspaper and charcoal with fresh stuff every day for about a week or until the smell is gone. A single treatment is rarely enough.

Newspaper

Shelf support

Charcoal briquettes

ABSORB THE ODOR WITH NEWSPAPER AND CHARCOAL
Smash about 12 charcoal briquettes used for grilling and spread the chunks on two trays. One goes in the fridge, the other in the freezer. Then crunch up newspaper and fill the shelves with it. Close the doors and walk away. Repeat every day for a week.

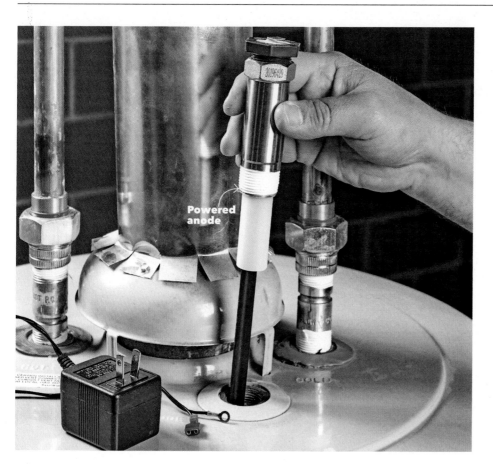

Powered anode

Does your hot water stink?

The smell is caused by hydrogen sulfide gas. This gas is produced in a couple ways. First, your water heater is a nice, warm place for sulfur bacteria to thrive. Second, your water heater is an ideal host for a reaction between sulfate in the water and the water heater anode. If your hot water smells like rotten eggs, you don't have to live with it. Replacing your water heater's standard anode rod with a powered anode ($132 online) should stop that sulfur odor.

THE TROUBLE WITH WHOLE-HOUSE HUMIDIFIERS

Whole-house humidifiers make dry, brutal winters far more comfortable indoors. Unfortunately, if you have a manual humidifier, the problems might outweigh the benefits. With manual humidifiers, you need to know the outdoor temperature hours in advance and adjust the humidity accordingly, every day. Few people actually do this. Most people just select a middle setting and never touch it again. As a result, home inspectors regularly find frost- and mold-covered attics, damaged windows and ruined ceilings.

Automatic whole-house humidifiers, on the other hand, have an outdoor temperature sensor so they can adjust the humidity level for you. If you do have a manual humidifier, either leave it off or do the daily work of keeping it properly adjusted.

REUBEN SALZMAN
HOME INSPECTOR,
STRUCTURETECH1.COM

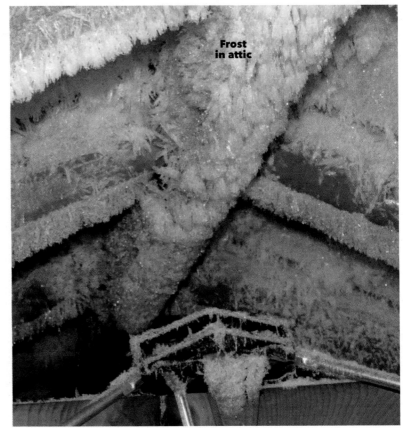

Frost in attic

What's the plastic cap on my hose bib?

Many building codes require hose bibs, also called sillcocks, to include an anti-siphon feature. This feature prevents the formation of a vacuum that could pull water from the outside into the clean water supply. While you can retrofit backflow preventers to standard spigots, frost-proof hose bibs have one built in, and that's what you'll find beneath that plastic cap.

The two main components are a bonnet, or port, and a spring-loaded disc called a poppet. These are sealed with rubber gaskets. Over time, water can leak from under the cap, but the repair for that is simple. Just remove the cap, either by prying it off or unscrewing it, then remove the components inside. Flush the opening to eliminate any debris that could prevent the poppet from sealing tightly. If any parts are broken or missing, replace them using one of the repair kits offered by most manufacturers.

Backflow preventer

Under-Sink Water Filtration

The water you cook with can affect your family's health, so consider installing a filtering system to eliminate pesticides, algae, heavy metals and chlorine. You'll reduce your exposure to toxins and gain peace of mind.

In-line filter or reverse osmosis?

I've always considered reverse osmosis (RO) to be the more effective water treatment system, but it does have some negative aspects. When I had well water, it was certainly the best choice, but RO systems can waste up to 5 gallons of water for every gallon filtered, and they can remove beneficial minerals as well. In the city, where I pay for every gallon used, I wanted to find a better alternative. In recent years, in-line filtration systems have really stepped up their game and boast similar filtration statistics without wasting water.

What's in your water?

A wide variety of organic and inorganic contaminants are a cause for concern, including chloramine or chlorine, water-soluble heavy metals (cadmium, chromium VI, lead, mercury), herbicides, pesticides, sediment, algae, mold and others.

Knowing how your local water is treated is also important when you're choosing a filtration system for your home. If you get city water, call or visit your municipal water provider's website and review the Annual Water Quality Report. This will tell you whether your water is treated with chlorine or chloramine, and if fluoride is added. If you get your water from a well, a whole-home RO system can be a great choice.

JAY CORK, ASSOCIATE EDITOR

Micro sediment membrane

Acid-washed coconut shell activated carbon

Micro sediment membrane

KDF-55 filtration media

Outlet connects to faucet

Inlet connects to cold water supply

NO PLUMBER NEEDED
At about $250, the UC-200 from CuZn is an affordable bacteriostatic filter. Unlike carbon-only filters, bacteriostatic filters don't support bacterial growth. Water is purified selectively, which means it allows beneficial mineral content to remain. It requires virtually no maintenance and installs under the counter in about 10 minutes; you simply hook it up to the cold-water supply. Visit CuZn.com to find a solution that fits your needs.

REPLACE A TUB SPOUT

Bathtub spouts can go bad in three ways: First, the diverter can wear out so it no longer blocks the water flow or sends water to the shower-head. Second, the threads inside the spout can crack or corrode where the spout screws onto the pipe. Water can then trickle along the pipe and drip inside the wall. Finally, the spout's finish can flake off or corrode.

Replacement is the solution to any of these problems. A new spout ($20 to $40) and everything else you might need are available at hardware stores and home centers. But before you buy a new spout, determine what type you need. First look under the spout. If you see a setscrew (**Photo A**), you have a "slip-on" spout. The setscrew might be smaller and harder to see than the one shown here; you may need a flashlight to spot it.

Replacing a slip-on spout is easy: Just loosen the setscrew (usually with a hex wrench) and pull the spout off the copper pipe that protrudes from the wall. Twist the spout as you pull and be gentle so you don't loosen any pipe connections inside the wall. Then slide on the new spout and tighten the setscrew.

If the spout doesn't have a set-screw, it's a screw-on spout (**Photos B** and **C**). Twist the old spout counterclockwise to remove it. If the pipe that protrudes from the wall is copper with a threaded fit-ting (**Photo B**), simply cut off the fit-ting with a tubing cutter ($10) and install a new slip-on spout (**Photo A**). If the pipe coming out of the wall is steel (**Photo C**), you need a new screw-on spout.

Ideally, the new spout will fit per-fectly onto the old pipe. But there's a good chance that the pipe pro-trudes too far or not far enough. There's also a chance that the threads are too corroded for you to screw on a new spout. Either way, you'll have to remove the old pipe (**Photo 1**) and screw in a new pipe of the correct length (**Photo 2**). Short sections of threaded pipe (called "nipples") are usually avail-able in 1-in. increments. They cost less than $5 each, so buy a couple of different lengths and save your-self a trip back to the store.

A Slip-on spouts slide over 1/2-in. copper pipe and fasten with a setscrew. This "universal" version also has threads inside, so it can screw onto threaded pipe.

B Screw-on spouts have threads deep inside. They can connect to a copper threaded fitting or to steel pipe.

C Screw-on spouts may have threads at the back end. Most come with a bushing so they fit either 1/2-in. or 3/4-in. pipe.

TIP: Leg-shaving can lead to tub spout trouble. The spout makes a conve-nient footrest for shaving, but that can damage the diverter or loosen pipe connections. The rim of the tub or a stool makes a much better footrest.

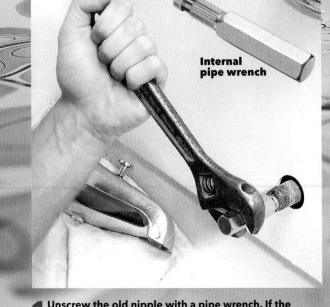

1 Unscrew the old nipple with a pipe wrench. If the nipple is too short to grab with a wrench, use an "internal" pipe wrench ($12).

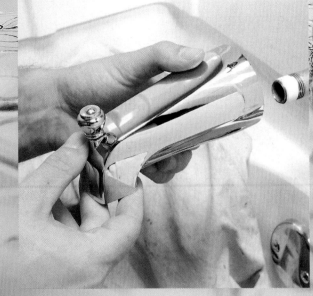

2 Wrap both ends of the new nipple with thread tape and screw it into the fitting inside the wall. Seal around it with silicone caulk and screw on the new spout.

22 INSTANT HEATING & A/C FIXES

Even a beginner can solve common problems—and save money!

BY BRAD HOLDEN

When your heating and cooling system isn't working properly, you might throw up your hands and call for help, thinking that whatever the problem is, solving it must be outside your skill set. Well, you might be surprised: The most common problems have simple solutions. Here are 22 extremely easy fixes that take minutes or less and can save you a wad of cash.

How's your filter?

A dirty filter causes your system to work harder, resulting in premature failure of parts. A dirty filter can also cause a shutdown. How often your filters need changing depends on many factors. Do you live in a high-traffic zone? Do you have pets? Do you leave the windows open? Write the date on your filter to help keep track of when it needs to be changed. Don't forget about furnace filters in the summer. They're also for the A/C.

MEET THE EXPERT
Tim Adams is the service manager at Standard Heating & Air Conditioning in Minneapolis.

Start at the thermostat

Most thermostats have a switch so you can set the system to "heat" or "cool." Make sure yours is set to the proper function.

Check the circuit breaker

A breaker can trip without fully moving to the "off" position, so flip it to the "off" position, and then back to "on," to be sure that's not the issue.

Run a quick power test

To see if the furnace is getting power, set your thermostat to the "fan" position. If you don't hear the fan turn on, there's a good chance there's no power to the furnace. If there's power to the furnace, it's time to check the furnace itself.

Check inside the furnace

New furnaces have fault codes, like cars. Check for codes or flashing lights, then look in your owner's manual or online to diagnose the problem. If you can't decipher the code or don't want to bother with it, send a video to the repair technician. It's helpful for the tech to know what the problem might be before coming out.

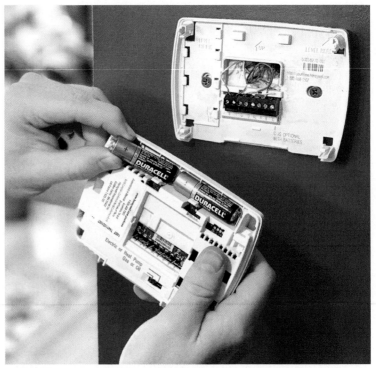

Replace thermostat batteries

If your thermostat doesn't seem to be working, try changing the batteries. They typically need to be replaced annually. After you've replaced the batteries, your thermostat might revert to its default settings and need to be reprogrammed.

Clean the igniter

Hot surface igniters are the most common ignition system on modern furnaces. They take the place of standing pilot lights and electronic igniters. Clean the dust off the hot surface igniter by leaving the igniter in place and blowing air through a straw. This part breaks very easily; don't even touch it. In fact, when you replace the furnace cover panels, do so gently to avoid breaking the igniter.

Pilot light

Clean the pilot

A dirty pilot can cause the flame sensor (or thermocouple) to get a false reading indicating the pilot isn't lit. Clean it off with a blast of air. Direct air to the exact spot with a drinking straw. Newer furnaces have hot surface igniters instead of pilots and electronic igniters.

Check the condensate pump

If you have a condensate pump, listen closely to make sure it runs. If not, try resetting the GFCI outlet that powers it. If that doesn't work, you may need a new pump (about $60).

Check for power

A furnace has a power switch nearby, often right on its housing. It looks just like a light switch. Check to make sure this switch hasn't inadvertently been switched to the "off" position.

Furnace access panel

Safety switch

Check the safety switch

Furnace cover panels often activate a safety switch when the panel is removed or left even slightly ajar. Check to see that the panel is fully closed.

CLOSED   OPEN

Is the gas valve on?

Find the gas line for your furnace, then find the valve. The valve's handle should be parallel to the gas line. If it's perpendicular, there's no gas going to the furnace.

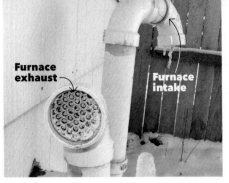

Furnace exhaust

Furnace intake

Check airflow

On the outside of your house, you may have a couple PVC pipes sticking out of the wall. One points downward (furnace air intake) and one points horizontally or upward (furnace exhaust). Drifting snow, ice buildup or nesting animals can block one or both of these pipes, causing a high-efficiency furnace to shut down.

Makeup air duct

Can your furnace breathe?

Your furnace room is likely supplied with a "makeup air" duct. It's a large, flexible, insulated duct that probably drops into a bucket. This duct supplies your house with fresh air to replace oxygen lost in combustion. Because furnace rooms often double as storage areas, it's easy to inadvertently block that duct. If it's blocked, kinked or squashed, it can cause your furnace to shut down, as there's no oxygen for combustion and it won't ignite. Typically, this isn't a big problem in old, drafty homes, but in new, super-insulated homes, it can be an issue.

A humidifier can cause your furnace filter to clog

If you use a portable humidifier, always use distilled water to fill it. Non-distilled water can cause a calcium buildup on your furnace filter and completely clog it in a matter of days. The buildup is white, so a white filter will still look clean when it's actually clogged.

Make sure water can drain

High-efficiency furnaces collect water as a by-product of combustion. In cooling mode, your A/C collects water from the air. In either case, that water needs to drain away. If not, your furnace will leak water or just shut down. First, make sure water is dripping from the end of the tubing when the system is running. If you don't see drips, clear the line by blowing through it with your mouth. Don't use a compressor; too much pressure can blow connections apart.

Check for blocked registers

Have you noticed large temperature swings in certain rooms or an unusually short furnace cycle time? Make sure there's nothing blocking the air returns. Returns pull air out of the room and back to the furnace, while supply registers blow air into the room. You can check the return airflow by holding a piece of paper against the return register. The paper should stick to the register. If it doesn't, there's an airflow problem.

Adjust the damper

If your heating ducts also serve as air conditioning ducts, they likely have dampers that require adjusting for seasonal changes. The seasonal settings should be marked on the duct. Two-story homes often have separate supply trunks to serve the upstairs and downstairs. To send more warm air downstairs (winter setting) or more cold air upstairs (summer setting), adjust the damper handle on each supply trunk.

Check for mice and other pests

Your condenser has an access panel behind which you'll find the wiring and connections. Because this is an outdoor unit, it's often an appealing residence for critters. After shutting off power at the breaker, remove the access panel and check for broken or chewed wires. Replace them as needed.

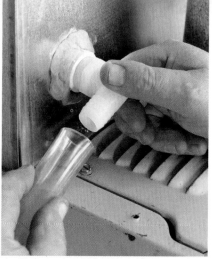

Does it seem like the A/C isn't working?

Condensation in your A/C attracts dust. When the condensation flows out the drain line, that dust can plug the line. Check the end of the drain line to see if water is coming out. If not, blow the line clear. Usually lung power is sufficient. Compressed air may cause something unseen to come apart. Also, remove the cap from the evaporator coil and clean out the tube with your finger.

Investigate your A/C's condenser unit

Is your A/C blowing air, but not cold air? Does the condenser seem louder than usual? If it's having to work too hard, it may just shut off. The condenser coil, located inside the outdoor unit, is probably dirty. To clean it, spray off the condenser coil. Don't use high pressure. Put your thumb over the end of the garden hose or use a sprayer nozzle. More pressure than that can bend the fins. The cleaning schedule for condenser coils—like the timing of filter changes—depends on environmental conditions. Cottonwood seeds can blanket your condenser coil in a day. Make a habit of cleaning the coil regularly.

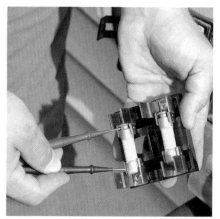

Check fuses in the disconnect block

These fuses are typically located in a box mounted to the house near the condenser. Set your multimeter to the lowest Ohms value and touch the red and black leads to opposite ends of each fuse. If you get a numerical reading, the fuse is good. But a zero, a minus symbol or an infinity symbol (∞) indicates a blown fuse.

Take your old fuses along to the home center to verify that the new ones match. Replacing a fuse can get you up and running again quickly, but if your unit regularly blows fuses, there's something else wrong with your system.

WHY PLUMBING NEEDS AIR

Understanding the dynamics of indoor plumbing

BY GARY WENTZ

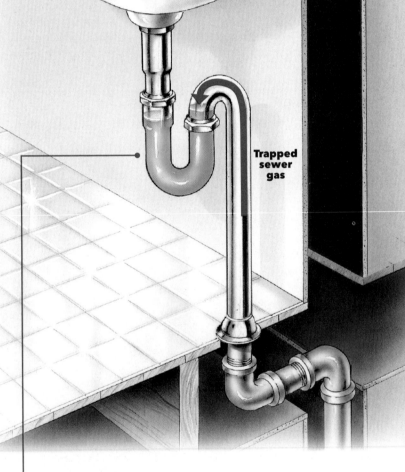

Trapped sewer gas

Your plumbing system is mostly made up of pipes that carry water or waste. That's easy to understand. But what about those "vent" pipes that just carry air? To understand them, let's return to the early days of indoor plumbing …

The answer begins with sewer gas, the smelly, unhealthy mix of vapors inside the sewer lines. If not blocked, sewer gas will waft up through drains and stink up the whole house.

Plumbing pioneers discovered this problem early on—and struggled to find a good solution.

1775: the S-trap

A bent pipe—brilliant! In 1775, Scottish inventor Alexander Cummings dreamed up the S-trap, which holds water and blocks sewer gas. But the S-shape also allows flowing water to create a siphon effect, which can suck water out of the trap, leaving a path for sewer gas. The solution was to manually refill the trap slowly so the siphon effect wouldn't occur. That was inconvenient. And if you forgot, you'd get a stinky reminder.

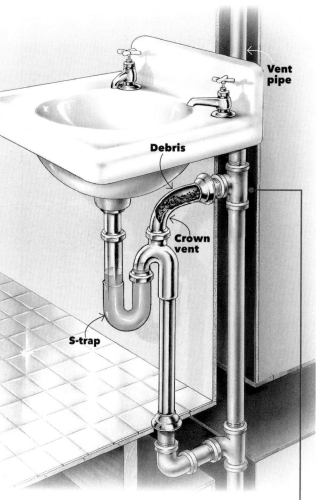

1880: Venting invented

About 1880, plumbers began adding a "crown vent" to the S-trap. The crown vent was connected to vent pipes that ran up through the roof. This allowed air into the S-trap, breaking the suction of the siphon effect. Water would remain in the trap, and sewer gas was blocked. But only temporarily. The problem with crown vents was that waste would often flow up into them and leave debris behind. Eventually, that debris would plug the vent.

1920s: The P-trap triumphs

By the 1920s, most vents were just upward extensions of the drainpipe, as shown here. The trap morphed from an "S" to a "P" shape. This configuration prevented the siphon effect just as well as a crown vent but didn't get clogged by debris. Plus, it was simpler to install. Today, only P-traps are allowed by plumbing codes, with one exception: Toilets contain a built-in S-trap. Therefore, urine passes through an S-trap rather than a P-trap. Plumbing irony.

Skip the vent pipes?

Installing a network of vent pipes running up through the roof is expensive and labor-intensive. But there is an easy alternative: an air admittance valve. AAVs let air in but not out, breaking the siphon effect without stinking up your house. And they cost only $15 to $40. But here's the catch: Your local plumbing code may allow an AAV under specific circumstances only or not at all. Check with your building inspector.

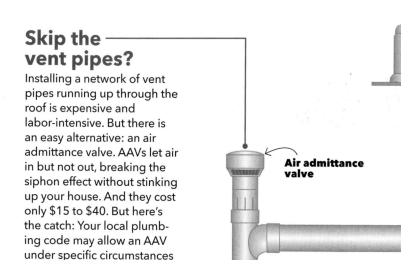

TIPS FOR AN EASY
FAUCET INSTALL

How to get a leak-free faucet with less stress

BY BILL BERGMANN

The instructions in the box with a new faucet tell you everything you need to know for a normal installation. Trouble is, there's no such thing as a normal installation. Every job has its complications.

To get the solutions to the most common problems, I sat down with a pro plumber who faces these faucet situations every day. Use these expert tips to make your faucet replacement an easy half-day job instead of an all-day ordeal.

MEET THE EXPERT
Joe Barnes is a second-generation master plumber with three decades of experience.

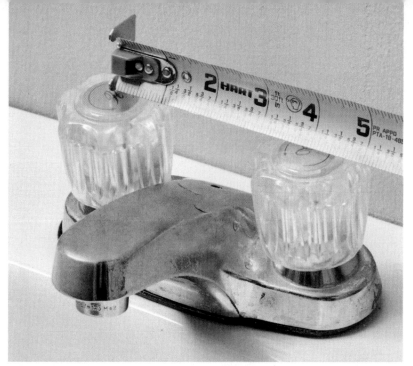

LOW-FLOW PROBLEMS?

If your faucet has weak pressure or flow, a new faucet probably isn't the solution. Here's how Joe tracks down the source of the trouble:

■ If both the hot and the cold are weak, the aerator is probably clogged. Simply remove it and clean it to solve the problem.

■ If either the hot or the cold (but not both) is weak, then faulty supply lines, shutoffs or supply pipes are the problem. Supply hoses or shut-off valves are easy enough to replace. Fixing faulty or antiquated plumbing is a larger job, but it can benefit other fixtures in the home that have low water pressure.

Measure before you shop

Before you choose a new faucet, check the configuration and spacing on your sink. If you have a three-hole configuration, measure from the center of each handle to determine your spacing. Standard spacing is typically 4 or 8 in. If you want a single-hole faucet but your sink includes three holes, no problem. Many faucets include a cover plate to conceal the other two holes.

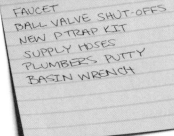

FAUCET
BALL VALVE SHUT-OFFS
NEW P TRAP KIT
SUPPLY HOSES
PLUMBERS PUTTY
BASIN WRENCH

Basin wrench

Ridgid EZ Change Faucet Tool

Get everything you need

When you go to pick up your new faucet, bring a list of every possible install item you could need. Joe says if he's headed to a job he hasn't seen, he'll be sure to have every potential part on board beforehand. One trip to return a few things is far easier than multiple runs for the stuff you thought you wouldn't need.

Get a basin wrench

A basin wrench ($15) gets at impossible-to-reach nuts below the faucet. Joe uses a basic version of this tool, but many plumbers like Ridgid's EZ Change Faucet Tool ($22). It will reach those difficult nuts and handle just about any other fitting you might encounter during a faucet install.

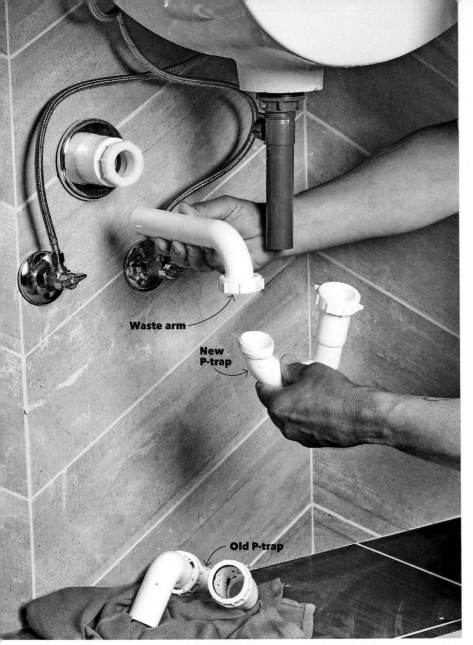

Waste arm

New
P-trap

Old P-trap

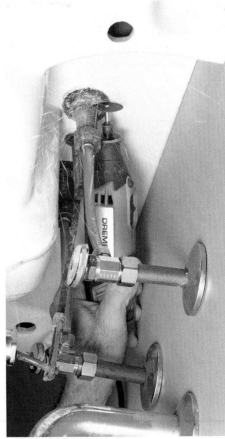

Replace your P-trap

Make space under the sink by taking out the P-trap. Reusing an old P-trap can be a messy ordeal, so Joe usually includes a new trap assembly on his installs. The cost of a plastic P-trap kit is less than $5, and you'll get peace of mind knowing all those fittings are new and clean. Keep in mind that most bath sink drains are 1-1/4 in., and kitchen sink drains 1-1/2 in. Joe sees a new P-trap as cheap insurance against callbacks.

Old supply line

New supply line

Replace your supply lines

Never reuse old supply lines. The last thing you want is water damage from a failed supply line. Even if the hoses are newer looking, Joe will replace them because the rubber washers can fail over time. Quality supply lines with a braided stainless steel casing may cost a bit more (about $8 each), but they're well worth it.

Cut stubborn connections

If you find rusted mounting nuts or other petrified connections that won't budge, go ahead and cut them. An oscillating tool or rotary tool with a metal-cutting blade works well for this.

Install the faucet first

If you're installing a new sink, mount the faucet to the sink before dropping the sink into place. Having everything in plain view always makes for better connections—and the less time you spend on your back under that sink, the better.

TEST THE SHUTOFFS

Almost every faucet is connected to shutoff valves beneath the sink. But those old valves often don't work, and it's best to know that before you begin. If your shutoffs don't stop the water flow, you can repair them or replace them. Or you could turn off the water to the whole house at the main shutoff valve while you replace the faucet. For help with those jobs, search for "shutoff" at familyhandyman.com.

Clean off your sink deck

To ensure a good seal between the sink and the new faucet, be sure to clean up the footprint of the old faucet. Scouring powder works well for soap scum and crud. For tougher lime or rust deposits, a pumice stone is the best remedy.

Pumice stone

Use plumber's putty

Some manufacturers suggest using silicone caulk to seal a faucet or drain, but beware: It can be difficult to apply and can stain natural stone. Joe prefers plumber's putty. It's easier to work with, and the non-staining variety won't leave blemishes. He also says it's far easier to repair a faucet assembly that was installed with putty. Silicone is as much an adhesive as it is a sealant and can make pulling things apart a pain.

Get leakproof connections

Each connection requires a different amount of torque to tighten. Over-tightening the slip nuts on a plastic waste line can strip the threads and make for a leaky connection. Always hand-tighten these connections. For flexible supply lines, the standard recommendation is to get them finger tight, then give them a quarter turn with a wrench. But Joe gives them a half turn and has never had an issue.

Don't skimp on the Teflon tape

A 40-ft. roll of Teflon tape costs about a buck, so don't be stingy with it. Make sure you wrap all your threaded connections clockwise several times. When you thread on that nut, it should feel tight, and the clockwise wrap will keep the tape from unraveling as you tighten the connection. Joe also wraps the threads for supply hoses even though they have a self-sealing rubber washer. Teflon tape is just more cheap insurance against any leaks, so don't skimp.

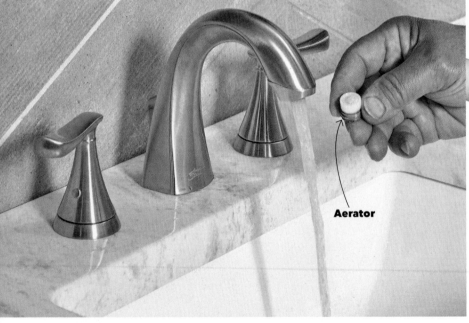

Aerator

Remove the aerator and flush out sediment

Plumbing work knocks sediment loose inside pipes. Be sure that sediment doesn't clog your aerator or valves. Joe always removes the aerator and then lets both the hot and the cold run for a minute to flush the lines before reinstalling the aerator.

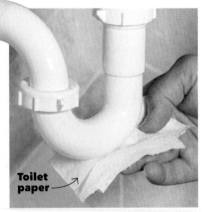

Toilet paper

The final step: Check for leaks

Once everything is connected and your water is back on, do a thorough leak check. Wipe it all down with a dry rag, and then blot your connections with toilet paper to see if there is any evidence of a slow leak.

14 COMMON PLUMBING CODE *VIOLATIONS*

A plumbing inspector helps you keep it legal

BY JAY CORK

I t's tempting to think of plumbing code as a collection of irritating rules that make projects more complicated. I'm guilty of this sometimes, but I also know that the code is a guide to good results, developed by thousands of experts over the course of more than a century. Ignoring it can result in leaks, damage, clogs, delays when you sell your home, or even an explosion.

When DIYers violate code, it's usually because they don't know the code. To help with that, we brought in plumbing inspector Eldon Rameaux to help us better understand the Uniform Plumbing Code (UPC) and to identify some common plumbing code violations. Here's what we learned.

WHAT IS CODE ANYWAY?

The UPC, or Uniform Plumbing Code, is basically a rule book for creating safe, reliable plumbing systems. It's updated every three years with input from the public, manufacturers and industry experts. State and local building departments then use it as a guide to write their own plumbing codes. Some simply accept the entire UPC as is, while others pick and choose which rules to adopt. These local codes—not the UPC—determine what you can and can't do on your next project.

MEET THE EXPERT
Eldon Rameaux is a journeyman plumber and plumbing inspector.

Don't cap your TPR valve

The temperature pressure relief (TPR) valve is one of the most important safety devices in your home. It releases excess pressure and prevents the water heater from exploding. But here's what sometimes happens: The valve releases some water because of high pressure, or it just leaks as it ages. To "fix" the drip, a homeowner then plugs or caps the TPR. And BOOM!

This wye fitting creates an S-trap—use a sanitary tee fitting instead

Beware the S-Trap

An S-trap is formed when the waste line curves down after the trap. That can create a siphon effect that sucks water out of the trap and allows sewer gas to flow up into the home. S-traps were commonplace in older homes. Today, they're sometimes created by accident, usually by using a wye fitting after the trap.

A SUMP PUMP CANNOT DRAIN TO THE SEWER LINE

Piping your sump pump into a plumbing drain is an easy way to get rid of water. But don't use the sewer line for this. Sending extra water to your local sewage treatment plant can get you in big trouble.

A CLEANOUT CANNOT BE USED AS A DRAIN

Some homeowners will use the cleanout as a drain for a basement toilet. This eliminates the only access to the main sewer line and becomes a major problem should a blockage occur. Keep the sewer cleanout properly capped, and only open it if you need to clear an obstruction.

Increase vent size at the roofline

In the winter, ice can actually form inside the vent that goes through the roof. If the vent is too small, it can easily become blocked. Avoid this in colder climates by using a 3-in.-diameter vent pipe.

PVC vs. CPVC

PVC and CPVC look alike and both are available at home centers. But don't get them mixed up. CPVC (chlorinated polyvinyl chloride) is code compliant for indoor water supply lines. PVC (polyvinyl chloride) isn't. CPVC is available in either standard NPS (nominal pipe size) or CTS (copper tube size).

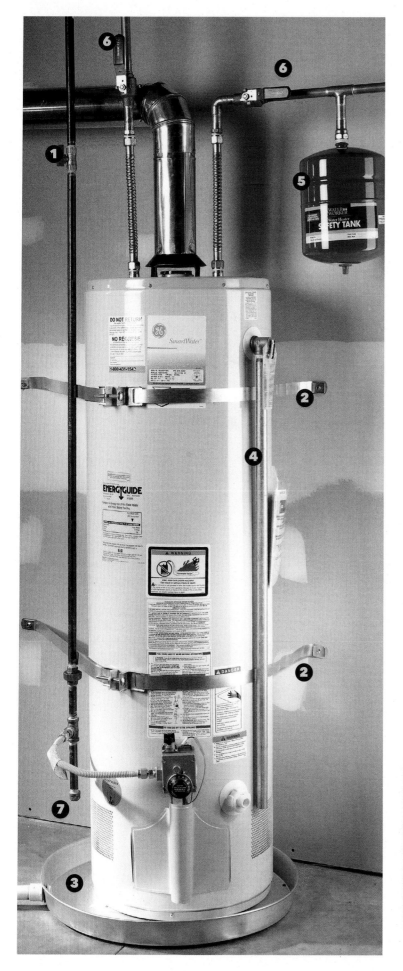

THE RULES FOR WATER HEATERS

1. GAS SHUTOFF
Code requires a gas valve near the water heater.

2. EARTHQUAKE STRAPS
These straps will prevent a water heater from shifting or tipping over and are required in earthquake-prone regions.

3. OVERFLOW PAN
It may not be required in all regions, but installing an overflow pan is a good idea for any location.

4. BLOW TUBE
The "blow tube" directs the scalding hot water that is released by the TPR valve toward the floor. The required distance between the blow tube and the floor is 18 in. or less.

5. EXPANSION TANK
If your home has a pressure regulator at the water main, a thermal expansion tank is also required. The tank may be installed vertically anywhere between the regulator and the water heater; however, it must have an additional support if it's installed horizontally.

6. ISOLATION VALVE
Code requires a valve on the incoming cold water line. A valve on the hot water line is not required, but installing one makes future water heater replacement much easier.

7. DRIP LEG
Any dust or grit in the gas line falls into this short section of pipe before it can reach the water heater's control valve. The required length of the drip leg varies.

CHECK WITH YOUR LOCAL INSPECTOR
The information in this article is based on the Uniform Plumbing Code, but local codes aren't always uniform; they can differ from one municipality to the next. So always check with your local building department.

Air-gap valve

Standard elbow

You might need an air-gap valve

Although the UPC calls for an air-gap valve between a dishwasher and the drain, many plumbers dislike these and some inspectors don't enforce this. Your local code may vary, so double-check with your plumbing inspector to be sure.

Changes in direction

When changing direction of drainage flow, the fittings allowed by code depend on the type of transition being made. Standard elbows are allowed only on horizontal to vertical transitions. Horizontal to horizontal or vertical to horizontal require a "long-turn" elbow.

VENTING NEEDS TO SLOPE, TOO

The purpose of plumbing vents is to carry air. But rain-water enters the vents on your roof, and condensation occurs in pipes. That's why vents have to slope down and drain into pipes below.

Choose the right rubber couplers

You've likely seen these black rubber couplers with a band clamp on each end. They seem great for odd plumbing situations, but they're also against code. Only fully sleeved fittings are approved and only for certain situations (see "Don't Glue PVC to ABS" below).

DON'T GLUE PVC TO ABS

Yes, a special glue is sold in the plumbing section of your hardware store for this purpose, but it's a code violation to join black ABS and white PVC plastics by solvent-welding. A fully sleeved transition coupling is the best way to get this done and remain code compliant.

Push-to-connect fitting

Never use saddle valves!

Saddle valves may seem like a remarkably handy invention, but they're trouble! When (not if) they start to leak, the damage caused can certainly outweigh the cost of installing a proper tee in the first place. If you're not up to soldering a new tee connection for your new ice maker, use a push-to-connect tee fitting made by SharkBite or Blue Hawk (as shown above).

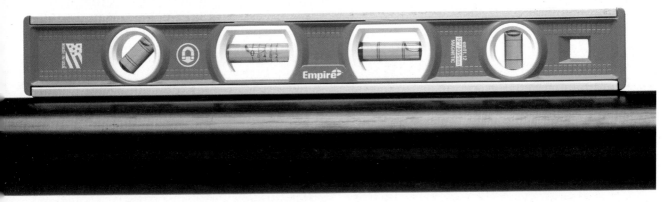

Proper drain slope is crucial

Drain slope that is less than 1/8 in. per foot, or more than 1/2 in. per foot, is a code violation. Aim for 1/4 in. per foot and you can't go wrong. Slope is easy to check with a spirit level.

VINTAGE
CAMPER
REVIVAL

HOW A SHABBY OLD TRAILER BECAME A SHOWPIECE

BY JAY CORK

For decades, the July/August issue of *Family Handyman* has focused on a yard shed project. But this year, we took on a different challenge, inspired by a daydream. Have you ever looked at an old, neglected thing and envisioned what it could be? That's how I felt when I first saw our camper. I looked past the dents and rust, the flat tires and the dull, oxidized aluminum.

Instead, I saw a mint-condition trailer rolling down the road, a traveling showpiece that would really turn heads. What's more, I imagined the freedom of a home on wheels. Go anywhere, anytime. Independent travel.

That freedom can come with a big price tag. A new camper of this size costs at least $20,000 and often twice that much. We got this relic for less than $7,000

and spent about the same on rehab. Not bad. But the real success goes way beyond economics. We got the best of old and new: a completely rehabbed camper, with a vintage style all its own; a little piece of history that grabs attention on the road and at campsites.

VINTAGE CAMPER REVIVAL

After almost 50 years outdoors in the sun, snow and rain, every exterior surface of this camper needed work.

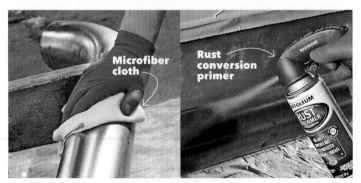

Coal slag

Pressure washer

▲ SANDBLASTING—WITH WATER

To remove old paint and rust, I first considered sandblasting. But that requires a big air compressor and creates a huge, dusty mess. So I gave "vapor blasting" a try. Like sandblasting, vapor blasting pummels a surface with sand or other abrasive media. But vapor blasting relies on water from a pressure washer rather than air. That reduces the mess and takes advantage of a tool you may already own. I tried a generic pressure washer vapor blasting kit ($30 online), and I learned three key things:

■ Match the gun to your pressure washer. There are different sizes available, with specific psi ratings. The pressure washer psi rating must match the range of the kit; the first one I bought, for $120, was too large and wouldn't function with my 2,700 psi pressure washer.

■ A bigger pressure washer is better. My 2,700 psi machine worked, but it was slow. A system in the range of 5,000 to 7,000 psi would produce results much faster.

■ Weight and size of the media make a difference. I tried three types of blast media before finding one that worked well. The coarse coal slag from Tractor Supply Co. ($10 for 50 lbs.) did the trick.

A CHANGE OF PLANS

My first plan was to restore the aluminum exterior to its original gleam. I talked to experts, amassed an arsenal of polishing gear and began experimenting. I was able to achieve a mirror-like shine, but progress was incredibly slow. Our schedule simply didn't allow for it.

So I searched for paint that would form a tough, shiny surface. The answer turned out to be easy: alkyd paint. Water-based acrylic paints are best for most DIY jobs, but old-fashioned oil-based alkyds generally level out better and form a harder film. Spraying paint in our work-space would be too messy, so I tried rolling. The results were great and better than spraying in one way: The slight texture left by the roller hid small dents and scratches.

Siphon wand

Vapor blasting attachment

Microfiber cloth

Rust conversion primer

▲ PREVENT "FLASH RUST"

Prepping steel for paint is a lot of work, so here's something you need to know: Moisture in the air will quickly cause "flash rust" on bare steel, and it might not even be visible. This will come back to haunt you after the paint has been applied. To prevent that, I immediately wiped everything down with denatured alcohol and then sprayed it all with a black rust conversion primer.

◀ PREP ALUMINUM FOR PAINT

This camper was dirty! If I wanted my paint job to last, I needed to thoroughly clean the surface. I tried soap and water, TSP and even muriatic acid, but they were completely ineffective against the camper's decades of exposure. Sold as a cleaner for aluminum watercraft, JJV's Best Aluminum Cleaner ($47 online) did an excellent job of preparing this old, anodized aluminum for paint.

It really helps having two people for this process. We used a spray bottle to apply the full-strength cleaner, and let it sit for 10 minutes. Then, with an industrial scrub brush, we worked the cleaner around as evenly as possible, spraying more where needed. Finally, using the fine spray setting on the nozzle, we rinsed it off with water.

Painting with a spray rig would have provided the smoothest finish, but that wasn't an option in our work- space. So I went with the next best approach and selected paint and tools that would give a smooth, tough finish.

▲ ADD A CATALYST

I used oil-based alkyd paint because it levels out well and forms a tougher finish than most water-based paints. I chose Krylon Farm and Implement paint ($40 a gallon at O'Reilly Auto). To make the paint even more durable and to speed curing, I added Krylon's cata- lyst hardener ($18 online).

Catalyst/ hardener

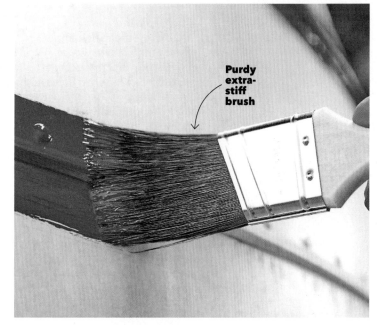

Purdy extra- stiff brush

▲ BRUSH, THEN ROLL

I brushed paint onto spots that the roller would miss, then imme- diately ran over them with the roller for a consistent texture. This paint is thick, so I chose an extra-stiff brush with natural bristles.

WEEKEND PAINTING PARTY

Our workspace was in a shop that produces concrete sinks and countertops—and tons of dust. To avoid painting while the concrete guys were stirring up a storm, I drafted a crew for a weekend painting marathon.

Getting it right would take some choreography: careful brushing around trim, then quickly rolling those areas to minimize texture mismatches. And we'd have to do it all twice for complete coverage. When we all got into the groove, our gray camper turned red fast. Two coats took less than six hours.

When we stepped back and looked at our work, there was a long silence, but then someone said what we were all thinking: "Red is so much better than polished aluminum!"

Yep. Just wish I'd known that before sinking so many hours into polishing experiments.

ENDLESS EXTERIOR DETAILS

We upgraded all the exterior lights to new LEDs, refurbished the name plates, installed a toolbox in the trailer's tongue... But the whitewall tires are my favorite detail. They cost four times as much as blackwall trailer tires, but the classic look was worth every penny.

▲ QUALITY ROLLERS ARE THE KEY

Don't buy cheap roller sleeves! High-quality sleeves are worth the extra cost because they give you much smoother results. I used a 3/16-in. Soft Woven Roller Cover from Sherwin-Williams.

PAINLESS RIVETING ▶

When the paint had cured and it was time to reinstall all the name plates and decorative pieces, I used POP rivets (aka blind rivets).

POP rivets are really simple; they're made of two pieces, the "hat" and the "mandrel." Rivets are inserted into predrilled holes and set using a rivet gun. The gun pulls the mandrel through the hat, mushrooming the end of the mandrel. The mandrel is then sheared off, leaving just the rivet head showing. The length of the rivet is important. It needs to be twice its width plus the thickness of the material. So, if you're using 1/8-in. rivets to join 1/4-in. material, the rivet needs to be 1/2 in. long.

Handheld rivet guns are common, but I always feel like I need a third hand when using them. I was dreading riveting by hand, but then I found the Milwaukee M12 battery-powered rivet gun. It handled all the rivet sizes I needed to use, and I could even use it single-handedly. At $230, the bare tool isn't cheap, but it makes this job much easier on your hands.

Hand-powered rivet gun

COOL COOLER SLIDE-OUT ▶

With the camper's old refrigerator gone, its access and venting door no longer served a purpose. So we decided to give it a new purpose. We built a lidded box/table just inside the door to house a cooler. The cooler sits on a platform that's mounted on heavy-duty 32-in. drawer slides. No need to heft a cooler full of ice or step inside to crack a fresh beverage. Just open the door and pull the cooler outside!

CUSTOM DECAL ▶

As much as we favor DIY, we chose to hire out the work on our camper's name badge. The front and back decals cost a total of about $200.

Leftover coal slag

▲ NONSLIP STAIR TREAD

This simple trick can add a nonslip surface to just about anything. I learned this technique making skateboards, using epoxy and clear grit. For the camper step, I used POR-15 OEM Bed Liner coating and coal slag left over from vapor blasting. I rolled the bed liner on the stair tread and then sprinkled the coal slag on top of it.

VINTAGE
CAMPER REHAB
BETTER THAN NEW!

MODERN MATERIALS AND TECHNOLOGY MAKE IT SMARTER THAN THE ORIGINAL

BY GARY WENTZ

Meet our camper: a 1972 Avion Voyageur. The Avion company produced campers for about 40 years, beginning in 1955. Like many other businesses, it was a child of the WWII industrial boom. It adapted materials and expertise from aircraft manufacturing to build campers. And not just any campers, but sleek, luxurious beauties. One vintage camper expert calls them "the best travel trailers ever made." In 1972 our Voyageur sold for about $8,000. In today's dollars, that's almost $50,000.

Our first plan was pure restoration, making the camper look factory-new. But as we got deeper into the details, that plan seemed less and less realistic. That's partly because finding exact replacement parts could have turned into a yearlong quest; a tiny camper sink in avocado green isn't easy to find. We also realized we could make our camper better than the original, with less expense and effort. With today's superior building materials and technology, we could make our camper more comfortable, convenient and durable inside. This make-it-better approach turned out to be a smart choice.

VINTAGE CAMPER REVIVAL.

CAMPER CABINETS

REDESIGNED TO CREATE AN AIRY, OPEN SPACE

BY BRAD HOLDEN

THE CABINETS THREW US A CURVE

Our cabinetry plan called for a new sink-base cabinet and a cabinet/bench combo that would provide extra seating and storage without losing open space. In a house, those are simple projects. But unlike a house, our camper doesn't have walls that are flat, straight and square; all the surfaces are curved. Building curved cabinets is a bit time consuming, but the simple tricks shown here make it doable for DIYers.

The curved cabinets we built are unique in other ways too. They're made largely from MDO, a material that's been around for decades but is unfamiliar to most builders. The smooth, uniform surface makes it a great choice for painted cabinets and doors. For the

Gap between wall and cabinet

Cardboard scribe tool

▲ NEW CABINETS ON CURVED WALLS

To accommodate a new cooktop, I tore out the old sink-and-stove cabinet and built a new one. Mostly, it was a standard cabinet project. But the concave walls threw me for a bit of a loop. There are a number of tools and techniques designed for scribing cabinets and countertops to perfectly fit a wall. My method involves whatever I happen to have on hand—in this case, a piece of cardboard.

■ MAKE A MARKING TOOL

I cut a scrap of cardboard, making a point at one end. With the cabinet as close to the wall as possible, I poked my pencil through the cardboard at the widest gap between the cabinet and the wall.

■ FOLLOW THE CURVE OF THE WALL

Holding the cardboard level, I followed the wall with the point, allowing my pencil to transfer the wall's contour onto the cabinet's side.

■ CUT THE CURVE

I followed the line with my jigsaw, then perfected the curve with a belt sander.

■ TEST THE FIT

My cabinet fit the wall perfectly. But that doesn't always happen. Sometimes I have to tweak the curve a few times with a belt sander.

Scribed line

countertops, we chose Richlite, another old but unfamiliar material.

We decided to paint our cabinets, mainly to brighten the camper's interior and make it feel more open. But paint has other advantages too: Our old cabinets had taken a beating over the years and required a lot of wood filler. Unlike a natural wood finish such as stain and polyurethane, paint makes those repairs completely invisible. And since cabinets in a small space can be expected to suffer damage, paint will make our cabinets easier to touch up.

Finding cabinetry solutions for the unusual spaces was a fun challenge!

REUSE OR REMOVE?

Every element in this camper required a decision: Fix it or replace it? Mostly, we decided that replacement was best. The countertops, base cabinets and all the cabinet doors, for example, were easier to replace than to renew. We also removed the fridge, stove and a cabinet that housed a propane furnace. It was a giant space hog that could be replaced with a small electric heater. There was a lot of breaking up, cutting up and carrying out.

Demolition work often feels like a step backward, making things worse before they get better. But clearing things out of our camper made an immediate improvement. The effect was incredible. Suddenly, the claustrophobic camper felt open, airy, a pleasant place to be, no longer a cramped cave. That resulted in changes to our original plans. We all wanted to retain the spacious feel. Overall, that meant fewer cabinets, trading some storage space for open space.

▲ MY FAVORITE FILLER

With decades of dents and dings, our cabinets were in need of wood filler. There are lots of wood fillers available, but most have a gritty texture, making it difficult to fill the smallest imperfections and achieve a perfectly smooth finish. If I'm painting cabinets or doors, I use MH Ready Patch instead. Ready Patch has the texture of joint compound, but it's harder and more durable when it dries. It sands smooth, leaving no trace of the dent or hole being filled.

▲ CABINET DOORS FROM MDO

Our cabinet doors were in rough shape. Since they were just slabs of birch plywood, I decided it would be easier to make new ones than to repair them. And since they would be painted, I chose to use MDO (medium-density overlay). MDO is basically plywood with a layer of resin on both faces. Developed for sign making, MDO is smooth, holds paint well and stands up to moisture. Like most plywood, MDO has ugly gaps in the edges. I filled them with my favorite filler (see above). MDO isn't carried by most home centers, but you can special-order it. I paid about $50 for each 4 x 8-ft. sheet of 1/2-in. MDO.

Resin

Plywood

Resin

Brad nails

▲ FASTEST FINISHING STANDOFFS

When I was painting all the cabinet doors, standoffs allowed me to coat the backs, then immediately flip the doors over to coat the edges and fronts. You can buy finishing standoffs, but why? I used to run screws through blocks or strips of plywood, but this is even quicker. Using 3/4-in.-thick plywood strips, just shoot 1-1/4-in. or 1-1/2-in. brad nails through the strips, spaced somewhat evenly.

▲ A SMOOTH PAINT JOB

Flat cabinet doors like these are much easier to paint than raised panel doors; all you need is a roller. But which roller will give you the smoothest finish? I tried flock foam and microfiber rollers but found that a cheap foam roller (and high-quality paint!) gave me the best results. The only downside is that foam doesn't hold as much paint as the others, so you have to dip it in the tray more often.

DOOR PULL DRILLING JIG ▶

Got a bunch of pulls to install? A drilling jig makes it fast and easy. Carefully lay out and drill the holes on a scrap of plywood and attach a fence to the edge for easy alignment. Just clamp the jig on the door and drill away!

Fence

LAB-GRADE COUNTERS

If our Richlite countertops look familiar, it may be a high school memory. This tough material was the tabletop of choice for many chemistry labs. But we chose it because the slatelike slabs look great combined with plywood.

VANITY REVIVAL

We couldn't find a replacement bathroom sink that would fit in a camper—and we certainly couldn't keep the avocado green version—so we gave the old one a fresh coat of white. We chose Rust-Oleum Tub & Tile, an acrylic epoxy ($15 online).

The results were great; not as smooth as the original glazing, but you have to look hard to find imperfections. The finish is also surprisingly tough. We were able to scratch a test area with a screwdriver, but it took some effort.

◀ HOT "NEW" COUNTERTOP SURFACE

Richlite has been around for about 70 years. It was originally used for industrial tooling and patternmaking. Recently, because of its extreme durability, it's being used in many other products, ranging from guitar fretboards to sunglasses to high-end countertops.

Richlite is 65% recycled paper and 35% phenolic resin. The surface is smooth, but the random pattern of the natural fibers in the paper imparts an eye-pleasing texture. Richlite is easily workable with standard woodworking tools, comes in a wide variety of colors and thicknesses, and can be used alone or bonded to a substrate.

For this countertop, 1/4-in. Richlite was bonded to 3/4-in. Baltic birch. Bonding to a substrate is best done with a vacuum press, but you can also glue it down with contact cement.

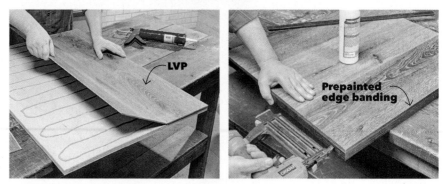

LVP

Prepainted edge banding

▲ FLOORING AS TABLETOP

Thinking about a durable table surface for a rec room or an RV? We used luxury vinyl plank (LVP). Made to endure heavy foot traffic, it's super-durable and comes in many colors and patterns. LVP is only about 3/16 in. thick, however, as it's always installed on a subfloor. So, we installed it on 3/4-in. plywood and used a Liquid Nails adhesive called Fuze-It to bond it to the plywood. To finish the edges, we glued and nailed on prepainted 1/4-in. hardwood edge banding.

RENEW FILTHY WALLS

TWO-STEP PREP FOR A FRESH COAT OF PAINT

BY MIKE BERNER

▲ EXTRA PREP FOR GRIMY OLD WALLS

The original wall color in our camper was a light beige. But years of grime and nicotine had turned the walls a brownish-yellow. To give the space an open feel, we chose white paint. But I knew from experience that you can't paint filthy walls without doing special prep work. That meant two things: thorough cleaning and stain-blocking primer.

■ SCRUB THE WALLS

I first doused the walls with Krud Kutter Tough Task Remover and scrubbed with a stiff brush. And scrubbed. And scrubbed. Then I wiped away the filth with a sponge and scrubbed more. Removing the buildup from those old walls left my arms stiff for a couple days.

■ SEAL IN STAINS

Stains like rust and nicotine will bleed through paint no matter how many coats you apply. To seal in any deep grime that wasn't scrubbed off, I applied two coats of stain-blocking primer. For this job in an enclosed space, I chose KILZ 3 Premium because it's water-based. Stain-blocking primers also provide good adhesion on problem surfaces like the vinyl on our camper walls.

KILZ 3 PREMIUM
INTERIOR | EXTERIOR PRIMER
HEAVY-DUTY HIGH HIDE SEALER & STAIN BLOCKER

A NEW FLOOR OVER THE OLD

TIPS FOR INSTALLING LUXURY VINYL, IN A CAMPER OR ANYWHERE!

BY MIKE BERNER

Luxury vinyl is easy to install and clean, and hard to damage. And since this vinyl can go right over many types of flooring, I didn't have to tear out the old floor. However, I did have to make a couple quick fixes.

▲ STAPLE THE EDGES

There's no need to remove the old flooring if the subfloor isn't squishy or soft. But take care of any curled-up flooring. If it's brittle enough to break if stepped on, cut it away, then staple down the loose edge.

▲ FILL THE GAPS WITH FLOOR PATCH

Fill holes and voids with floor-patching compound. This will harden and support the new floor and help prevent wear marks in those areas later. Use a mudding knife to smooth and level the compound to match the old flooring.

▶ EASY CURVED CUTS

There were a lot of rounded cuts and notches to make! I tried using an angle grinder with a cutoff wheel. The grinder worked great but created a lot of dust. I wore a respirator and had to wipe the dust off each plank before I installed it.

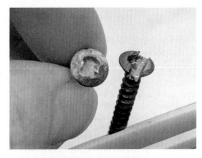

Secure your workpiece

Transition strip

▲ CHANGE DIRECTIONS

It can be difficult to wrap vinyl planks around doorjambs. If you need to lay flooring through a doorway, plan to end the flooring in the opening and change the plank direction in the next room. Then add a transition strip for the finishing touch.

▲ SOLUTION FOR TRICKY SCREWS

Our camper had hundreds of odd-ball screw heads. We couldn't find a bit to fit them, so I cut slots into the heads using a rotary tool fitted with a cutoff wheel. That allowed me to remove screws with a regular flathead screwdriver. This solution works for corroded screws too. I learned this trick while restoring an old motorcycle. Works every time!

IT'S LUXURY VINYL FOR THE WIN

Luxury vinyl was a slam dunk for our camper floor because it's one of the most DIY-friendly options available. Unlike most types of flooring, it isn't attached to the subfloor with adhesive or fasteners—it's a floating floor. That saves installation steps up front and eliminates huge

replacement hassles later. It can be removed in minutes rather than hours or days.

Another advantage of luxury vinyl is that it's relatively thin, so you can install it right over existing flooring without removal or building up the floor to the point where it

interferes with doors.

Luxury vinyl comes in two forms. Luxury vinyl planks (LVP) generally have the look and shape of wood boards. Luxury vinyl tile (LVT) mimics tile or stone in shape and pattern. We chose LVP for its warmer color tone.

EASY LIGHT ANYWHERE

SUPER-VERSATILE LEDs PROVIDE BRIGHTNESS, AMBIENCE—OR BOTH!

BY MIKE BERNER

LED strips in original fixture

LED light channel

12-volt bulb in modern fixtures

Under-cabinet puck lights

LEDs: THE SMART CHOICE

Upgrading the lighting in this camper reminded us just how inefficient lighting used to be and how great it is today. As expected, LED lighting gave us more light.

But the other advantages of LEDs are particularly helpful in a camper. First, they draw less power. That means less load on a generator or battery pack. Second, they produce less heat. In a small space on a warm day, that matters. That also allows you to use LEDs in creative ways like we did, tucking them into tight spots, where heat buildup could lead to fire.

Power source: 12V transformer or 12V battery

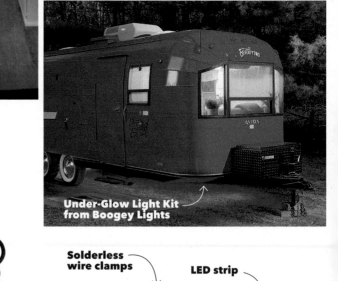

Under-Glow Light Kit from Boogey Lights

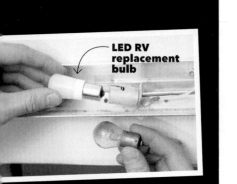

LED RV replacement bulb

Solderless wire clamps

LED strip

LED controller

PEEL-AND-STICK LIGHTING ▶

Our camper lighting was completely outdated incandescent bulbs: excessive energy and low light. To get more light and less heat while using less power, I chose LED strips. I used DynamicColor lights, but there are many similar products. I bought strips, controllers, wire and clamps. Buying the components separately gives you the flexibility to put them anywhere.

Figuring out what components you need is the hardest part. Here's what you need (p. 114) and how to put everything together. With these strips, I could dim the light or change it to a variety of colors.

■ CUT STRIPS TO ANY LENGTH

Cut the strip right on the line going through the copper contacts so the connection is maintained; on my LED strip, there was a line every three LEDs. Connect the strip to the cable with solderless clamps, attach the controller, then hook it up to the power. I didn't have to solder a single wire.

■ STICK STRIPS ANYWHERE

Peel away the adhesive backing and stick them wherever you need light. For the camper, I stuck them to the back of the curtain valance for accent lighting.

■ ENCLOSE THE STRIPS

I also placed the strips above the beds. I wanted them to be concealed, so I put them in an aluminum channel and mounted it. The channel came with a frosted lens, which provided a finished look.

Peel and stick

Aluminum channel

◀ MODERN TECHNOLOGY FOR AN OLD FIXTURE

We liked the old ceiling light fixture in our camper and wanted to keep it. My solution was to stick an LED strip around the inside circumference of the light fixture. Before I mounted the fixture, the strip worked. But when I attached the light fixture to the ceiling, it didn't work.

It turns out the contacts on the back of the LED strip were making a connection to the metal fixture. When I mounted the fixture to the ceiling, I created a short in the circuit. I took down the fixture and put a piece of double-sided tape (not shown) between the strip and the fixture and got it up and running again.

portable PREP CENTER

Running water and a work surface for convenient outdoor cooking

BY GARY WENTZ

WHAT IT TAKES

TIME	COST	SKILL LEVEL
1 day	*$250*	*Beginner*

TOOLS & MATERIALS
Basic hand tools, drill/driver, jigsaw, circular saw

Even when you've left behind the comforts of your kitchen, you still need to wash vegetables or season the steak before mealtime. This table makes those tasks a whole lot easier. The sink serves up running water, while the countertop gives you a convenient work surface. When you head for home, the whole thing folds up for easy transport. And when you get home, you just might find it perfect for the patio.

1 BUILD THE BOX

Arrange the box parts with the best-looking sides facing outward, and join the corners with trim-head screws. Choose the top and the front of the box and label them to prevent confusion later.

2 DRILL THE LEGS

A drill press is best for making the bolt holes in the legs. But if you don't have one, a homemade drill guide will help you bore the holes straight. All you need are a couple blocks cut at 90 degrees.

Drill guide

Leg

PLANNING AND BUILDING TIPS

■ This prep table is intended for outdoor use and will withstand a little rain, but it isn't built for constant exposure to the weather. When you're not using the table, protect it with a tarp or grill cover.

■ I used poplar because it's knot-free, fairly hard and mid-priced. The countertop panel is aspen.

■ I cut the legs from 1x6 stock, but some home centers carry 2-1/2-in.-wide material, which would let you skip that step.

■ The upper ends of the legs must be rounded. I traced around a can of spray paint and cut the curves with a jigsaw.

■ The sink is optional. Without it, you'll gain more work surface, making the table useful for other tasks.

■ The lower shelf is optional. It's handy and it adds strength and stability, but it's not absolutely necessary.

■ To position the shelf cleats, set the shelf on the stretchers, trace along them and then screw the cleats along the traced lines.

■ I finished the table with a couple coats of spar urethane. It will hold up to water and is easy to renew with a fresh coat.

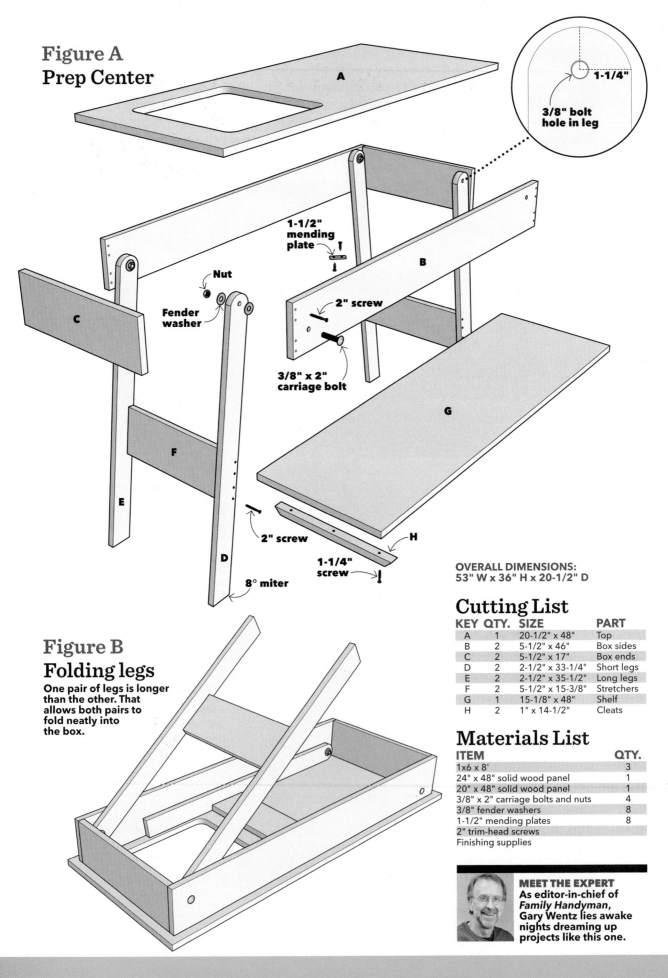

Figure A
Prep Center

3/8" bolt
hole in leg

1-1/4"

A

1-1/2"
mending
plate

Nut

B

Fender
washer

2" screw

C

3/8" x 2"
carriage bolt

G

F

E

2" screw

D

1-1/4"
screw

8° miter

H

Figure B
Folding legs

One pair of legs is longer
than the other. That
allows both pairs to
fold neatly into
the box.

OVERALL DIMENSIONS:
53" W x 36" H x 20-1/2" D

Cutting List

KEY	QTY.	SIZE	PART
A	1	20-1/2" x 48"	Top
B	2	5-1/2" x 46"	Box sides
C	2	5-1/2" x 17"	Box ends
D	2	2-1/2" x 33-1/4"	Short legs
E	2	2-1/2" x 35-1/2"	Long legs
F	2	5-1/2" x 15-3/8"	Stretchers
G	1	15-1/8" x 48"	Shelf
H	2	1" x 14-1/2"	Cleats

Materials List

ITEM	QTY.
1x6 x 8'	3
24" x 48" solid wood panel	1
20" x 48" solid wood panel	1
3/8" x 2" carriage bolts and nuts	4
3/8" fender washers	8
1-1/2" mending plates	8
2" trim-head screws	
Finishing supplies	

MEET THE EXPERT
As editor-in-chief of
Family Handyman,
Gary Wentz lies awake
nights dreaming up
projects like this one.

3

3/4" spacer

Short leg

Long leg

1/16" spacers

1/2" spacer

Carriage bolt

3 DRILL THE BOLT HOLES

Assemble the leg sets. Lay the longer set in the box against a 3/4-in. spacer. Drill through the box, using the leg holes as a guide. Bolt the legs to the box. Then place the short legs on the long legs against a 1/2-in. spacer. Slip 1/16-in. spacers between the legs, then drill and bolt the legs into place.

4 INSTALL THE COUNTERTOP

Place each 1-1/2-in. mending plate at an angle on the top of the box, and screw it into place. Center the countertop and screw the plates to it. The plates will allow the top to move slightly as it shrinks and swells with changes in humidity.

5 CUT THE SINK HOLE

Place the sink upside down on the countertop and trace around it. Then mark your cutting lines 1/4 in. inside the traced lines. Drill a starter hole and cut along the inner lines. Install the sink according to the manufacturer's instructions. **Tip:** Drive a screw into the cutout to provide support as you finish the cut.

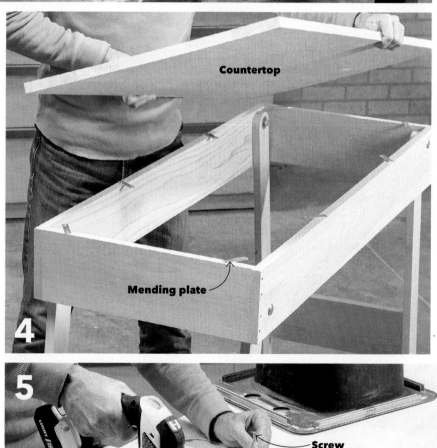

Countertop

Mending plate

4

5

Screw

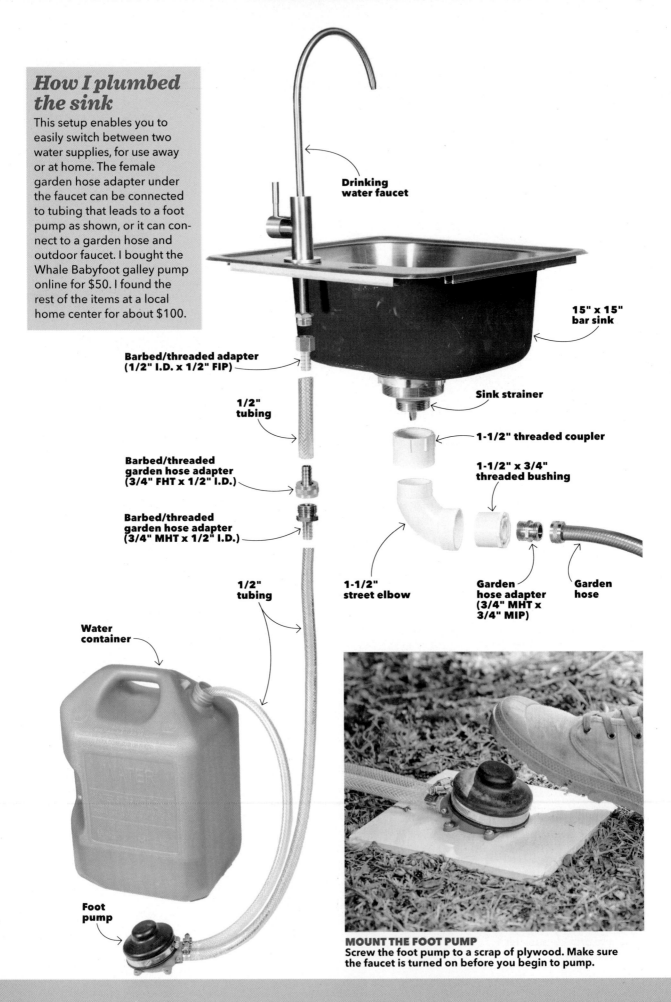

How I plumbed the sink

This setup enables you to easily switch between two water supplies, for use away or at home. The female garden hose adapter under the faucet can be connected to tubing that leads to a foot pump as shown, or it can connect to a garden hose and outdoor faucet. I bought the Whale Babyfoot galley pump online for $50. I found the rest of the items at a local home center for about $100.

Drinking water faucet

15" x 15" bar sink

Barbed/threaded adapter (1/2" I.D. x 1/2" FIP)

1/2" tubing

Sink strainer

Barbed/threaded garden hose adapter (3/4" FHT x 1/2" I.D.)

1-1/2" threaded coupler

1-1/2" x 3/4" threaded bushing

Barbed/threaded garden hose adapter (3/4" MHT x 1/2" I.D.)

1/2" tubing

1-1/2" street elbow

Garden hose adapter (3/4" MHT x 3/4" MIP)

Garden hose

Water container

Foot pump

MOUNT THE FOOT PUMP
Screw the foot pump to a scrap of plywood. Make sure the faucet is turned on before you begin to pump.

4 Woodworking & Workshop Projects & Tips

the smartest END TABLE

Modern style on the outside, modern technology hidden within

BY BRAD HOLDEN

When I was browsing for end tables, I saw this sleek, simple design that I loved, and then I saw the price tag: $800! I decided to build my own and add a high-tech twist: My table has a hidden wireless phone charger to help eliminate cords and clutter. I built the table from plywood and tempered hardboard and then covered it with adhesive-backed walnut veneer. For about one-fourth the price of the end table at the store, I was able to make a matching pair!

WIRELESS CHARGING BUILT IN

To charge your phone with a wireless charger, you just set your phone on it. These chargers cost $20 or less but are finicky; some don't work if the phone is in a case or if the phone isn't centered perfectly on the charger. For this project, my charger would need to work through 1/8-in.-thick tempered hardboard and a layer of veneer. With that in mind, I bought a few chargers to test. All the chargers worked through the hardboard and veneer. Some of them even worked through two thicknesses of hardboard, so to be on the safe side, I chose one of those (the Anker brand).

Charging station

Peel-and-stick veneer makes it easy

This end table looks like it's made from thick slabs of solid wood, but it's actually just plywood and hardboard covered with adhesive-backed veneer.

PSA (pressure-sensitive adhesive) veneer is easy to work with. You just cut your pieces to size, peel off the backing, stick them into place and trim the excess.

Veneer comes in many different species at lumberyards and online. I chose walnut for this project. When you're applying veneer, follow this rule: Apply the least visible parts first. For example, this table's top is veneered on all the edges and the top face. So apply veneer in this order: back edge, side edges, front edge and finally the top. This way, each piece of veneer covers the thin edge of the previous piece, making the edge less visible.

To cut veneer, you'll need a scissors and a utility knife. The only other tools are a J-roller ($20 at home centers) and a flat sanding block. For that I use a piece of 3/4-in. plywood, sized to fit a sanding belt.

Figure A
Smart End Table

Overall Dimensions:
20" High x
15-3/4" Wide
x 24" Deep

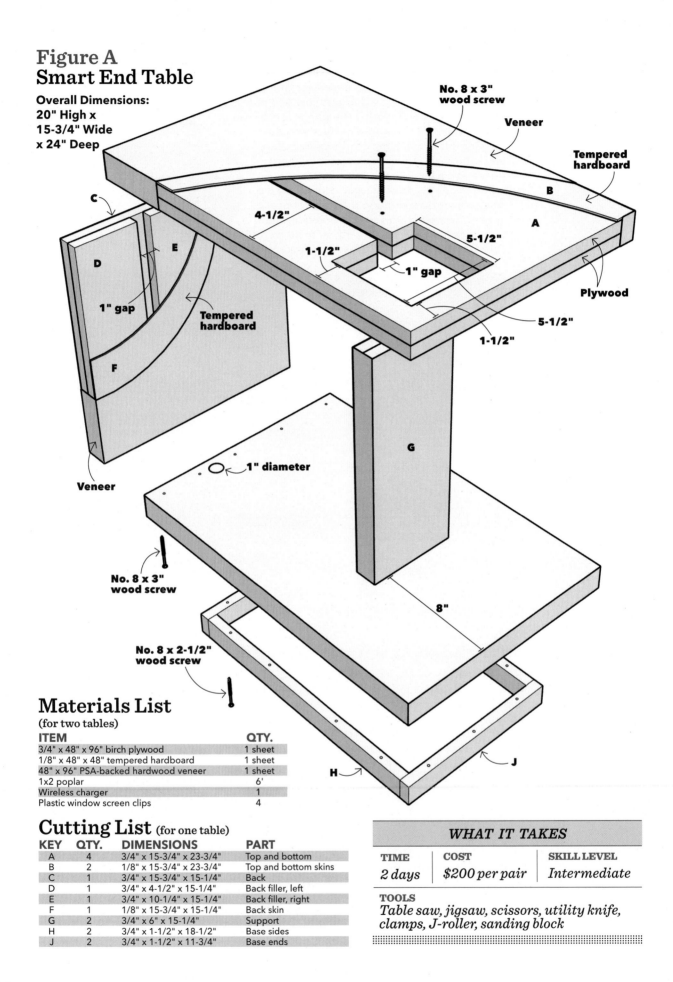

No. 8 x 3" wood screw

Veneer

Tempered hardboard

4-1/2"

1-1/2"

5-1/2"

1" gap

5-1/2"

1-1/2"

Plywood

C

D

E

F

1" gap

Tempered hardboard

Veneer

1" diameter

No. 8 x 3" wood screw

No. 8 x 2-1/2" wood screw

G

8"

H

J

A

B

Materials List
(for two tables)

ITEM	QTY.
3/4" x 48" x 96" birch plywood	1 sheet
1/8" x 48" x 48" tempered hardboard	1 sheet
48" x 96" PSA-backed hardwood veneer	1 sheet
1x2 poplar	6'
Wireless charger	1
Plastic window screen clips	4

Cutting List (for one table)

KEY	QTY.	DIMENSIONS	PART
A	4	3/4" x 15-3/4" x 23-3/4"	Top and bottom
B	2	1/8" x 15-3/4" x 23-3/4"	Top and bottom skins
C	1	3/4" x 15-3/4" x 15-1/4"	Back
D	1	3/4" x 4-1/2" x 15-1/4"	Back filler, left
E	1	3/4" x 10-1/4" x 15-1/4"	Back filler, right
F	1	1/8" x 15-3/4" x 15-1/4"	Back skin
G	2	3/4" x 6" x 15-1/4"	Support
H	2	3/4" x 1-1/2" x 18-1/2"	Base sides
J	2	3/4" x 1-1/2" x 11-3/4"	Base ends

WHAT IT TAKES		
TIME	**COST**	**SKILL LEVEL**
2 days	*$200 per pair*	*Intermediate*

TOOLS
Table saw, jigsaw, scissors, utility knife, clamps, J-roller, sanding block

Cord cutout

Charger cutout

1

Hardboard skin

Back

Filler

Cord channel

2

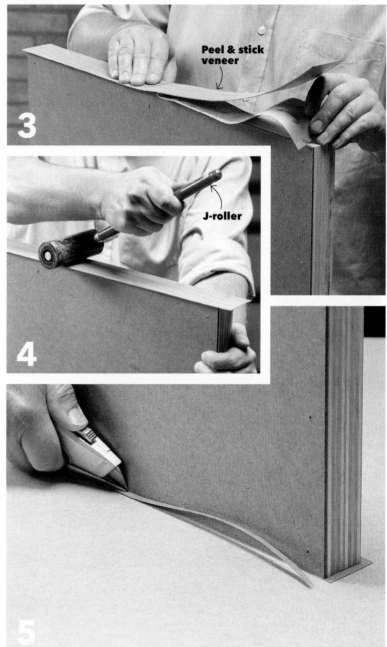

Peel & stick veneer

3

J-roller

4

5

1 CUT THE PARTS

Cut all the parts 1/4 in. oversize in length and width, then cut the recesses for the cord and charger in the tops. Glue up the two layers of plywood for each top and bottom (A) and each support (G). Glue the skins (B) onto each top and bottom.

2 ASSEMBLE THE BACK

Glue the back fillers (D and E) to the back (C), leaving the 1-in. wire channel between them. Glue the back skin (F) to the back assembly. Cut all glued-up assemblies to finished size. Trim all the edges, leaving smooth, flush surfaces for applying veneer.

3 VENEER THE EDGES

Cut a strip of veneer about 1 in. longer than the edge. Peel back one end of the backing and line up the veneer on the edge. Press down the end, lightly at first in case you need to reposition it, and then pull the backing off as you press the veneer onto the edge. Take care with positioning. Once you apply serious pressure, there's no turning back! Veneer all edges of the top and bottom, and then just the vertical edges of the back and support.

4 ROLL THE VENEER

After applying veneer, use a J-roller to apply firm, even pressure to the entire surface. Be careful as you get near the ends; if you go over the edge, the veneer can break off and cause unsightly tears.

5 TRIM THE EXCESS

Set the veneered edge face-down and trim off the excess with a utility knife. I laid a piece of MDF on my workbench to use as a surface for trimming. Unlike plywood or a hardwood bench surface, MDF doesn't have grain, so it won't pull your utility knife off course.

6 SAND THE ENDS

Sand the veneered ends flush before applying veneer to adjacent edges, keeping the sanding block perfectly flat. This is my favorite sanding block for this purpose. It's just 3/4-in. plywood cut to fit a sanding belt. If you don't have a sanding block like this, make one. You'll use it all the time.

7 SAND THE FACES

Once all the necessary edges are veneered, sand the veneer edges flush with the faces. Keeping your sanding block flat, sand toward the center of the part so the sanding block doesn't pull off the veneer.

8 VENEER THE FACES

Veneer the faces of the bottom, back and support. Just as you did with the edges, peel back one end of the backing and then position the veneer. Once it's in the right place, with a little overhang on all the edges, press down the peeled portion, and then peel off the rest of the backing, pressing down the veneer as you go. Finish up with a J-roller, then trim off the excess.

9 SAND THE CORNERS

Sand the edges of the face veneer flush with the faces of the edge veneer. Use a sanding block at an angle, sanding only downward or side to side. This also breaks the sharp corner. Sand until the edge of the face veneer is just flush with the face of the edge veneer. If you go farther than that, you risk sanding through the veneer. This takes a little practice, so go easy until you get the hang of it.

All veneer pieces cut slightly oversize

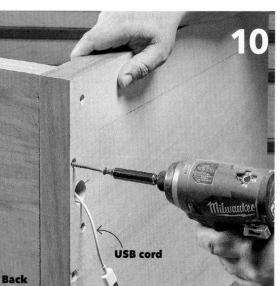

Back

USB cord

Bottom

Utility knife

Inlay taped in place

10 ATTACH THE BACK
Drill a 1-in. hole for the cord through the bottom, lining up the hole with the channel in the back. Run the cord through the back and through the hole, and then screw the back to the bottom.

11 FASTEN THE TOP
Screw the support to the bottom, then feed the cord into its slot in the top. Screw the top to the back and support, countersinking the screw heads below the surface. Sand the top, making sure all the veneer edges are flush with the surface.

12 CUT THE INLAY
Mark the location of the charger in the top veneer. Clamp a can to the veneer and carefully cut around it with a small utility knife. Rotate the inlay 90 degrees and tape it in position with painter's tape.

13 VENEER THE TOP
Apply the top veneer just as you did with the other face veneers. Remember to peel the backing from the inlay, too. Press the veneer down with the J-roller, trim the excess, and then sand the corners. Sand the whole table with 220-grit. Use a light touch so you don't sand through the veneer.

14 ADD THE BASE

Assemble the base (H and J) using glue and finish nails. Fill the nail holes, then sand and paint the base. I used flat black so the base would "disappear" under the table. Center the base on the bottom and attach it with screws.

15 INSTALL THE CHARGER

Wireless chargers aren't made to be mounted, so I had to improvise. I cut small blocks the same thickness as the charger and glued them to the hardboard. Then I installed plastic window screen clips to hold the charger in place.

Screen clip blocks

Screen clips

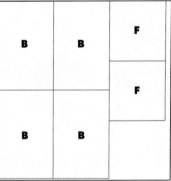

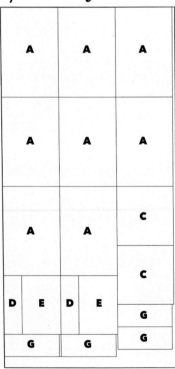

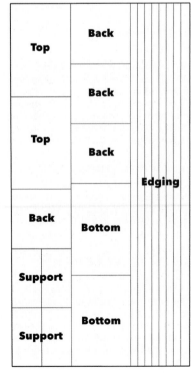

Figure B
3/4-in. Plywood

A	A	A
A	A	A
A	A	C
		C
D E	D E	G
G	G	G

Figure C
1/8-in. Hardboard

B	B	F
B	B	F

Cut all the hardwood veneer pieces slightly oversize. Once the veneer is in place, you'll trim and sand off the overhang flush with the edges of the part. ▶

Figure D
Hardwood Veneer

Top	Back	
	Back	
Top	Back	Edging
Back	Bottom	
Support		
Support	Bottom	

clamping TIPS

Clever solutions, better results

BY DAVE MUNKITTRICK

First things first. Here are three basic types of clamps that belong in any workshop:

Pipe clamps are the everyday high-pressure workhorses of woodworking. They cost just $15 per set, plus a few bucks more for pipes. Because you can quickly screw the clamps onto different lengths of pipe, one set of pipe clamps does the same work as several lengths of bar clamps. Buy pipes in 2-, 3- and 4-ft. lengths and you'll be ready for most situations.

Bar clamps are quicker and easier to use than pipe clamps. Light-duty bar clamps are perfect when you need a long reach and moderate pressure. They cost $10 and up.

Spring clamps are the fastest helpers for holding your work in place or doing light-pressure clamping. They're cheap, too: Most cost less than $5.

Bar clamps

Spring clamps

Pipe clamp

Wax paper

Reynolds CUT-RI WAX PA

Reynolds CUT-RITE

Prevent clamp stains with wax paper

The moisture in glue triggers a reaction between iron and chemicals in wood (called "tannins"). The result is black stains on the wood, especially with tannin-rich woods like oak or walnut. A strip of wax paper creates a barrier between the clamp and the wood. I also use wax paper to keep glue off my cauls.

Hand screw clamp

Extension

Long-jaw hand screw

Extend the reach of your hand screw clamps with a couple of lengths of scrap wood. Screw the jaw extensions to the side of your hand screw clamp and away you go. Works great and couldn't be easier.

No-clamp veneer trick

Gluing down veneer is tough. You have to apply even pressure over every square inch. There are fancy tools for this, but for small veneer jobs, try this trick: Apply a thin coat of wood glue to both the substrate and the back of your veneer. Let the glue dry. Then position the veneer and use a hot iron (no steam) to reactivate the glue. Then press the veneer into place. The bond is almost instant and very strong.

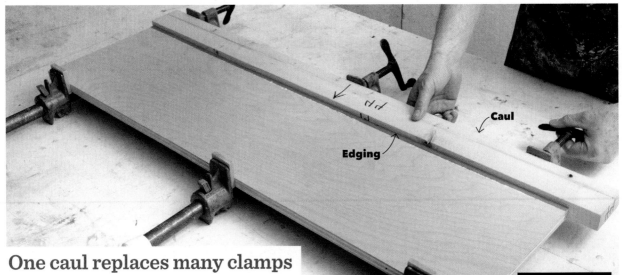

Edging

Caul

One caul replaces many clamps

Thin, flexible parts require lots of clamps to achieve a consistently tight fit. Or you can use a caul. This solid-wood edging on plywood would have required a clamp every few inches. But with a stiff caul to spread the clamping force, you can use fewer clamps, spaced far apart.

WHAT'S A CAUL?
If it's designed to spread clamping pressure over a wide area, you can call it a caul.

Cauls keep glue-ups flat and flush

As you squeeze boards together with pipe clamps, they sometimes arch or slip out of alignment. Pairs of upper and lower cauls are the solution. Lightly squeeze the cauls with bar clamps, then tighten the pipe clamps, then tighten the cauls a bit more. Repeat these adjustments until the boards are joined flush and flat.

Two-by-fours make great cauls. I carefully select ones that have a slight bend, or "crown," along the 1-1/2-in. edge—but no twist or warp. A crown is an advantage because it creates extra pressure in the middle of the caul. Label all your cauls with an arrow marking the direction of the crown and the length of the caul.

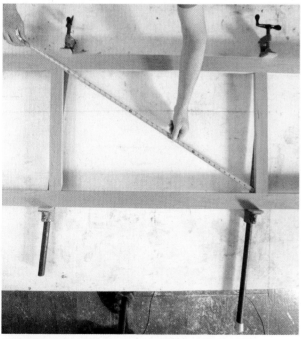

Shift clamps to square

To check the squareness of a cabinet frame or box, take diagonal measurements. If the measurements aren't equal, shift the position of the clamps. In this photo, I exaggerated the shift for clarity. In most cases, a slight shift will do the trick. Sometimes, shifting just one clamp will pull the assembly into square.

Water pressure

Some woodworkers keep a stack of bricks in the shop for those times when weight is better than clamps. But I think plastic buckets make the best weights. Filled with water, they provide a lot of weight. When empty, they're light, easy to store and handy for other jobs.

ROOM
TRANSFORMER

From home office to guest room in seconds

By Brad Holden

If you're tight on living space or you want your guest room to double as an office, here's a piece of furniture you'll want to check out. This bed quickly converts to a desk without increasing its footprint. When you switch it back to a bed, the desk stays level, so you can leave all your stuff on it!

A company called Hiddenbed sells bed kits with all the parts precut and ready for assembly. You can also purchase just the hardware kit, which includes the plans, and that's the option shown here. Building the bed yourself instead of buying the precut kit can save you about $1,200! To make this furniture even more user-friendly, I added a strip of LED lights and attached corkboards to the bed's underside.

Shopping for materials

The hardware for a twin bed costs about $300 at hiddenbedusa.com. There are also versions for double- and queen-size beds. All the other hardware, fasteners and supplies are available at home centers.

I used maple lumber and plywood from a specialty lumberyard and finished it later with a couple coats of polyurethane. You could save money buying materials from a home center, but the quality won't be as good.

BED POSITION

DESK POSITION

Tip: The hardware kit includes everything needed for the folding mechanism, but not the fasteners used to assemble the bed/desk. The company offers a fastener kit, which I ordered. But, the fasteners in the kit are large-diameter screws with heads that show after assembly. I wanted a cleaner look, so I used glue and trim-head screws instead.

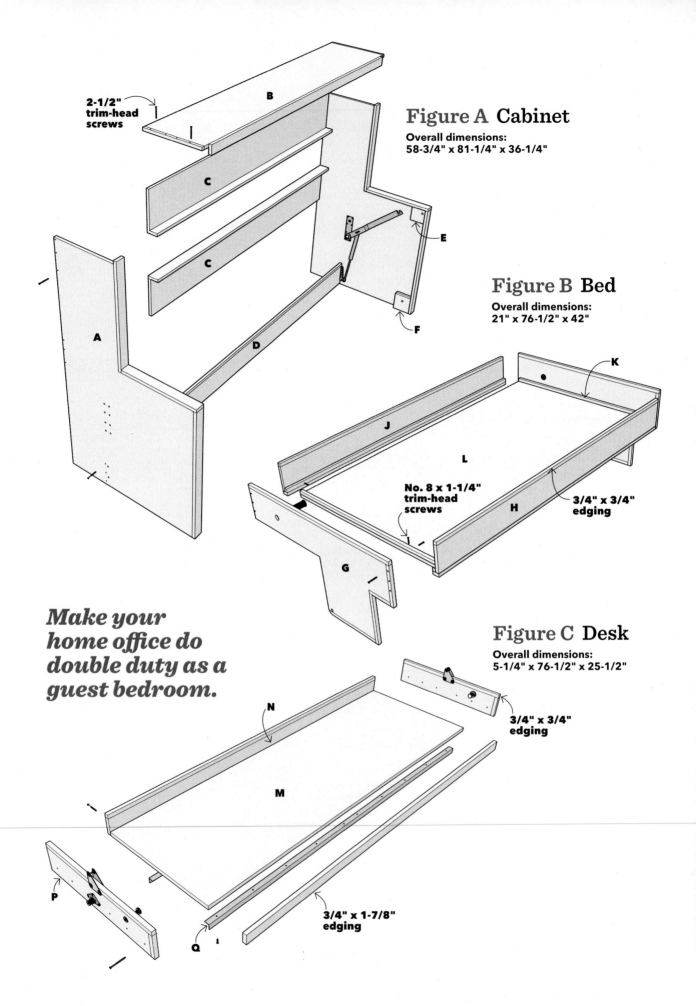

**2-1/2"
trim-head
screws**

Figure A Cabinet

**Overall dimensions:
58-3/4" x 81-1/4" x 36-1/4"**

B

C

C

A

D

E

F

Figure B Bed

**Overall dimensions:
21" x 76-1/2" x 42"**

K

J

L

**No. 8 x 1-1/4"
trim-head
screws**

H

**3/4" x 3/4"
edging**

G

*Make your
home office do
double duty as a
guest bedroom.*

Figure C Desk

**Overall dimensions:
5-1/4" x 76-1/2" x 25-1/2"**

**3/4" x 3/4"
edging**

N

M

P

Q

**3/4" x 1-7/8"
edging**

1 CUT THE PARTS

Most of the parts are simple plywood rectangles. But the sides and bed ends have inside corners, requiring stopped cuts. To make these cuts, mark out the cutting lines on plywood. Cut close to the corners using a circular saw with a cutting guide. Finish the cuts with a handsaw, then smooth the cuts with a file or sanding block.

2 APPLY THE EDGING

Cut all the edging about 1/16 in. wider than the thickness of the parts being covered, so it'll just barely overhang both faces. (Plywood and lumber thicknesses vary slightly, so standard 1-by lumber may not cover the edge of 3/4-in. plywood.) Apply the edging to all parts before assembly using glue and finish nails.

3 SAND THE EDGING

When the glue is dry, sand the edging flush with the plywood faces. To avoid sanding through the plywood's veneer, scribble a pencil line down the joint. Stop and check your progress frequently.

4 DRILL THE HOLES

The sides, bed ends and desk ends require accurately placed holes and recesses for hardware. The original plans for this bed were in metric, and because the hardware hole locations are critical, I recommend using a metric tape measure (less than $20 online). I also recommend using Forstner bits because their guide points make it much easier to center holes precisely.

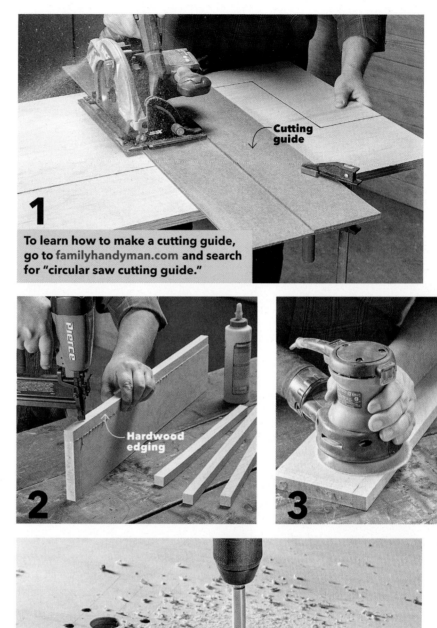

1

To learn how to make a cutting guide, go to familyhandyman.com and search for "circular saw cutting guide."

Cutting guide

2 Hardwood edging

3

4 Forstner bit

Materials List

ITEM	QTY.
4' x 8' sheets of 3/4" maple plywood	4
1x6 x 96" solid lumber for edging	4
1x4 x 96" solid lumber for edging	2
1' x 1' x 72" angle iron	2
1/4-20 x 3/4" hex-head bolts	16
1/4-20 x 2" hex-head bolts	4
1/4-20 cap nuts	20
1/4" lock washers	20
No. 10 x 3/4" flat-head wood screws	6
2-1/2" trim-head screws	
1-1/4" trim-head screws	
Polyurethane	1 qt.
LED strip lights	
Corkboard	
Wood glue	
Hardware kit, available from hiddenbedusa.com	

Cutting List

KEY	QTY.	PART	DIMENSIONS
A	2	Sides	3/4" x 35-1/2" x 58"
B	1	Top	3/4" x 18-3/4" x 79-3/4"
C	2	Backs	3/4" x 10" x 79-3/4"
D	1	Stretcher	3/4" x 6-1/4" x 79-3/4"
E	4	Upper lock blocks	3/4" x 4" x 4"
F	4	Lower lock blocks	3/4" x 5" x 5"
G	2	Bed end	3/4" x 19-1/2" x 40-1/4"
H	2	Bed rails	3/4" x 6" x 75"
J	2	Rail cleats	3/4" x 7/8" x 75"
K	2	End cleats	3/4" x 3/4" x 39-1/2"
L	1	Bed platform	3/4" x 39-1/2" x 75"
M	1	Desk top	3/4" x 24" x 75"
N	1	Desk back	3/4" x 3-5/16" x 75"
P	2	Desk ends	3/4" x 4-7/16" x 24-3/4"
Q	2	Desk stiffeners	1" x 1" x 72" angle iron

5 ASSEMBLE THE CARCASS

Prop up the sides on their back edges, then fasten the top to them with glue and trim-head screws. Attach the back shelves and bottom stretcher the same way. Because of the applied edging, you'll often be driving screws through solid lumber. Trim-head screws are self-drilling, but don't risk it. Drill clearance holes first. Glue and nail the locking pin blocks into place.

6 APPLY THE FACE FRAME

The edging on the front of the carcass is wider to hide the hardware. Apply this edging using glue and finish nails. When the glue is dry, sand the edging flush with the outer faces. Fill nail and screw holes with wood putty, sand the whole carcass to 180-grit, then apply a finish of your choice.

7 ASSEMBLE THE DESK

Glue and screw the desk back and ends to the desk platform. Drill and countersink screw holes in the angle iron desk stiffener. Flip the desk over and attach the stiffener to the underside using 3/4-in. wood screws.

8 BUILD THE BED

Cut and sand the radiused corners of the bed ends, then attach the front and back rails to the ends. Glue and screw the platform cleats to the rails, and then screw the platform to the cleats. The plans don't call for cleats on the bed ends to help support the platform, but I installed some anyway. Instead of attaching these to the underside, where they would show, I attached them above the platform, and then screwed the platform to them.

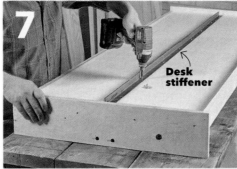

Desk stiffener

Gap for finger pull

Link pivot

Tribearer

9

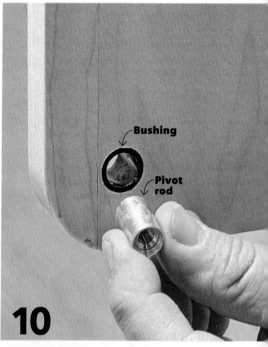

Bushing

Pivot rod

10

9 INSTALL THE DESK HARDWARE

Fasten the "tribearers" to the desk ends with No. 8 x 3/4-in. flat-head screws. Attach the link pivot to the desk ends using the provided threaded pivot rods and screws. Make sure you orient the plates correctly. I put them on wrong the first time. Thinking the holes were mismeasured, I drilled new ones. Eventually, I found my mistake and had to make new ends!

10 INSTALL THE PIVOT PINS

Press the plastic bushings into the holes in the bed ends, and then insert the pivot rods.

11 ATTACH THE SIDE HARDWARE

Attach the pivot arm plate and spring bracket using hex-head bolts and flat hex-drive cap nuts. I was tempted to use screws for this so no hardware would show on the exterior. Because of the torque applied to these parts, however, I decided through-bolts were a better choice. You could use carriage bolts, but the cap nuts ($10 for a 12-pack online) give a tidy, finished look. Then insert the locking pin bushings into their holes.

11

Cap nut

Link pivot

Tribearer

12

13

Trunnion

14

Locking pin

12 ATTACH THE BED TO THE DESK

Set the desk on the floor. With a helper, slide the bed ends into place in the pivot links on the desk. Install the pivot rod screws, securing the bed and desk together.

13 ATTACH THE BED/DESK TO THE CARCASS

Insert the bushings and trunnions into their holes in the bed ends, and then slide the bed/desk assembly into the carcass. Line up the trunnion screws with the threaded holes in the pivot arm plates and thread them in. Hook the pivot arms under the tribearers.

14 INSTALL THE LOCKING PINS

Insert the locking pins into their holes in the desk ends, and then mark the pin locations in the locking pin blocks. Drill the locking pin holes in the blocks, then fasten the locking pins in place using the provided screws.

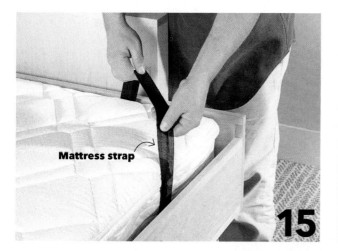

Mattress strap

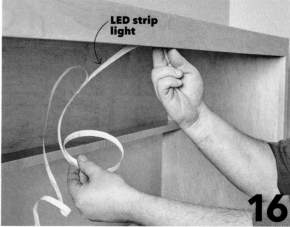

LED strip light

15 SECURE THE MATTRESS

To keep the mattress from tipping against the narrow shelves when you fold up the bed, secure it with elastic straps at the corners. Attach the straps to the bed platform with wood screws and flat washers.

16 INSTALL STRIP LIGHT

The LED strip light is optional, but it's a nice feature. It's adhesive-backed, so you just stick it into place, plug it in and set up the app on your phone.

An LED strip light is perfect for reading in bed, or just to have fun changing colors and creating a mood. This 78-in. strip light from LIFX costs $90 online.

Plywood Cutting Diagrams

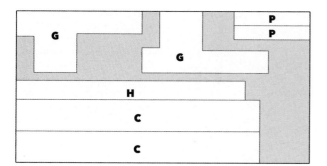

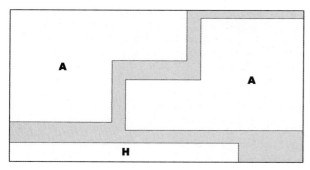

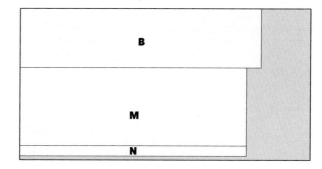

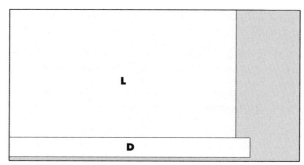

TABLE
IN A DAY

Peel-and-stick veneer makes it stunning and simple

BY GARY WENTZ

When it comes to woodworking, I'm a cheater. I want masterpiece results, but I love shortcuts. That's why I like to build tables using hollow-core doors and veneer. This method is faster, easier and cheaper than solid wood construction, and the table is lighter and more stable. The first table I built this way is as flat and flawless as it was 20 years ago.

I spent about $500 on materials because I chose high-grade zebrawood boards and veneer. Built from a species like oak or cherry, a table could cost well under $300. I completed the construction in a day, then spent a few more hours applying a finish.

WHAT IT TAKES

TIME	COST
1–2 days	*$250–$600*

SKILL LEVEL
Intermediate

TOOLS & MATERIALS
Basic hand tools, circular saw, clamps or pneumatic nailer

EASY RECIPE FOR AN ELEGANT TABLE

A HOLLOW-CORE DOOR is flat, strong, lightweight and inexpensive ($40 to $60), making it the perfect foundation for a table.

"SKIN" glued to the door provides a tougher tabletop. The faces of a hollow-core door are super thin and easy to puncture. The skin can be plywood, MDF or hardboard.

PEEL-AND-STICK VENEER costs a few bucks more than standard veneer, but it gives you perfect results without special tools or skills.

SOLID WOOD gives the table a durable edge. Veneered edges look just as good, but they aren't nearly as tough. Any thickness will do, but thin stock costs less and is easier to apply. This edging is 3/8 in. thick.

MATERIALS, TOOLS AND TIPS

■ Hollow-core doors are available at home centers, typically in widths of 28, 30, 32 and 36 in. You can cut them down from their standard height (80 in.) for a table of a different length. You can also cut them to width, but that's a bit more work.

■ I bought the 28-in. hairpin legs online for about $60. There are lots of styles and finishes available. For a dining table, I strongly recommend hairpin legs formed from three columns rather than two.

■ This project requires lots of wood glue, at least 16 oz. To give yourself more working time, consider a slow-setting glue such as Titebond Extend, or add about 10% water to standard glue.

■ My plywood skin had some flaws—tiny lumps that telegraphed through the veneer and became visible only after the veneer was finished.

To avoid this, examine your plywood carefully. Better yet, choose hardboard or MDF for the skin.

■ When you add a skin over the door, don't cut it to fit the door; an exact match is almost impossible. By starting with an oversize skin (**Photo 4**) and then trimming (**Photo 5**), you'll get a perfect fit.

■ When the edging is complete, make sure its top is flush with the skin. If you find any uneven spots, sand them flush. But be careful not to round the outer corner of the edging.

■ Veneer requires only a light sanding before finishing. I always sand by hand only. The veneer is micro-thin and easy to sand through with a random-orbit sander.

■ I finished my table with two coats of polyurethane, followed by two coats of wipe-on poly.

Endless options

Veneer, a super-thin layer of wood, has been used by woodworkers for centuries because it eliminates hours of labor and can overlay a base material that's more stable than solid wood. More than that, it's an opportunity to use gorgeous wood without spending a fortune. I found more than 100 wood species options online, including a dozen I'd never heard of. A 4 x 8-ft. sheet of peel-and-stick veneer costs from $70 to $700. My zebrawood veneer came from veneersupplies.com.

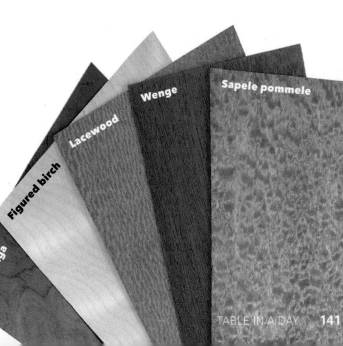

Bubinga Figured birch Lacewood Wenge Sapele pommele

MEET THE EXPERT
Gary Wentz is editor-in-chief of *Family Handyman*, where he shows off his successful projects. Failures stay hidden in his garage.

Hollow-core door

Straightedge

Webbing

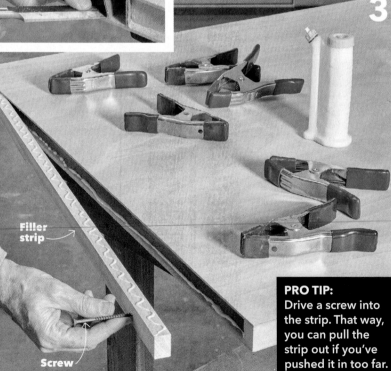

Filler strip

Screw

1 CUT THE DOOR

To get a straight cut, run your circular saw along a straightedge. I used a scrap of plywood. Your table can be any length you want. Just remember to account for the thickness of the edging when you determine the door length.

2 MAKE SPACE FOR THE FILLER STRIP

Hollow-core doors have cardboard webbing inside. Use a chisel or sharp putty knife to slice through the glue that fastens the webbing to the faces of the door. Then shove the webbing inward.

3 GLUE IN THE FILLER STRIP

Cut a strip of 3/4-in.-thick wood or plywood to fit into the door. The strip has to be perfectly straight, so choose straight stock. Fasten the strip with wood glue and spring clamps.

PRO TIP:
Drive a screw into the strip. That way, you can pull the strip out if you've pushed it in too far.

4 ADD A SECOND SKIN

Cut 1/4-in. material 1/4 in. larger than the door. Coat the door with wood glue and position the plywood, letting it overhang on all four sides. Nail down the perimeter of the plywood and set heavy objects on the interior area.

COOL TOOL: A notched putty knife, found in the flooring tools aisle at home centers, makes a great glue spreader.

5 TRIM THE SKIN

Cut off the overhanging skin with a flush-trim router bit. The bearing guides the bit, leaving the skin perfectly flush with the door.

6 ADD THE EDGING

Wrap the door with solid-wood edging. Start on the short ends, then cover the long sides of the door. I skipped the clamping process and fastened the edging with 23-gauge pins instead. **Note:** Use a straightedge to position the edging. It has to be perfectly flush with the skin.

EDGE FASTENING OPTIONS:
There are a few ways to fasten the edging. The best approach is clamping, but that's time-consuming and requires a pile of long clamps. So I went with glue and a 23-gauge pin nailer. The tiny nails are easy to hide with a smidgen of filler. An 18-gauge brad nailer would also work, but the larger nail holes are harder to camouflage later.

Flush-trim bit

Straightedge

Edging

Veneer

Paper

7 APPLY THE VENEER

Cut the veneer 1 in. larger than the tabletop, using a utility knife with a fresh blade. Peel off the protective paper and set the veneer in place. Don't apply any pressure until the veneer is centered on the tabletop.

8 ROLL THE VENEER

Peel-and-stick veneer uses pressure-sensitive adhesive. For a strong bond, apply lots of force and roll the whole table twice; with the grain and across the grain. Veneer rollers cost $20 online.

Roller

9 TRIM THE VENEER

With a helper, set the tabletop on a cutting backer such as hardboard or MDF. Be careful not to damage the overhanging veneer. Trim it with a fresh, sharp blade. To avoid splintering, cut in two or three light passes rather than one deep cut. **Note:** Don't use plywood as a cutting backer. The grain can pull your blade off course.

10 ATTACH THE LEGS

Screws won't hold well in a hollow-core door, so first glue on leg bases cut from 1/2-in. or 3/4-in. plywood. Screw the legs on and you're done!

Materials List

- Hollow-core door
- 1/4" x 4' x 8' plywood, MDF or hardboard
- Solid wood for edging
- 4' x 8' peel-and-stick veneer
- 28" hairpin legs
- Wood glue
- Finishing supplies

ESSENTIAL:
After trimming the veneer, ease the sharp edges where the veneer covers the edging. Sand them lightly, or profile the edges with a router. Just be sure to use a sharp bit to avoid splintering the veneer.

Backer

Veneer

10

Hairpin leg

Leg backer

Apply poly with a roller—really!

Coating a large table-top with a brush is a high-stress speed test. You have to move fast to coat the whole surface before the poly-urethane become gooey. But haste often leads to missed spots, uneven coverage or ugly brush marks.

So instead, I use a mini roller. Sound crazy? I thought so too until I watched a friend do it. Since then, I've done it a dozen times, and even my worst results were better than I could have achieved with a brush. Here's what I've learned:

■ Slower dry times are better, so heat is bad.

You'll get smoother results at 70 degrees than you will at 80 degrees.

■ Rollers work well with oil-based poly; with water-based poly … a disaster.

■ I've had the best results with microfiber rollers, though foam rollers are fine too.

■ When the surface is perfectly smooth, finish up with two or three coats of wipe-on poly, which is much less problem-prone than regular poly.

■ Apply at least two coats, more if you want

more protection. Sand lightly between coats.

■ Light coats are best. Heavy coats lead to stubborn bubbles.

■ The poly will look terrible at first. You'll be tempted to roll it again to "fix" it. Don't. Left alone, the bubbles will pop and the tiny bumps will level out.

■ When you've built up the desired thickness, give the finish at least a day to fully harden. Then wet-sand to smooth out any little imperfections. I use 600-grit wet/dry sandpaper and soapy water as a lubricant.

Quick & simple
PHONE STAND

On the phone's screen:

3:22 PM
🔒 tasteofhome.com

Share | 📌 Save on Pinterest | Next Recipe >

Pizza Margherita

A classic Pizza Margherita, named for Queen Margherita of Italy, shows off the colors of the Italian flag with red tomatoes, white mozzarella and fresh green basil. It's so scrumptious that you'll be glad the recipe makes not one but two 13-inch pizzas! —Loretta Lawrence, Myrtle Beach, South Carolina

Make a dozen great gifts in one afternoon

BY TRAVIS LARSON

If you have a lot of people on your gift list, we've got you covered. Here's a simple item everyone will appreciate. And you can crank out 12 of them in an afternoon—finishing time included!

Test groove

1 CUT A TEST GROOVE

Assemble a 3/8-in.-thick dado set in your table saw and adjust it to cut 3/8 in. deep and 1 in. away from the fence. Set the angle to 20 degrees, then cut a groove in a piece of 2x6 to test the fit of your devices.

2 CHECK THE FIT

Rest your devices in the groove. They should feel firmly secure when you tap the screens. If not, adjust the depth and/or width of the groove and retest until they do. When the fit is right, cut the groove in your project board.

WHAT IT TAKES

TIME	COST
Once you're set up, you can make at least 10 an hour	25¢ to a few dollars each, depending on wood species and thickness

SKILL LEVEL *Beginner*

TOOLS *Table saw*

3 RIP THE BEVELS

Set your saw's blade to 20 degrees. Cut parallel bevels on the edges of the board. A ripping blade is best for ripping solid lumber, but a combination blade is fine.

4 CUT TO LENGTH

Crosscut the stands to length using a miter gauge with a stop block clamped to the saw's fence. Clamp it a few inches behind the blade. As you slide the workpiece past the block, there's a gap between the fence and the workpiece so it doesn't bind. Cut a bevel at the end of the board, then slide the beveled end against the block to cut successive stands to length.

5 SAND THE EDGES

Glue sandpaper to a flat board using spray adhesive, and then sand all four beveled edges up to 180 grit.

Choose any wood, any thickness

Our photos show how to make a device stand suitable for holding either a tablet or a phone. All you need is a length of wood of any species that's at least 3/4 in. thick. A 3-1/2-in.-wide board works fine for phones, but you'll need a minimum width of 5-1/2 in. to make a stand for a tablet. The cutting angles and steps are the same for any width or thickness.

We used walnut to make the phone stand shown on p. 146. But this would be the perfect project for an eye-catching exotic species like bubinga, teak or purple heart. They're all available at woodworking stores and online. With a project this small, you can get a beautiful, unique look without breaking the bank.

You'll need a table saw

This project involves cutting grooves (**Photo 1**), ripping beveled edges (**Photo 3**) and cutting the stands to length (**Photo 4**)—tasks best done on a table saw. We cut beveled edges parallel on opposite sides, but you can cut opposing bevels or go with square edges and rout decorative profiles if you wish. The groove dimensions don't factor in any protective case you may have. They're just a starting point; you'll likely need to adjust them. The test shown in **Photo 2** will help you fine-tune the grooves.

Sand the boards first

If you're using construction or rough-sawn lumber, sand the top face of the boards up to 180 grit before doing any cutting. It's much easier than sanding small parts later. When you're done, spray on a finish of your choice. If you're in a hurry, shellac is a good choice because it dries quickly between coats.

Best Pro Tips

Expert advice from the job site. By Jay Cork

LINT-FREE APPLICATOR
Terry-cloth staining pads work great for gel finishes too.

GET A GLASS-SMOOTH FINISH

My early wood-finishing results weren't pretty: I refinished musical instruments I had no business even touching and ruined some valuable furniture. I've learned a lot since then, working with some of this country's top experts in wood finishing. Now I'd like to share some of that knowledge with you.

If there's one thing I've learned about wood finishing, it's that patience is always rewarded; there are very few shortcuts to achieving great results. But that's not a bad thing. In fact, I find that it's really enjoyable to slow down and pace myself. When I get in a hurry and cut corners, I always regret it.

MEET THE EXPERT
Jay Cork is an associate editor at *Family Handyman*. He began his wood-finishing career as a teenager.

Jay's Finishing Kit

Technique is important for achieving consistent results, but quality tools and materials play a major role too. Here are some I've come to rely on:

MAGNIFYING GLASS/LIGHT
A magnifying glass with a light helps me spot blemishes.

TACK CLOTH
Tack cloths are meant to clean the surface between coats. I've never liked the store-bought ones, but a microfiber cloth dampened with solvent has never failed me.

SANDING BLOCKS
I love this sanding block! It's $12 at woodcraft.com. The block uses the same 5-in. discs as my sander, and it's form-fit for my hand.

SPATULA KNIVES
With some types of grain, the color difference requires two or more tones of filler. I use small art knives to achieve that detail.

RUBBER SQUEEGEE
For larger areas, a rubber squeegee will help spread the filler into the grain. This grout tool that I found at a hardware store does the same job.

COLORED PENCILS/ MARKERS
Use colored pencils or markers to create grain lines on a repair.

VERSATILE WOOD DYE
TransTint wood dye ($22 at Rockler) is soluble in both alcohol and water. I use it to tint shellac or a water-based finish. Go easy—a little goes a long way!

STEEL WOOL
Used between coats, Briwax "0000" oil-free steel wool ($13 at Woodcraft) won't contaminate the finish. I never use steel wool on bare wood; the iron can cause little black stains that will never come out.

FESTOOL SANDPAPER
Festool "Granat" is hands-down the best sandpaper I've ever used. It's more expensive, but you'll save money using it.

EPOXY PUTTY
Epoxy putty is a great choice for repairing damaged furniture, but beware—it doesn't take stain exactly like wood. See my tip about faking grain.

BRUSHES
I find that a very stiff, natural-bristle brush gives me greater control for brushing polyurethane.

PAINTING PYRAMIDS
Painting pyramids keep your project elevated and stable—but be careful! I once sanded a piece while it was still on the pyramids and the points dug in on the back side! Oooops!

NITRILE GLOVES
In the past I've used blue latex gloves. But I discovered these ultra-durable Venom Steel nitrile gloves ($10 for 50 at Menards). I'll be using these from now on.

TWEEZERS
Dust, hair, brush bristles and even insects can all ruin your finish. If you catch the culprit quickly with a pair of tweezers, the finish should level back out.

BLOXYGEN
Bloxygen ($13 at Rockler) displaces oxygen with an inert gas. Spraying it into a can of finish as you put the lid back on keeps the finish from going bad.

CHISEL
A sharp chisel is for more than just wood! I use one to shave off drips and runs after the finish has dried.

PREVAL SPRAYER
When topcoating with epoxy, I like to have a Preval sprayer ($5 at Menards) filled with denatured alcohol. A little spritz will help settle bubbles and other surface imperfections.

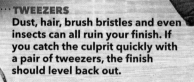

TIMBERMATE WOOD FILLER
Timbermate ($9 at Woodcraft) is a water-based wood filler made from wood flour. It can be thinned out with water for use as a grain filler, and it shrinks less than any other filler I've used.

MINERAL SPIRITS AND DENATURED ALCOHOL
Certain finishes require specific solvents. I use denatured alcohol for thinning shellac and epoxy. Mineral spirits can be used for thinning oil-based finishes and for cleaning.

Jay's tips for a fantastic finish

DE-WHISKER BEFORE WATER-BASED STAIN

Water-based stains and finishes can cause the grain to rise like whiskers. To avoid this, "de-whisker" the wood before staining. Mist it with water, but avoid oversaturation; just spray and wipe with a towel. After it dries completely, sand with 220 grit and it will be ready to finish.

■ START WITH GLOSS

A satin finish is simply a gloss finish with tiny particles in it. Those "flatteners" make the finish less shiny. But, too many layers of satin can obscure the grain, causing the finish to appear dull. To avoid this, I start with at least two coats of gloss then apply one last coat using satin. That gives me the depth and luster I love to see in a finish.

■ SAND BETWEEN COATS

Modern polyurethanes don't require sanding between coats for adhesion, but I still recommend it. Dust nibs need to be removed before the next coat. It might be tempting to use a random orbital sander. Don't! Block-sanding by hand with 320 grit is the way to go.

■ NEVER USE COMPRESSED AIR TO REMOVE DUST

Compressed air is very good at blasting away dust after sanding, but it's a really bad idea. Here's why: Compressors often contain moisture, oil and small particles of rust. All it takes is a microscopic drop of oil to produce "fish eye" in a finish. Instead, use a lint-free rag with mineral spirits.

SHAVE AWAY RUNS

When you see a run, your first instinct may be to grab a piece of sandpaper. Don't! Sandpaper can damage the area around a run and make things worse. I prefer using a very sharp chisel to remove drips or runs in finish. If you spot a run as the finish is drying, wait! Let the finish dry first.

HIDE A REPAIR WITH FAKE GRAIN

Sometimes repairs don't blend in because the grain lines have been interrupted. I use colored pencils and markers to make fake grain to disguise the repair. This skill takes time to master, so my advice is to practice! It's a really fun challenge. Buy many brown shades, not just a couple, and don't forget red and yellow. Most important, start with lighter colors. You can always go darker, but not the other way around!

SET UP LOW-ANGLE LIGHT

In the shop, proper lighting for finishing is one of the hardest things to get right. It might be perfect from one perspective but useless from another. I've used floor lamps or utility lights as a source of reflected light, but the reflection was too small. Then I had a better idea—I attached a 4-ft. LED light fixture vertically to a stand. It stands opposite me as I work, always giving me a long, solid line of reflected light in the finish.

MY FAVORITE FINISHES

When finishing a tabletop, I prefer oil-based polyurethane. I just love the classic amber hue that oil provides. Another advantage: Oil-based finishes can be thinned much more than water-based poly. I find thinning the final coat 50/50 really helps level it out. For highly figured wood, rubbing in a few coats of boiled linseed oil (and letting it dry completely) before the polyurethane topcoat can give the figure even more depth.

I use shellac on virtually every finishing project. Zinsser SealCoat is a wax-free clear shellac that works very well as a sanding sealer or prestain conditioner. I love General Finishes Arm-R-Seal because I can apply it with a brush, wipe it on or even spray it. General Finishes Gel Topcoat in satin gives an attractive, hand-rubbed sheen.

RUB OUT WITH STEEL WOOL

Gently rubbing out the final coat of satin finish with "0000" steel wool and a little soapy water will produce the silkiest, smoothest finish you've ever felt.

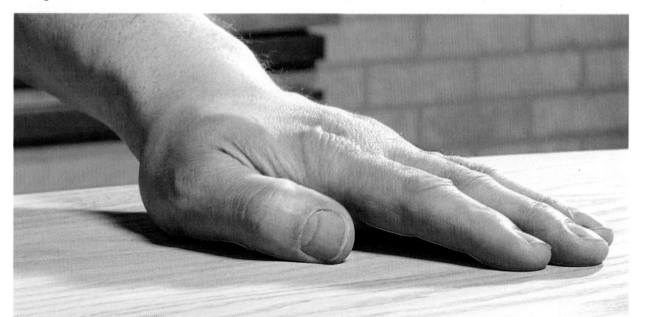

SEE WITH YOUR FINGERS

The most important lesson I learned when cutting my teeth refinishing cars, furniture and musical instruments was to not trust my eyes. Our fingers are far more capable of sensing minute details. Even before the finishing process begins, my fingers will tell me very quickly if my joints are all glued evenly, or if there are any rough spots that need to be addressed.

Grain filling: What, why and how?

Red oak, hickory and ash are the most common species with "open grain." While beautiful in their own right, they don't take a finish evenly. No matter how much you sand, that bumpy texture will show in the finish. That texture can be attractive, but if you want a perfectly smooth finish, you'll have to fill the grain. I usually fill the grain on tabletops and musical instruments.

MY FAVORITE FILLER

I've tried many grain filler products, but the only product I use now isn't even a grain filler; it's marketed as a water-based wood putty. Timbermate is made from wood flour and available in many species. It'll accept stains, dyes and finishes just like the wood around it. It ages the same as wood, which makes me confident that my project will look good the day I complete it as well as years down the line.

1 MIX IT BY HAND

I start with two big scoops of Timbermate wood putty in a plastic food container. Wearing nitrile gloves, I slowly add water and mix it with my fingers. This takes time; mix until those last little clumps are dissolved.

2 SPREAD IT OUT!

When the slurry is the consistency of yogurt, I scoop it up with my hands and spread it on the wood. Just like I do when I stain, I'll rub in circles and across the grain, working the filler into the pores of the wood.

3 GET THE SPOTS YOU MISSED WITH A SECOND COAT

Applying a second coat produces the best results; it covers little spots that were missed. I'll even start the second coat before the first one is completely dry so the slurry remaining in my container doesn't dry out.

4 SAND LIGHTLY!

I like to wait a day before sanding so the moisture has a chance to evaporate. I've achieved the best results using a random orbital sander that has effective dust collection, and variable speed so I can slow it down. I start with 80-grit paper and stop at 220.

TIP: I use only Festool sanders because they have the best dust collection of any random orbital sander on the market. More important, the complete absence of vibration means my hand and wrist won't hurt after hours of use.

5 SEAL WITH SHELLAC

Shellac is very versatile! Because it's compatible with all finishes, it can be used as a barrier between water- and oil-based stains and topcoats. I use thinned shellac as a prestain conditioner. I'll also use it after grain filling to even out the absorption rate of the filler and wood, so the stain or topcoat lies down evenly. In addition, shellac can be used alone as a stunning topcoat, but that's for another article (or three).

1 Aim for the consistency of yogurt

2 Quart-size plastic container

3 Missed spots

4 Festool RO125

5

Handy Hints®

Clever solutions from our readers

GRIP ODD SHAPES

Holding a spindle or other odd-shaped part in a bench vise is tricky. To hold the part firmly without marring it, I sandwich it between two pieces of rigid foam.

ANNE HANSEN

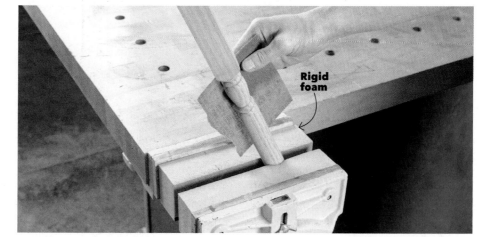

Rigid foam

Precision Dado Adjustments

Once in a while, my dado set matches the size of my material perfectly, but usually not. That's when playing cards come in handy for dialing in the dado's width. Instead of removing the dado stack several times to find just the right combination of shims and cutters, I install the dado set as close as possible to the right size, but slightly under. Then I clamp an auxiliary fence to my saw's fence, set the fence to cut precisely on the dado layout line farthest from the fence and make the first pass. Next, I slip cards behind the auxiliary fence until the dado set lines up with the layout line closest to the fence and make the second pass. One playing card equals about 1/64 in. This is more accurate than making micro adjustments to my saw's fence.

LES BEEKMAN

Zip-tie tail

INSTANT PHONE STAND

Need to prop up your phone to watch a video or look at project plans? A couple of zip ties are all you need. Secure one zip tie around each end of your phone, using the excess "tail" to keep the phone upright.

ERNIE COYLE

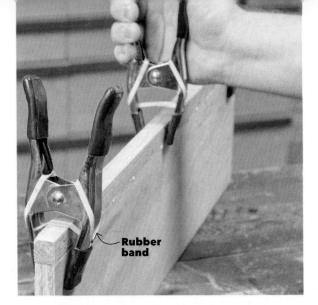

Rubber band

DIY EDGE-BAND CLAMPS

I could buy clamps ready-made for gluing on edge banding, but I came up with a way to make my own while working on a project recently. All you need are spring clamps and rubber bands. Poke the rubber bands through the holes in the jaws of the spring clamp, and then loop them around the end of the clamp to hold them in place. It works great!

TOM KRAMIN

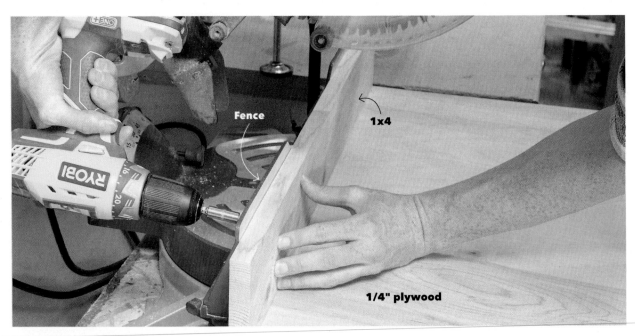

Fence

1x4

1/4" plywood

SAFER SAW FENCE

Cutting small parts on a miter saw is dangerous. There's typically a wide gap between the fence halves and another in the throat plate. Without full support for the workpiece, small offcuts can (and will) go airborne. To solve this problem, attach a sacrificial fence.

Make the fence by gluing and nailing a length of 1x4 to a piece of 1/4-in. plywood. Attach the 1x4 to your saw's fence. Miter saw fences usually have holes predrilled, but if yours doesn't, just drill a few. Two holes on each fence section is sufficient. The fence greatly increases safety and makes it super easy to get accurate cuts. After you've made one cut, the kerf tells you exactly where your saw will cut. Just mark a cutting line on your workpiece and line it up with the kerf.

BRAD HOLDEN

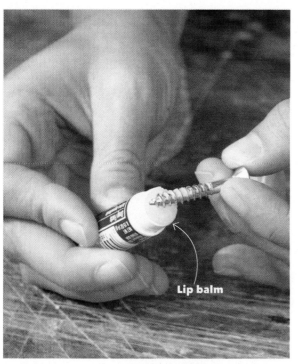

HANDY SCREW LUBE

If you enjoy working with hardwoods, you know how important it is to lubricate screws. It makes driving the fasteners easier and reduces the amount of heat produced. But what if you don't have a bar of soap or a pile of beeswax nearby? Reach for a tube of lip balm. It does a fine job of lubricating screws, and it fits in your pocket.

DEAN GUTHRIE

PAPER TOWEL CLAMP

I like to keep a roll of shop towels at hand when I'm at the workbench. To prevent the towels from rolling off the bench, I clamp a quick-grip-style clamp to the edge of the bench and slip the paper towel roll over the clamp's rod.

BRAD JOHNSON

MAKE YOUR OWN POCKET HOLE PLUGS

Instead of buying pocket hole plugs, use this jig to make as many as you need. Drill a pocket hole into a 2x4. Then insert a 3/8-in. dowel and slice it off flush with the face of the 2x4. After making the angled cut, push the dowel through, cut the end at 90 degrees and repeat.

JACK OWEN

Cool hardware organizer

Whether you're taking something apart for repair or getting ready to assemble some flat-pack furniture, having all the hardware neatly organized and not rolling around on your workbench is super helpful. I keep a couple ice cube trays in my workshop just for this purpose.

JAMIR BARBER

Stop block

1x4

A STOP BLOCK FOR LONG CUTS

Setting up a stop to make repeat cuts is definitely a time-saver. Here's my solution for cuts that extend beyond my saw's fence. I attach a long 1x4 to my saw fence and use a stop block I made from a short piece of 1x4 and a 1/4-in. plywood lip. I just slide the stop block to where I need it and clamp it into place.

TED KANON

Cut the top corner of the triangle

PERFECTLY SQUARE, HANDS-FREE!

Holding parts square while clamping and fastening can be tricky. These plywood triangles make it easy. Using a miter saw or table saw, cut the triangles, taking care that your setup is perfectly square. Drill a hole at each corner, large enough for your clamp heads. Be sure to cut off the triangle's top corner, so it doesn't get glued to your workpiece.

JOE SKIBA

Cheesecloth pad

STAIN DABBER

For a quick touch-up, pour some stain into a condiment bottle. Leave the cap off and cover the top with multiple layers of cheesecloth or cotton, and secure them with a rubber band. When you tip the bottle, the stain flows through the pad. The thicker the pad, the easier it is to control the flow.

CORA JIMINEZ

What plants can *poison* my pet?

The list of household plants that can sicken cats and dogs is long, but list-making can exaggerate the danger.

In 2018, of the 213,773 calls to the ASPCA's poison control center about possibly poisoned pets, fewer than 11,000 involved plants. The top three causes were OTC medicines (19.6 percent), human Rx medicines (17.5 percent) and human foods (11.4 percent). Plants accounted for just 5.5 percent of all poisoning cases. To play it safe, any time you bring plants or flowers into your house, find out how toxic they are. Lilies, including calla lilies and peace lilies, are poisonous to cats. Even a small amount of a sago palm is toxic to dogs.

Another plantlike toxin is blue-green algae. It often appears as viscous mats along the shore of more stagnant water and may have a rusty brown color. The blooms contain a neurotoxin that can kill a dog within one hour. But most poisonings aren't from plants, and most aren't fatal.

If you suspect poisoning, seek help immediately from an emergency vet. Bring the packaging or any remnant of the poison you suspect. The ASPCA operates a poison hotline: (888) 426-4435. The group also offers a searchable database of toxic and nontoxic plants, as well as a free mobile app about toxins focused on dogs, cats, horses and birds.

COMMON PLANTS THAT ARE TOXIC

ALOE

CARNATION

DAISY

EUCALYPTUS

GARLIC

HYDRANGEA

LILY

Slow Feeder for Puppies

My puppy was eating his food so fast that he vomited it back up. Instead of buying a slow-feed bowl, I drilled holes into a 12-in. length of 2-in. PVC pipe and capped the ends. I fill the tube with puppy food, and he has to roll it around to get the food to fall out of the holes. My puppy gets all the food he needs, and I don't have to clean up the mess that comes from eating too fast. Be sure the holes are large enough for the food to come out!

CHARLIE MAY

PVC pipe

33 DIY PEST CONTROL TIPS

Sealing your house on the outside beats fighting pests inside

BY MIKE BERNER

Insects, spiders and rodents all have their place. OUTSIDE! It's faster and easier to keep pests out than it is to remove them. The exterior of your house is full of paths for pests to find their way in. So we called on our expert to help us find those paths and give us some tips and tools to lock pests out.

MEET THE EXPERT
Joe Stampley would be the first to say that he'd rather not make a trip to your house. He says prevention is the best pest control advice.

Seal them out!

1 TRIM TREES: Overhanging branches make your roof accessible for tree-scaling pests like squirrels and chipmunks.

2 CAP YOUR CHIMNEY: Any vents on your roof that lead into your home should be covered with a cap and screen.

3 SEAL VENTS: Gable, soffit and crawl space vents need a mesh backing to keep out critters. When it's missing, these are good spots for birds and bats to call home.

4 REMOVE STANDING WATER: The stagnant water in rain barrels, wheelbarrows, pools and birdbaths can become a breeding ground for insects such as mosquitoes.

5 SEAL YOUR GARAGE: A broken garage door seal will allow pests to move into your garage Replacing it is easy.

6 TAKE CARE OF ANTHILLS: If the ants on your driveway don't bother you, use a perimeter spray to keep them outside. If you want them gone, use granular bait.

7 FILL HOLES: Use hydraulic cement to patch small holes from old conduit or cable entry points, as well as gaps and cracks in your block or concrete foundation. Use caulk for gaps and cracks around trim and siding.

8 FLAPPER CHECK: Make sure the flapper for your dryer vent opens easily and closes all the way.

9 INSPECT DOOR AND WINDOW SEALS: Check that the weather stripping and sweeps are intact, and repair them if they aren't.

10 PROTECT YOUR GARDEN PRODUCE: If you don't want to fence the garden, try a raised bed. If rabbits are eating your garden, sprinkle powdered fox urine around the plants.

11 GUTTER DETERRENT: Keep critters from clogging gutters by using a downspout guard and retractable downspout.

12 BAG YOUR BURNERS (NOT SHOWN): When grilling season is over, wrap the burners and any other openings to keep bugs out.

Take your time inspecting

The first step on your pest prevention patrol should be to walk around your house armed with a mirror, kneepads and a roll of masking tape. Plan to spend about an hour noting and marking spots where pests could find a way in. A good place to begin is the front door, and move your way around the house. Start low and look for cracks and holes in the foundation. Then look for gaps where the siding starts and work your way up to the roof.

Check vent flappers

Check the flappers on your dryer and range vents. They're designed to open as air gets pushed out of these appliances, but if the vents become clogged, the flappers will get stuck open. This is especially true for dryer vents. Remove any debris or lint buildup and make sure the flapper closes when the appliance isn't exhausting.

Setscrews

Flue pipe

Cap the chimney and vents

Chimney caps and furnace exhaust vents are easy to seal. Chimney caps have setscrews that snug the cap to the flue pipe. PVC vent caps with mesh come in different sizes and fit right over the end of the exposed pipe.

Repair screens

If you have insects sneaking into a small tear in a window or door screen, a quick patch will do the trick.

Cut a square hole around the tear with a straightedge and a sharp utility knife. Keep the hole as small as possible and leave at least 1/2 in. of old screen next to the metal frame.

Cut a patch of fiberglass screen that will lap 1/2 in. over each edge. Lay wax paper under the window screen to keep the glue from sticking to the workbench. Apply a bead of glue around the hole, and spread the glue through the patch and window screen with a flat wooden stick.

Cracked vent boot

Quick fix for a roof boot

After years of exposure to weather, roof vent boots can dry and crack, leaving an inviting opening to the warmer air inside. Bees and other insects, as well as rain and snow, can get in and cause havoc. You don't need to replace the boot; just buy no-caulk thermoplastic flashing and slip it over the vent. They cost less than $5 at home centers.

No-caulk vent flashing

Replace weather stripping

If your weather stripping is allowing big drafts to get through your windows and doors, chances are bugs can find a way into your house as well. Check that the weather stripping is sound and replace it if necessary. For older doors and windows, an adhesive-backed option is quick and easy. For newer doors, the weather stripping has a built-in barb that fits into a kerf on the doorjamb. Pull the old one out and press a new one in.

Seal your garage door

If your garage door can't seal tight, it may as well be open. Remove the bad seal from its track, then scrape and brush away the dirt and corrosion with a screwdriver and a stiff brush. Install the new seal, using a little dish soap and water to slide the new garage door seal into the track.

Caulk gaps in siding and trim

There's often a gap where two different types of building materials come together, and pests will come right in. To seal the gap, first fill it with backer rod (sold in many different sizes), then mask off a nice, clean line for caulk, squeeze it in and smooth it out.

How NOT to attract pests

■ **REMOVE PEST HOMES**
Woodpiles, garbage cans, wheelbarrows full of dirt or water, and children's sand tables can all make nice homes for pests. Move them away from your home, cover them or remove them altogether.

■ **ELEVATE YOUR PLANTS**
Pests love vegetation, but if the plants are on a stand, they're a lot harder to get at. Potted plants can also collect water, which is a breeding ground for insects.

■ **TAMPER-PROOF PET FOOD**
Your pet isn't the only one who likes dry kibble. Don't store pet food in the bag you buy it in. When you open the bag, dump it into a sealed, tamper-proof container.

■ **UPGRADE PORCH LIGHTS**
Ever notice the flock of insects at your front door light? It's not necessarily the light they are attracted to; it can be the heat from the bulb. Swap your incandescent bulb for an LED option that's approved for wet locations.

■ **NO-VACANCY A/C**
It's smart to protect your A/C unit from snow and ice during the winter. Instead of creating a nice, warm home by wrapping it with a tarp, protect it with a piece of plywood and a few bricks.

■ **PEST-PROOF YOUR GRILL**
When you store your grill for the winter, make sure it's clean and free of grease and burnt bits of food. If the burners are removable, take them off, wrap them and plug the hose ends to keep bugs out.

■ **CLOSE THE GARAGE DOOR**
It's obvious, but when you're not going in or out of your garage, make sure it's closed—or you'll find yourself fostering birds, mice and squirrels.

■ **CLEAN THRIFTING**
If you like the thrill of bargain hunting, make sure you also enjoy cleaning whatever furniture or clothing you find before you bring it in. You never know where it came from or if it sat in a garage for years before someone decided to donate it.

Our favorite sealing weapons

COPPER AND EXPANDING FOAM

Stuff a generous amount of copper mesh into the larger gaps around your home. Use a screwdriver to press it in, leaving about 1/2 in. of space to fill with expanding foam. The foam will keep out small pests, and the copper mesh will act as a second layer of defense in case the foam is chewed by pests.

HYDRAULIC CEMENT

To fill holes in your block or concrete foundation, use hydraulic cement. Regular cement shrinks as it cures, making it difficult to get a good patch. Hydraulic cement expands as it cures, so it can fill voids tightly. **Note**: After you mix hydraulic cement with water, it will start to harden after about three minutes, so mix up only what you can apply in that time.

SIDING, WINDOW AND DOOR CAULK

Caulk is the gold standard for filling small gaps and cracks up to about 3/8 in. deep and wide. When you're buying caulk to fill gaps outside, look for the words "paintable" and "flexible" on the tube. If you can't find a matching color, go with clear so it doesn't stand out.

DOWNSPOUT GRATES AND RETRACTABLE DOWNSPOUTS

Mice and squirrels can find a home inside your gutters and downspouts. Prevent this at the top with a downspout grate and at the bottom with a retractable downspout.

FIBERGLASS MESH

This is the go-to screen door patch, but it's also great for attic and crawl space vents, which have larger spaces that birds and bats can get through. Most vents will have it already, but if it's missing, glue or staple a layer of mesh on the back of the vent.

WIN THE WAR ON PESTS

Tools and tricks of an expert

J oe Stampley does battle with home invaders every day. And wins. Some of it is dirty work: crawling under decks, squeezing into attics, cleaning out traps and removing wasp nests. But there is a lot more to pest control than dirty work. Joe's skills in identification and prevention and his experience outsmarting pests are what really make Joe successful. To help you win the war, he opened his toolbox and shared some tricks of the trade.

MEET THE EXPERT
Joe Stampley is a technician for Plunkett's Pest Control (plunketts.net).

MORE SMARTS = LESS CHEMICALS
"It's more practical than spraying a chemical." Joe uses chemicals as as a last resort— only about 10% of the time.

IDENTIFICATION IS KEY
Understanding what you're up against is the first step to getting your pest problem under control.

MICE ARE THE WORST
Joe's toughest foes are mice. They reproduce and populate quickly, making them hard to eliminate.

Joe's Pest Tool Chest

Joe carries a lot of gear to jobs. He needs to be prepared with tools to identify, contain and exterminate pests safely. We dumped out all his tools and asked about each of them.

DISINFECTANT SPRAY + DUST BRUSH + TOILET BRUSH
Joe makes sure the area he leaves behind is cleaned up and sanitary for the homeowners. Disinfecting spray and a dust brush are the perfect tools for small droppings and other messes. He wields a toilet brush for bigger messes.

HEADLAMP
Frequently encountering dark spaces, cracks and crevices, Joe finds a light mandatory, and having both hands available to plug holes and set traps, priceless.

Kneepads

BAIT GUN
This gun can apply bait, insecticide and rodenticide gels with pinpoint precision. Joe prefers using the bait gun because chemical sprays drift around.

RESPIRATOR
Joe doesn't often use chemicals—only when all his other options have failed—but when he does, he protects himself with a mask and respirator. He changes the filters regularly and makes sure his mask is cleaned every day so he doesn't have to smell yesterday's cheeseburger.

LATEX GLOVES
You might think these are for protecting Joe's hands from the chemicals, and you'd be right, but they also keep scents from giving Joe away. Many pests have a strong sense of smell and run for cover when they smell humans.

Safety glasses

EXPANDING FOAM

Joe uses window and door foam instead of foam formulated to stop pests. Anti-pest foams work, but Joe would rather avoid chemicals in areas where kids might poke and pick at foam.

COPPER MESH

Forget steel wool; it can rust and crumble away. Use copper mesh instead. It will last forever, and the interlocking design makes it difficult for rodents to gnaw through and pull out of cracks.

DID YOU KNOW?

Ants are the ultimate pest: They are found on every continent except Antarctica and have been around for more than 50 million years. They don't have eyelids, so they never sleep. They also snack on rodenticide without harm.

Specimen tray

ZONE MONITOR

These sticky cardboard tents attract and trap insects. They allow Joe to identify the pests and know the quantity he's dealing with. And that helps him decide what to do next.

Inspection mirror

HANDY STICK

This is a home-made tool consisting of a hook screw and a dowel. Joe uses it to reach into small crevices and ones he'd rather not stick his hands into. And sometimes, he uses it to scoop something up off the ground to avoid bending over.

INSECT BULB DUSTER

Joe uses a bulb duster to gently apply powdered pesticides in cracks and on other surfaces. He also has one for nontoxic powders like flour or baby powder that he uses to track pests in areas where chemicals should be avoided, such as kids' rooms and daycare centers.

BRUSH MULTI-TOOL

Joe has fashioned this trap cleaner into his own pest multi-tool. It not only cleans out the traps he empties daily but also contains the keys for opening them.

First aid

Bait station

PETS & PESTS

Joe's tips for outsmarting pests

HEED THE WARNINGS ON PESTICIDES

The labels on insecticide and rodenticide products have important information on how to use them safely, including where to spray, when to spray, how much and how often. Keep yourself, your family and the environment safe by strictly following these guidelines.

ASK GOOD QUESTIONS OF POTENTIAL EXTERMINATORS

When hiring a pest control service, ask:
- How do you plan to identify the pests?
- What removal methods do you use, and how do you keep pests out?
- When do you decide to resort to chemicals, and what products do you use?

The answers can help steer you to a professional, safety-minded company. For more info about hiring a pro, visit pestworld.org.

DON'T EXPECT INSTANT RESULTS

Pest control is a process, not a set-it-and-forget-it solution. Joe often makes several trips to identify, monitor and solve problems. In some cases, you'll need ongoing service to keep pests from returning.

OVERDO TRAPS

Joe always puts out more than the required number of traps. If the situation calls for 15 traps, he puts out 20. This ensures that he catches all the rodents. For extra insurance, he leaves a few traps behind.

PROTECT OTHER ANIMALS

When targeting pests, you can accidentally harm other animals. This is called secondary poisoning, and birds and other animals that make a snack out of pests can get caught in the crossfire. Joe uses pesticides that contain warfarin or bromethalin because they pose less risk to birds and mammals through primary and secondary poisoning.

Oily rub mark left by rodents

DOUBLE UP

Mice can nibble away expanding foam, and tiny insects can sneak past copper mesh. When possible, use both. Stuff in the mesh then seal it in with foam.

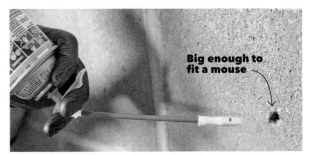

Big enough to fit a mouse

DON'T SKIP TINY HOLES

Mice can fit into a hole as small as 1/4 in. If their elongated skulls can fit through, the rest can too. Plus, filling those holes will also keep bugs out.

Possible entry point

KEEP THE LIGHTS OFF

To find pest entry points, head to the basement, crawl space or garage and keep the lights OFF. Light shining through gaps and cracks will show you where pests can get in. And you'll have better luck tracking down rodents and other pests because many are nocturnal and sensitive to light—when a light goes on, they will scurry!

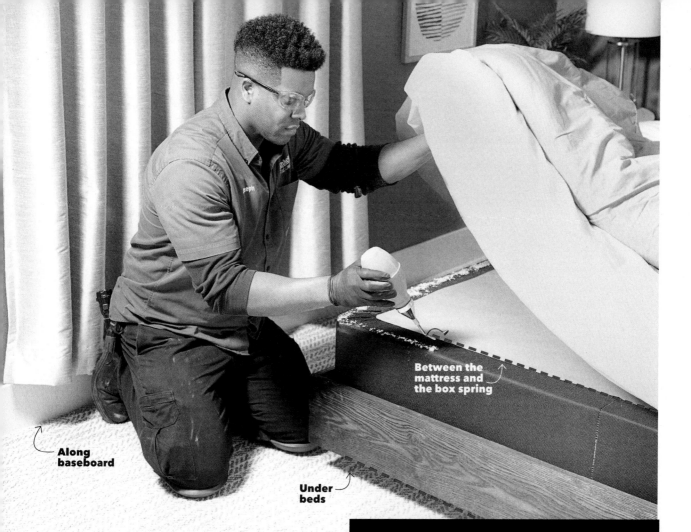

Between the mattress and the box spring

Along baseboard

Under beds

SAFE, EFFECTIVE PESTICIDE

Diatomaceous earth is harmless to humans; some brands are even considered safe for consumption (although there's no reason to eat it). Here's how it works: When insects like bedbugs or ants crawl over diatomaceous earth, this abrasive powder scratches off the waxy layer of their exoskeleton. The bugs then become desiccated and die. Joe spreads diatomaceous earth with his bulb duster under mattresses, bed frames and at the baseboard trim.

12 simple steps to prevent pests

Sometimes it doesn't take a pest pro to keep out pests. There are many quick and easy steps you can take yourself:

- ■ Install a squirrel guard on your bird feeders. It will keep rodents from spilling the food and attracting more pests.
- ■ Clean outdoor grills and cooking areas.
- ■ Use city-issued trash bins, and if they get cracked or the lid goes missing, ask for a replacement.
- ■ Move stacks of firewood away from your house. They make perfect homes for pests. If you don't want a pest nest, don't stack wood at all.
- ■ Take out the trash more often.
- ■ Don't store paper bags or an excess of household cleaning products under cabinets, near trash or next to your fridge.
- ■ Run a dehumidifier to remove moisture.
- ■ Go through your storage area twice a year and move things around. If nothing jumps out at you and you see no signs of pests, you're fine—but you probably will.
- ■ Remove clutter.
- ■ Eliminate standing water.
- ■ Get rid of mold and bacteria.
- ■ And finally, Joe says, "If you see a hole and you can plug it, plug it."

YARD PESTS?

16 proven solutions from a pro

BY JASON INGOLFSLAND

There are hundreds of ways to deal with yard pests. But what works and what doesn't? For expert guidance, we talked with Derrick Benz, who battles pests every day, all day (and wins!). He told us that few solutions work every time.

Sometimes, small deterrents are enough. If you just make food or shelter a little harder to find, critters will often move to friendlier areas. But if animals are especially hungry or stubborn, you may have to try several solutions. Here are some of the strategies that have worked the best for Derrick.

❶ Lock down your trash

Raccoons are especially good at opening trash cans, but a bungee cord is usually enough to foil them. Also deal with trash odor. Garbage may smell bad to you, but to many pests it smells like dinner. Put trash in plastic bags and seal them. If your trash can is dirty, wash it out with soap and water.

❷ Pick up nuts and fruit

Lots of animals love nuts and fruit. Removing these treats while they're on the tree usually isn't practical. But gathering fallen apples or raking up nuts is an effective way to send critters elsewhere for dinner.

❸ Eliminate hiding places

Small animals seek out hiding places—in open spaces, they feel exposed to predators. So trim the shrubs around your foundation. Also check around your property for any other hiding spots, like wood piles, and move them away from your house.

❹ Let your dogs out

Animals are less likely to come near your yard if they know a potential predator is around. Your dog may show you where the invaders are hiding out—and leave scents that ward off unwanted visitors.

❺ Kill off clover

Clover isn't the worst weed in most lawns, but Derrick says it's one of the most attractive to rabbits and deer. There are a few ways to eliminate clover, but the best defense is healthy grass.

❻ Cut the grass

Tall grass in a neglected lawn isn't just an eyesore; it makes an attractive haven for insects and rodents. Even if those grass dwellers don't bother you outdoors, some will find their way into your house. They'll also attract predators that you may not want in your yard.

❼ Contain compost

Uncovered grass or leaves are fine, but any compost that contains food scraps needs a pest-proof container or cover. Otherwise, you're inviting animals to a feast.

❽ Install plastic predators

Plastic owls often scare off rodents. The key is to mount them up high, usually on the roof or in a tree—that's where animals expect to see predatory birds. You can get a plastic owl for $20 or less online.

❾ Remove squirrel nests

Squirrels can be a yard nuisance, but it gets worse: Eventually, they'll look for ways to get into your house, seeking nesting sites in your attic or eaves. To make them feel unwelcome, it's best to knock down their nests. Sometimes, you can do that with a long pole. In other situations, it's easier to cut off a tree branch to bring down the nest. Either way, removing squirrel homes is a great incentive to make them seek friendlier yards.

❿ Wipe out grubs

Grubs living in soil are yummy to some rodents. Little cone-shaped holes in your yard are usually evidence that raccoons or skunks are digging for grubs. Moles and voles also go where the grubs are. Eliminate your grub problem with grub killer, available at home centers for $15 to $25.

⓫ Scare them with scents

Derrick says a few drops of coyote, fox or wolf urine is a good deterrent. He recommends a light application, just around the perimeter of your yard and garden. You won't notice it, but animals will smell it from a distance and go elsewhere. You'll find predator urine at home centers and online for $25.

⓬ Fence out rabbits

Keeping rabbits out of gardens with chicken wire is an old idea, but Derrick says patience is the key to their departure. It may take months for the bunnies to give up and move to other feeding grounds.

Loves grubs!

⑬ Close the backyard buffet

Pests are like people: If you're serving up their favorite meal, they'll keep on coming back. Knowing what attracts pests is often the first step toward keeping them away. Want to discourage a particular type of pest? Check this list to see if there are food sources you're willing and able to remove.

PEST	COMMON FOODS THEY EAT
SQUIRRELS	Walnuts, acorns
COYOTES	Mice, squirrels
DEER	Hostas, leafy shrubs and bushes
MOLES	Grubs
RABBITS	Clover, berry bushes, berry trees
RACCOONS	Grubs, trash
SKUNKS	Grubs
TURKEY	Grass, insects, berries

Motion sensor

⑭ Spray them away

Motion-activated sprinklers often discourage deer, rabbits and raccoons, according to Derrick. Just keep in mind that animals may get used to the sound and spray and eventually ignore them. Motion-activated sprinklers are available at home centers and online for about $45.

⑮ Catch and release—far away

Derrick is a believer in live trapping but says homeowners often make mistakes. Here are a few tips for success:

- When handling the trap with an animal inside, wear Kevlar gloves.
- Choose a trap with a metal plate under the handle to protect your hand from teeth and claws.
- Call a wildlife preserve to see if you can release the animal there.
- Release animals at least 10 miles from your home; their ability to find their way back is incredible.
- When finished, clean the trap with a bleach solution to eliminate scents that may scare off the next critter you want to trap.

⑯ Install a chimney cap

Various animals will occasionally find their way down a chimney, but Derrick says raccoons especially like chimneys as nesting sites. Chimney caps cost as little as $20 at home centers and online.

5 Exterior Repairs & Improvements

DIY CURB APPEAL

Mike and Steph Berner are busy people. Aside from full-time jobs, they have two preschool kids, a baby on the way and a new home. It's a good house—no serious problems. But like most older homes, it needed updates, especially for curb appeal. Since Mike is an editor at *Family Handyman*, the whole crew saw an opportunity to get outside and show what we can do. On the following pages, you can see the projects that made Mike and Steph's house look better than new.

MAKE YOUR ROOF LOOK LIKE NEW P. 188

CUSTOM SHUTTERS THAT COST LESS P. 179

A BOLD, UPDATED FRONT DOOR P. 182

BEFORE!

AFTER!

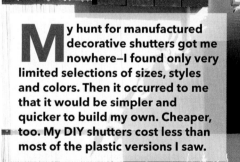

CUSTOM SHUTTERS

The size, style and color you want—for less than the cost of plastic shutters

BY JEFF GORTON

My hunt for manufactured decorative shutters got me nowhere—I found only very limited selections of sizes, styles and colors. Then it occurred to me that it would be simpler and quicker to build my own. Cheaper, too. My DIY shutters cost less than most of the plastic versions I saw.

MEET THE EXPERT
Jeff Gorton is a carpenter, remodeler and former *Family Handyman* editor.

Figure A
Custom Shutter

EACH SHUTTER IS 14" WIDE.
THE HEIGHT IS DETERMINED BY
THE WINDOW HEIGHT.

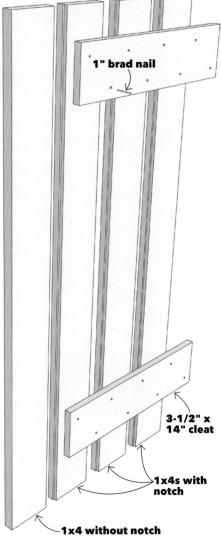

1" brad nail

3-1/2" x
14" cleat

1x4s with
notch

1x4 without notch

Figure B
Notch

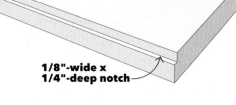

1/8"-wide x
1/4"-deep notch

Materials
In addition to 1x4 boards, you'll need 1-in. nails,
2-in. exterior screws, waterproof wood glue and
painting or finishing supplies.

My design is simple, just four 1x4 boards joined by a cleat. The details are what make the shutters special. I'll show you how to cut notches in the boards to create attractive shadow lines and how to reduce the thickness of the cleats for a refined appearance.

Measure, then buy materials
Before going to the home center, measure your windows to determine the height of the shutters so you can figure out the length of boards you need. For the most authentic look, measure from the top of the window frame (not including the window trim) to the top of the windowsill and build your shutters this height. Use these measurements to make your lumber list. Each pair of shutters requires eight 1x4 boards and an additional 5 ft. of 1x4 for the cleats.

I chose Boral TruExterior trim boards for my shutters.

Inexpensive pine boards would also be fine, but you'd have to be vigilant about repainting them in the future. Any moisture entering the wood would quickly lead to rot. If you prefer a rustic look, cedar with a transparent or semi-transparent stain would be a good choice. Whatever you choose, be careful to pick out straight boards with undamaged edges.

Mounting the shutters
I used 2-in. exterior trim-head screws to mount my shutters (one screw in each corner). This approach will work with most wood, vinyl, aluminum and steel siding. If you have a stucco or masonry exterior, you'll have to mark the screw hole locations on the exterior and drill holes to accept plastic masonry anchors. Light-duty anchors are fine for this job. For more information, search for "masonry anchors" at familyhandyman.com.

WHAT IT TAKES

TIME	COST	SKILL LEVEL
2 hours per pair of shutters	$25 to $35 per pair	Intermediate

TOOLS
Basic hand tools, drill, table saw, miter saw

1x4 board

1

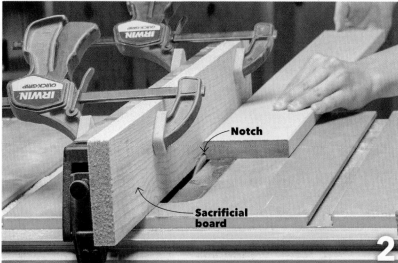

Notch

Sacrificial board

RESAW SAFELY

You'll have to remove the blade guard to resaw boards, so it's essential that you use a push block to keep your fingers well away from the blade. Also mount a featherboard to the saw just in front of the blade. You can make a featherboard or buy one. This Kreg model (Photo 3) costs about $25 online.

2

Push block

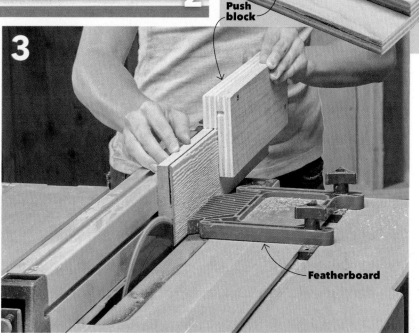

3

Featherboard

1 CUT BOARDS TO LENGTH

Every pair of shutters requires eight boards of the same length. For fast, accurate cuts, use a stop block. Screw the block to a board that's about 6 in. longer than your shutter height. Clamp the board to your miter saw fence so that the distance from the blade to the block equals the shutter height. Then simply slide the end of the board against the block and make your cut.

2 NOTCH THE BOARDS

Six of the eight boards are notched along one edge, creating an attractive shadow line between the boards. To cut the notches, clamp a sacrificial board to your table saw fence. Position the board against the blade and set the blade height at 1/4 in. Run the boards across the blade, move the fence slightly away from the blade and then run them across a second time to get a notch 1/8 in. wide.

3 RESAW THE CLEATS

You could use 3/4-in.-thick stock for the cleats, but I think thinner cleats look better. To "resaw" the cleats to 1/2 in. thick, set the blade height at 1-7/8 in. and the fence 1/2 in. from the blade. With the board on edge, make the first cut. Then turn the board over and make the second cut.

4 ASSEMBLE THE SHUTTERS

Arrange the boards on your workbench and clamp them together. Measure the width across the four boards and cut cleats to that length. Then, using one of the cleats as a guide, draw lines 3-1/2 in. from each end. Apply waterproof wood glue to the cleats and fasten them with 1-in. nails. Let the shutters rest for at least an hour before painting or finishing.

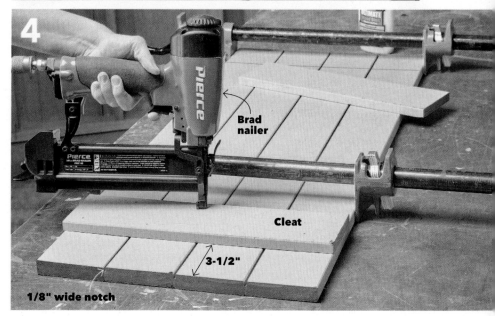

4

Brad nailer

Cleat

3-1/2"

1/8" wide notch

FRONT ENTRY
FACE-LIFT

Update your front door the easy way

BY MIKE BERNER

The usual way to replace a door is to tear out the old jamb and install a new "prehung" door. Often that's a good way to go. But in my older house, that would have meant ordering a custom jamb width, fussing with tricky interior trim for hours and cutting back the hardwood flooring. So I chose to put a new door in the old jamb. This did require some extra work; I had to move hinges and strike plates for the latch and dead bolt. But I still think it was faster and easier.

You can skip those steps If you're lucky when you hang your new door and the new hardware locations match the old. I'll show you how to change out a door slab and trim and how to solve problems along the way.

BEFORE

To complete the new look, we replaced the dated light fixture, house numbers and mailbox with modern matte black options.

4 things to know before you buy a door

Purchasing a door isn't an open-and-shut decision; there are many things to consider before opening your wallet. Here's how I break it down:

1 Most doors are sold "pre-hung," which means they come attached to a doorjamb. The hinges are installed and the dead bolt/latch holes are bored. Because pre-hung doors are readily available, it might be easiest to buy one and scrap the jamb.

2 Less common are slab-only doors. They require boring holes for hardware and cutting mortises for new hinges.

3 Measure your existing door—height, width and thickness—and buy one to match.

4 Door swing is important. Most doors swing inward; a left-hand inswing door has hinges on the left and opens to the left. A right-hand inswing door has hinges on the right and opens to the right.

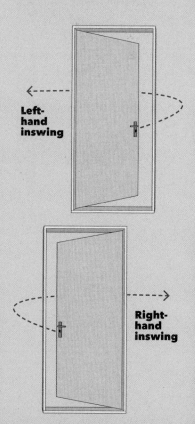

Left-hand inswing

Right-hand inswing

1 REMOVE THE OLD DOOR

Unscrew the hinges from both the new door and the existing door, then set the new door in place to find out if the strike plates and hinges line up with the old ones. If they do, screw the hinges into the jamb and consider yourself lucky—and skip to **Photo 6**. If the new hinges don't line up, draw a line from the bottom hinge to the top that connects the back edges of the hinges. It will help you place the new hinges later.

2 PLUG THE HOLES

Glue pine blocks into the latch and dead bolt holes. When the glue sets, cut the blocks flush with a chisel. Glue thin strips of pine into the hinge mortises.

Dead bolt plug

Latch plug

WHAT IT TAKES

TIME	COST	SKILL LEVEL
1 day	*$350 and up*	*Intermediate*

TOOLS
Drill, pry bar, oscillating tool, router plus a bit/sharp chisel, circular saw or miter saw

MATERIALS
All-purpose wood filler, two 8-ft. 1x2s (plugs plus jamb extensions), Z-flashing

3 FILL THE GAPS

Smooth over the plugs with auto body filler. The filler hardens fast; you can apply two coats if needed and sand it flat, all in about 30 minutes.

4 MARK THE HINGE LOCATIONS

Cut two blocks of scrap wood to the height of the threshold plus 1/8 in. Set the door onto the blocks and move the door into position. Make sure the new hinges are on the line you drew along the old hinges. Then temporarily attach the door with one screw in each hinge. Trace the hinges with a sharp pencil and remove the door.

5 CUT MORTISES

Follow the traced line with a utility blade, making this cut as deep as the hinge is thick. Then, with a chisel at the edge of the jamb, establish the depth of the mortise and work your way from the top down. Cut with the bevel of the chisel down to keep the blade from digging in. When you reach the knife line, the chips should fall away. Hinge-mortising router jigs make this job easy and fast, but if I have only one door to do, I cut the mortises by hand.

3

Line up new hinges here

Mortise plug

4

Threshold block

5

Score with knife

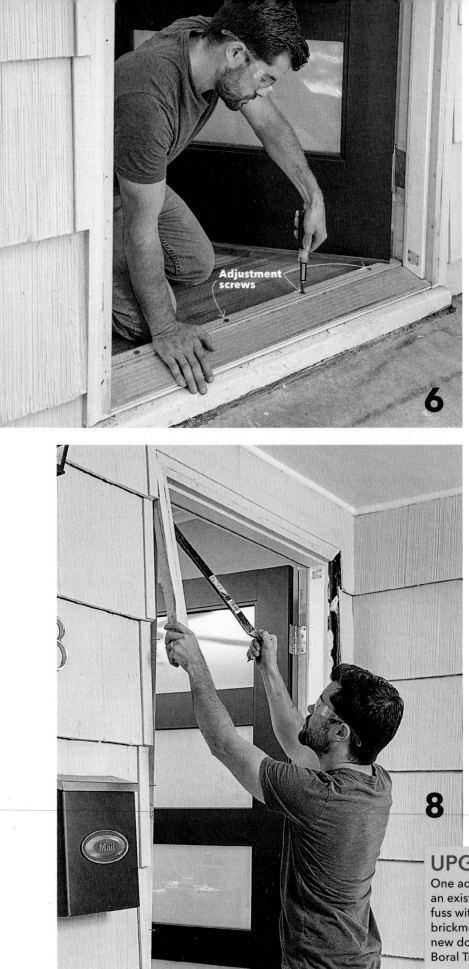

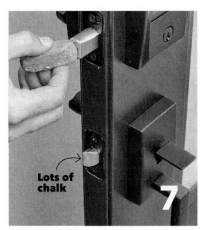

Lots of chalk

Adjustment screws

6

8

6 INSTALL THE DOOR AND ADJUST THE THRESHOLD

Place the door back on the blocks, predrill and screw the hinges in the new mortises. To make the fit air-tight, turn the adjustment screws to move the threshold up or down. You want the door sweep to be pinched slightly when the door is closed.

7 LINE UP THE DEAD BOLT AND LATCH

Use chalk or lipstick to coat the ends of the dead bolt and door latch. Retract the dead bolt and latch as you close the door all the way, then turn the handles to let them contact the jamb. Use a 7/8-in. Forstner bit to drill holes where the latch and dead bolt touched the jamb. Place the strike plate over the hole and trace and cut mortises as you did for the hinges.

8 REMOVE THE OLD TRIM

Cut any caulking between the trim and the siding with a utility knife. Otherwise, you might lift the siding as you pull off the trim. Take care to not dent the doorjamb as you pry the trim away.

UPGRADE YOUR TRIM

One advantage of putting a new door in an existing jamb is that you don't have to fuss with the trim. But, I didn't think the old brickmold trim fit the sleek style of the new door. So I replaced the old trim with Boral TruExterior trim. Here's how I did it.

9 CUT THE SIDING

If your new trim is wider than the old, you'll need to cut back the siding. I used 3-1/2-in.-wide trim and wanted a 1/4-in. reveal on the doorjamb as well as some wiggle room for caulking, so I traced a line 3-7/8 in. in from the doorjamb. An oscillating tool worked well to cut my cedar shake siding.

10 INSTALL NEW TRIM

Cut a length of Z-flashing 1/4 in. wider than the top piece of trim. Tuck the flashing under the existing tar paper or house wrap. The sheathing on my house was about 1/4 in. proud of the jamb, so I cut a 1/4-in. jamb extension to let the trim sit flat. I tacked the extension 1/8 in. from the edge of the jamb.

11 FASTEN THE TRIM

Screw the trim to the sheathing and doorjamb with trim-head screws every 24 in. Since my trim is wider than the sill, I cut a notch around the sill. To finish up, caulk along the siding, fill the screw holes and paint.

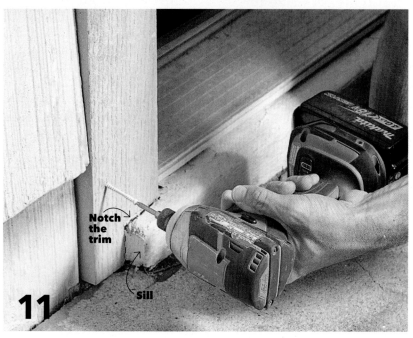

Roof Stain SOLUTIONS

Remove and prevent ugly roof algae

BY JASON INGOLFSLAND

Roof stains make any house stand out—but not in a good way. Luckily, these stains aren't inevitable as a roof ages. They're caused by algae growth in humid, shaded areas, usually with lots of tree cover. While algae won't damage your roof, it will hurt your home's curb appeal.

Fortunately, it's easy and inexpensive to remove and prevent stubborn algae stains yourself. Here's how to clean your roof and make your home stand out in the best way.

HOW TO REMOVE ROOF STAINS

To see an immediate improvement, you'll need to climb onto your roof, spray it with a cleaning solution and rinse with water. A cleaning solution and water will remove most algae stains right away, but some can be especially difficult. If you have a steep roof, it's best to call a pro. Here's how I cleaned my roof.

1. MIX A HOMEMADE SOLUTION

To save money, I opted to make my own solution. Commercial roof cleaners are available at most home centers, but they're expensive and won't work any better than a homemade solution. Plus, it's easy to make your own. Mix 15 oz. of an oxygen bleach powder (I used OxiClean Stain Remover, available at home centers for about $12) with 2 gallons of warm tap water in a garden sprayer. Don't use chlorinated bleach; it'll kill the lawn and plants on the ground below.

2. SPRAY THE SHINGLES

Once you're on the roof, start at the edge and spray the shingles with your homemade solution, working your way up to the ridge. A wet roof is a slippery roof, so leave a dry path back to your ladder. Allow the solution to sit for 20 minutes before rinsing. Tough stains may require an additional application and a mild scrubbing with a stiff-bristle brush.

3. RINSE WITH A GARDEN HOSE

After you've waited for the solution to do its work, douse the roof with a garden hose, clearing suds and algae off the shingles. You'll see a big improvement unless your stains are especially stubborn. Never use a pressure washer to clean the algae; the roof will be clean, but its life will be shortened by the loss of granules.

MEET THE EXPERT
Andy Lodge has been in the industry since 1981 and has worked on hundreds of roofing projects around the world. He is now a consultant for IKO Industries.

BE SAFE!
Climbing a roof is dangerous. Use a safety harness, wear boots or shoes with good traction and consider installing a slide guard. For more information, search "roof safety" at familyhandyman.com.

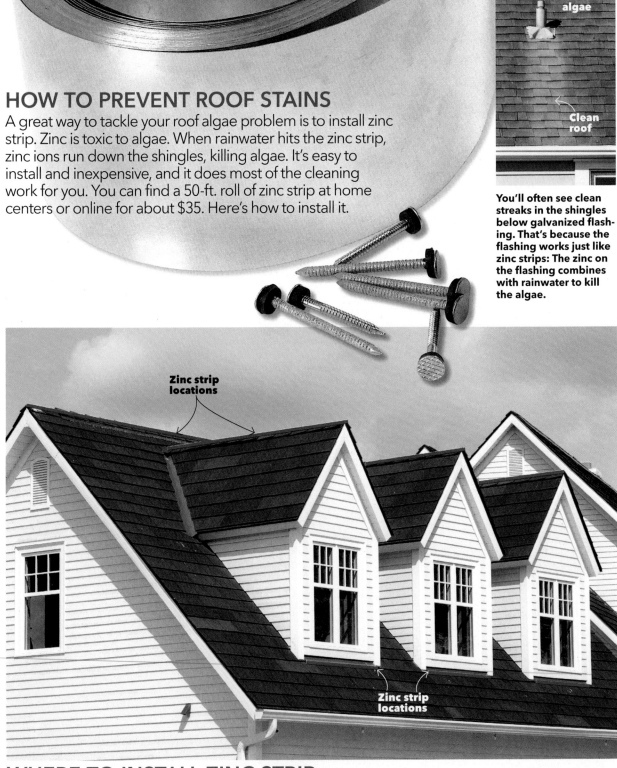

HOW TO PREVENT ROOF STAINS

A great way to tackle your roof algae problem is to install zinc strip. Zinc is toxic to algae. When rainwater hits the zinc strip, zinc ions run down the shingles, killing algae. It's easy to install and inexpensive, and it does most of the cleaning work for you. You can find a 50-ft. roll of zinc strip at home centers or online for about $35. Here's how to install it.

Black algae

Clean roof

You'll often see clean streaks in the shingles below galvanized flashing. That's because the flashing works just like zinc strips: The zinc on the flashing combines with rainwater to kill the algae.

Zinc strip locations

Zinc strip locations

WHERE TO INSTALL ZINC STRIP

Zinc strips work only on areas directly downhill. So if you have dormers, ungalvanized roof vents, valleys, roofs under gables or any other sections that could obstruct the flow of zinc, install zinc strip in those locations too.

HOW TO INSTALL IT

1. SLIDE IT UNDER THE SHINGLES

Start at the beginning of the ridge and gently pry up the cap shingles with a crowbar. Roll out 2 ft. of zinc strip and slide it no more than 1 in. under the cap shingles.

2. FASTEN UNDER THE SHINGLE

Fasten with galvanized rubber washer nails under the shingles. You can also use an exterior construction adhesive. Continue to fasten the zinc strip every 12 in. until you've reached the end of the ridge and then clip it to length with scissors. I found cutting the zinc strip at the end saved time and kept it from flapping around in the wind.

Zinc strip test

Zinc strip is often marketed as a moss, fungus and algae preventer, but not as a remover. However, expert home inspector Reuben Saltzman installed zinc strip on a moss-covered roof to see if it would remove the moss over time. As you can see in the before and after photos, it significantly reduced the moss and algae. So, if you don't mind waiting, you can skip the cleaning and let zinc strip do the job.

SHINGLES BEFORE

18 MONTHS LATER

Replace your roof with algae-resistant shingles

If you're in the market to reshingle your roof, consider installing algae-resistant shingles. They'll keep your roof looking great and cost about the same as standard shingles.

INSTALL AN
OUTDOOR HANDRAIL

Add safety and style with a custom railing

BY JEFF GORTON

A new iron handrail on the front steps will enhance your home's curb appeal, but the real benefit is the safety it provides. Whether you need to replace a wobbly old railing or add a railing where there isn't one already, we'll show you how to order and install a new one.

Iron handrails range in price from $50 to $150 and up per running foot. In addition, some companies charge several hundred dollars to measure for and install the railing. Here's where you can save cash. We'll show you how to measure a simple set of steps so you can order a custom railing. If your entry steps are curved, have jogs or are an unusual shape, ask the railing company to measure for you. Either way, we'll also show you how to securely bolt the completed railing to your concrete steps.

Order a custom railing

Careful measuring is the key to a successful handrail order. **Photos 1 - 4** show how to take the measurements you'll need to order the railing. Record the measurements on a sketch as we show at right. Take the sketch to the railing fabricator to place the order.

Most large cities have an iron railing fabricator that will be glad to show you the railing designs it sells. There are a few standard styles—you just have to choose between straight and twisted spindles, and perhaps between a top rail that starts with a "lamb's tongue" and a scroll.

We added a few upgrades to the basic railing to come up with our design (**Photo 5**). First we chose to install a brass cap rail. Then we added a second rail 4 in. below the top. We also increased the size of the straight spindles from the standard 1/2-in. width to 5/8 in. for a heavier appearance. For an easy do-it-yourself installation, ask the railing company to weld 3-in.-square stainless steel plates to the bottom of each post and drill 3/8-in. holes in all four corners. Then you can simply bolt the rail to the stairs as we show here. Get a quote from your fabricator for your railing design.

After ordering your custom railing, you'll probably have to wait a few weeks for it to be completed. But once you get the railing home, it'll take you only a few hours to do a top-notch installation. The only special tool you'll need is a hammer drill with a 3/8-in. masonry bit. You can rent a large hammer drill for about $30 for four hours, and the bit will cost about $10. Purchase 3/8 x 1-7/8-in. sleeve anchors and 5/16-in. cap nuts for each. Make sure you wear safety glasses and hearing protection when you're drilling.

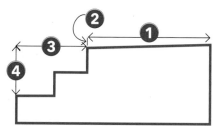

Make a simple sketch and jot down four measurements to help the fabricator build a perfect railing.

1 MEASURE THE LANDING

If you're installing railings on both sides, make separate sketches and take separate measurements for each side.

2 MEASURE THE SLOPE

Lay a level on the landing and shim it until the bubble is centered. Then measure the gap between the level and the landing.

3 MEASURE THE RUN

Hold a level against the lowest step and adjust it until the bubble reads plumb. Then measure from the edge of the level to the edge of the landing.

4 MEASURE THE RISE

Lay a level on the landing and adjust it until the bubble is between the lines. Measure from the level to the top of the bottom step to determine the total rise of the two steps.

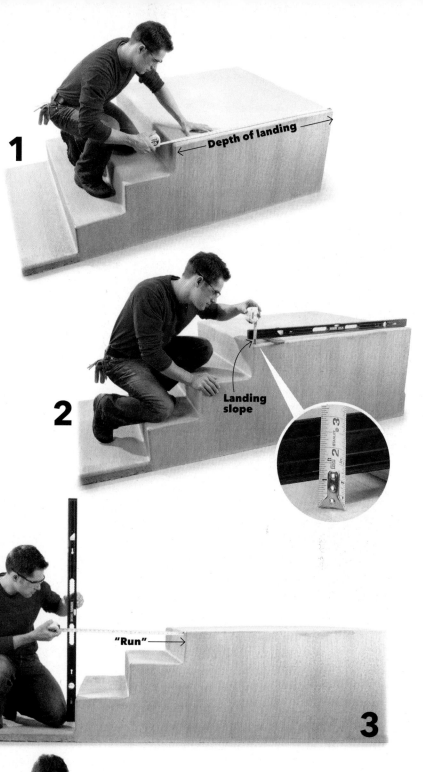

Hammer drill

Mounting plate

5

6

Depth gauge

3/8" masonry bit

7

Strong anchors make for a sturdy railing

Sleeve anchors provide strong support in solid concrete. But the pressure exerted by the anchors as you tighten the nuts can crack or "blow out" concrete that's not structurally sound. Before you order a new handrail, be sure the concrete is solid—that is, free of cracks and surface deterioration.

If your steps are covered with brick or stone, materials that can easily crack, you may have to use a different anchoring method, such as a two-part epoxy anchoring system. Ask the railing fabricator for advice before you order the rail.

Photos 5 and **6** show how to locate and drill for the anchors. Set the railing on the steps with the edge of the plates at least 1-1/2 in. from both the front and the side of the step. Adjust the railing position until the mounting plates are parallel with the side of the steps. Then mark the hole locations with the drill while the railing is in place to ensure accurate bolt placement.

Start by drilling one starter hole through each of the end brackets and dropping an anchor bolt into the hole. This keeps the railing from shifting while you mark the remaining holes. When all the holes have been marked, remove the railing and complete the holes by drilling them 2-1/2 in. deep. Drill vertical holes; otherwise, the plate may not fit over the bolts. Set the gauge on your hammer drill for accurate hole depth.

When all the holes have been drilled, tap anchor bolts into each one and set the railing into place (**Photo 7**). Snug up the bolts, but don't fully tighten them until you've checked the posts for plumb (**Photo 8**).

5 LOCATE THE ANCHOR HOLES

Position the railing with the plates an equal distance from the edges of the steps. Drill one hole at each end and drop in anchors to hold the railing in place. Then mark the remaining holes by drilling shallow starter holes.

6 DRILL ANCHOR HOLES

Set the railing aside and drill 2-1/2-in.-deep holes.

7 INSTALL THE ANCHORS

Tap in the anchors. Then remove the nuts, set the railing into place and snug up the nuts.

Sleeve anchor

Shim posts for a perfect installation

Out-of-level steps can cause the handrail posts to lean. **Photo 8** shows how to check for and solve the problem. We used stainless steel washers because they're thinner than galvanized washers and won't rust. They're readily available at hardware stores and home centers. As an added precaution against corrosion, spread a layer of high-quality caulk under each plate before bolting them down. This keeps water out of the bolt holes and provides a little extra strength.

For a neater-looking job, we cut off bolts that were too long and replaced the hex nuts with decorative cap nuts (**Photos 9** and **10**). The railing company painted the cap nuts to match the railing.

8 CHECK THE POSTS

If a post leans, loosen the nuts and slide a washer under the side it leans to. Snug the nuts and recheck the post.

9 CUT THE BOLTS

Saw the bolts flush to the hex nuts with a hacksaw. Then remove the hex nuts.

10 ADD CAP NUTS

Thread cap nuts onto the bolts and tighten them.

Mini hacksaw

Hex nut

9

Stainless steel washers

8

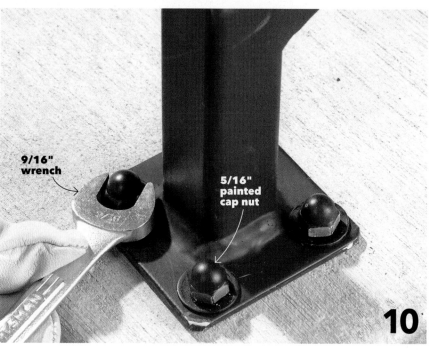

9/16" wrench

5/16" painted cap nut

10

Carpet deodorizers can kill your vacuum

Many carpet deodorizers contain baking soda because it's a good odor absorber. But a vacuum repair technician tells us that baking soda is harmful to your carpet as well as to your vacuum's performance and longevity. Here's how it can damage your carpet and your vacuum:

■ Baking soda particles, which are abrasive, work their way under the carpet where your vacuum can't suck them out. In heavy traffic areas, the resulting abrasion breaks down the carpet backing.

■ Baking soda gets into the vacuum's motor, gears and bearings, gradually destroying them.

■ Baking soda can quickly clog a vacuum cleaner filter. A clogged filter makes the vacuum work harder, wearing it out much sooner.

Better solutions

To remove odors, you need to clean them out, and baking soda doesn't clean. You wouldn't sprinkle baking soda on your clothes, vacuum it off and call them clean. Cleaning involves a carpet cleaning machine, liquid carpet cleaner and water.

To make your house smell good without harming your carpet or vacuum, try Fragrant Scent Vacuum & Room Freshener ($8 for a two-pack online). It's safe to vacuum, and you can put it in the vacuum itself to deodorize the vacuum, too.

SIMPLY CLEAN

Tools, tricks and recipes for a spotless home

Schar Ward cleans the old-fashioned way—with homemade cleaning solutions, rags made from sheets, and a little elbow grease. With decades of experience, she's tackled dirt, grime and stains that aren't for the faint of heart, and she doesn't think you need fancy new products to clean. With a little knowledge, you can get the job done with many of the household cleaners you probably have lying around. Here are some of her favorite techniques to make your house shine.

MEET THE EXPERT
Schar Ward has been professionally cleaning homes since 1973. She's the author of *Teaching Children to Clean* and loves to pass on her knowledge to the next generation.

Schar's Secret Weapons

Shown below are Schar's favorite commercial cleaning products—for removing stubborn mineral deposits, cleaning and protecting wood surfaces, and more. We were surprised to learn that for most cleaning tasks, she prefers to mix her own solutions. Check those out at right.

OLD ENGLISH
To clean and protect wood surfaces, Schar recommends Old English. Its nongreasy formula helps prevent water marks and stains.

PHOSPHORIC ACID CLEANER
For stubborn mineral deposits on natural stone, porcelain, concrete and masonry, Schar says phosphoric acid cleaner is a must-have. After applying, let it sit for 10 minutes, rinse and you're done. You could use vinegar, but it takes longer.

MURPHY OIL SOAP
Schar loves using this cleaner on wood floors, but she emphasized that you need to dry the floor afterward.

FOLEX
Schar has seen plenty of tough carpet stains. She says Folex carpet spot remover has never failed to take out a stain. You can find it online or at home centers.

USE ERASER SPONGES ON PAINT WITH CAUTION
Eraser sponges like the Magic Eraser have their uses, but be careful on painted surfaces; they can alter the sheen of the paint. Alternatively, use a mix of Murphy Oil Soap and baking soda to clean walls.

MAKE YOUR OWN CLEANING SOLUTIONS

Instead of loading up on expensive cleaners, make your own solutions with common household products like vinegar and baking soda. Here are a few of Schar's recipes:

SCRUBBING SOLUTION
- 1-3/4 cups baking soda
- 1/2 cup water
- 1/2 cup castile soap
- A few drops of essential oil

Mix in bowl and stir until it has the consistency of frosting. Store in a pump bottle. Shake well before use. It's effective on pots and pans, sinks, bathtubs and more.

ALL-PURPOSE SPRAY
Fill a spray bottle with half vinegar and half water. Add 10 drops of scented oil.

WINDOW CLEANER
Pour one bottle of club soda in a spray bottle.

HARD-WATER BUILDUP CLEANER
- 1 tsp. borax
- 1 tbsp. castile soap
- 2 tbsp. white vinegar
- 2 cups water
- 5 drops of essential oil

Mix and store in spray bottle.

ESSENTIAL OILS
Add an essential oil to your cleaning solutions for a fresh scent.

CLEANING

Tips to Clean Like a Pro

RUN THE DISHWASHER WITH VINEGAR

Dishwashers need to be cleaned if you have hard water. Place a half cup of vinegar on the top rack and run it normally. Do this every few weeks.

DITCH THE MOP

Schar doesn't use a wet mop. She says mops do more harm, spreading dirt everywhere. Instead, she says to clean floors on your hands and knees. First vacuum, then fill a bucket three-quarters full of warm water and 1 tbsp. castile soap. Wash with a terry cloth rag in a 4-sq.-ft. section, dry and repeat, working your way out of the room.

KNEEPADS Inexpensive, non-marring foam cap kneepads help keep you comfortable while you wash the floor.

- **■ MAKE YOUR OWN RAGS**
  To save money, Schar makes her own rags from sheets she buys at the thrift store. Cut them to size and if you like, hem them so they don't fray. You'll have plenty of rags without paying a premium.

- **■ WASH YOUR RAGS TWICE**
  If you want a clean house, you need clean rags. Dirty rags harbor all kinds of bacteria, so wash your rags twice—once with bleach and the second time without.

- **■ FORGET DISPOSABLE CLOTHS**
  Disposable dust cloths might seem like a good idea, but use a flannel cloth with a little Old English instead. It's just as effective and you'll save money.

- **■ ANYTHING YOU WASH, YOU DRY**
  Don't wash surfaces with a cleaner and let them dry on their own; it leaves a sticky residue. Dry everything after washing.

- **■ LIFT OBJECTS; DON'T SLIDE**
  When dusting, it's easy to move objects around without thinking about how you're moving them, but Schar emphasizes you must lift them rather than sliding. Sliding scratches the finish.

A PUMICE STONE GETS RID OF MINERAL BUILDUP

Use a pumice stone to remove mineral deposits from toilets, sinks, tubs and oven interiors. Pumice is abrasive enough to grind off the minerals but won't scratch porcelain. Just be sure to keep the end wet. You can use it on grill and oven grates, too. Pumice stones cost about $1.50 each at home centers and online.

Don't get overwhelmed

Faced with a whole house to clean, you're more likely to procrastinate, get sidetracked during the job or just give up. So Schar has developed a strategy to make cleaning manageable, approachable and efficient.

■ **START WITH THE DIRTIEST ROOM FIRST**
Tackle the big project first and everything else will seem easy in comparison. Plus, you'll feel better when it's done.

■ **WORK TOP TO BOTTOM, LEFT TO RIGHT**
When staring a dirty room in the face, you may feel at a loss to know where to start. Schar recommends you work top to bottom, left to right. When you're done, do a quick once over to see if you've missed anything.

■ **SET A TIME LIMIT**
Instead of telling the family it's a cleaning day, set a time limit and stick to it. Cleaning isn't so bad when you say you'll do it for two hours rather than all day.

Wax paper

USE HEAVY BOOKS TO HELP REMOVE CARPET STAINS

Spray the stained area with Folex or other carpet stain cleaner, blot it with towels, being sure not to rub, and cover the towels with wax paper. Then place heavy books or other weights on top of the towels. Leave the weights in place overnight and the stain will be gone.

BOWL SWAB
Schar uses a bowl swab to clean toilets. Standard toilet brushes don't work well for spreading toilet cleaner around the bowl—a little water rinses it right off the bristles. The swab, on the other hand, retains the cleaner and can reach underneath the rim and down the throat of the toilet bowl. Schar also uses a swab to clean tile.

RAGS
Schar uses three types of rags: cotton sheets, flannel and terry cloth. The cotton sheets are for drying windows, the flannel is for dusting, and the terry cloth is for scrubbing.

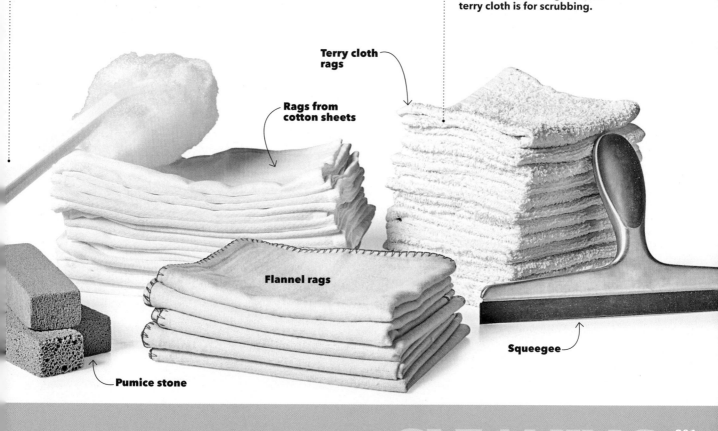

Terry cloth rags

Rags from cotton sheets

Flannel rags

Squeegee

Pumice stone

CLEANING

201

EASY STICKER REMOVAL

My son plastered his bedroom furniture with stickers. Once he moved out, I turned his bedroom into the guest room. To remove the stickers, I softened the adhesive with a blow dryer and scraped them off with a plastic putty knife.

STEVE WINTER

INSTANT INK REMOVER

Alcohol-based hand sanitizers do a good job of removing permanent marker ink. They reactivate the ink, allowing you to easily wipe the stain off. Cover the entire ink stain with hand sanitizer. Let it sit for about a minute and then wipe off the ink with a soft rag.

RAY WESTERHOFF

Steam-Clean Your Microwave

I've found that steam is the best way to clean my microwave. But I don't use just water. Here's my special mix: Combine 2 cups of water, 2 tablespoons of vinegar, and lemon rinds in a microwave safe bowl. Microwave the mixture on high for about five minutes, and then, with the door still closed, let it sit for three minutes more. Remove the bowl and wipe down the interior with a sponge.

KARY MURPHY

6 Outdoor Structures, Landscaping & Gardening

PERGOLA PARADISE
Like a traditional pergola, it shades the patio. But the slatted walls also provide privacy—without making you feel hemmed in.

LAZY DAY LOUNGER
Incredibly comfortable and easy to build, it's also practical with its huge, easy-access storage drawer.

MODERN CONCRETE PATIO
We got the trendy look of oversize porcelain pavers minus the oversize price tag.

backyard
ESCAPE

ALL-IN-ONE GRILLING STATION
Designed for style and convenience, this super-sturdy console will support the heaviest grill and last a lifetime.

MEET THE HOMEOWNERS

When Sara and Robert Stelfox bought their new home, the entire backyard was a blank space, a big, flat rectangle of grass. Anyone would have called it bland, but to Sara, Robert and the *Family Handyman* editors, it was also a perfect opportunity. After hours of sketching, debating and refining plans, we selected the projects shown here.

Sara's favorite feature is the roomy lounger. Tucked into a corner, it's a private getaway where she can relax with a book. For Robert, the pergola has transformed the backyard the most. It blocks the Florida sun but allows a cooling breeze to flow through. For details on these projects and more, check out the following pages.

PERGOLA
PARADISE

Shade and privacy with a modern twist

By Mike Berner

Create an escape in your own backyard by building this beautiful pergola. The horizontal slats block the sun and harsh wind while keeping the space open enough for you to enjoy a breeze. It's the perfect spot to enjoy your morning coffee or wind down after work.

The angled rafters nicely complement the ceiling slats and eliminate the need for bracing. This pergola may look big and complex, but only a few details separate it from a traditional pergola. Once the posts are placed, the rest is easy.

WHAT IT TAKES

TIME	COST	SKILL LEVEL
4 days	$2,000 to $4,000	Intermediate

TOOLS & MATERIALS
Standard carpentry tools, drill/driver, circular saw, angle grinder, 15-gauge nailer

PLANNING AND BUILDING TIPS

- We built this pergola in Florida, where building codes are strict about hurricane-proofing. Really strict. We spent more than $3,000 on specialty hardware, engineered drawings and permits. Chances are, your local codes will allow you to skip some of these costly steps. You could downsize the beam to a double 2x8, opt for smaller, 4x4 posts and use bolt-down post bases rather than bases that are set in the concrete (**Photo 2**). Check with your local building inspector.
- This pergola was part of a project that included a new patio. If you already have a concrete patio, set the posts right on top. Again, check with your local inspector.
- Only two posts are needed to hold up the beam. You can position the other three for less privacy or more, or eliminate them.
- This pergola is built from treated lumber and cedar. Cedar drives up the cost substantially. Using treated slats and fascia will save you about $800.
- The diagonal rafters are supported by 45-degree joist hangers. If your local building code requires hangers, note that you'll need both left and right versions. If not, skip them and save $400.
- I nailed the joist hangers to the ledger before installing rafters. This made installing the rafters a major hassle. It would be better to tack the rafters into place and then add the hangers.
- The house we built the pergola onto had concrete walls. Attaching the ledger board required drilling into the concrete and $80 worth of wedge anchors, as well as extra labor.

Figure A
Modern Pergola
Overall dimensions:
19' 10" W x 9' 11" D x 8' 6" H

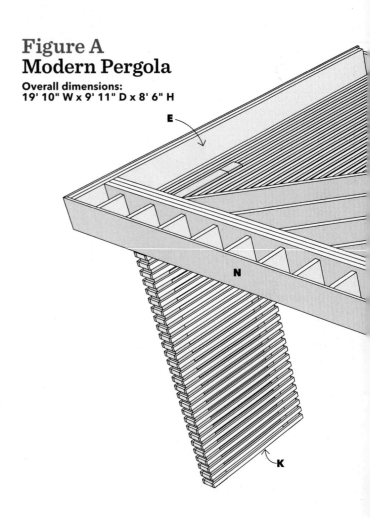

Figure B
Pergola Layout

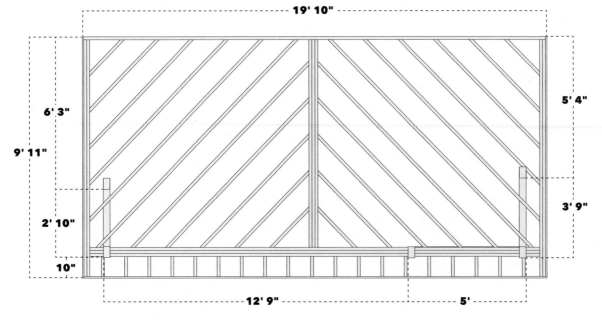

Materials List

ITEM	QTY.
Pressure-treated 2x8 x 14'	10
Pressure-treated 2x8 x 20'	1
Pressure-treated 2x10 x 20'	3
Pressure-treated 2x10 x 10'	7
Pressure-treated 4x6 posts	5
Pressure-treated 2x4 x 8'	5
Pressure-treated 2x6 x 8'	3
Skewed hangers (left)	22
Skewed hangers (right)	22
Post bases	5
Double 2x8 concealed hangers	2
Triple 2x8 hangers	2
2x8 joist hangers	19
90-degree framing angle	4
Cedar 1x2 x 8'	31
Cedar 1x2 x 10'	142
Cedar 1x12 x 16'	4
Wedge anchors	15
Hanger nails, stainless steel	
15-gauge nails and construction screws	

Cutting List

KEY	PART
A	2x8 ledger board
B	4x6 post
C	3-ply 2x10 main beam
D	2x8 fascia blocks
E	2-ply 2x10 side beam
F	3-ply 2x10 center beam
G	2x8 angled rafters
H	2x6 wall frame
J	2x4 wall frame
K	1x2 horizontal cedar cladding
L	1x2 ceiling cedar cladding
M	Cladding nailer
N	1x10 cedar fascia

1 LAY OUT THE POST LOCATIONS

Determining the post locations is the fussiest part of this project. I drove two stakes 109 in. from the house and stretched a string between them. Then I adjusted the stakes until the string was exactly parallel with the house.

2 PLACE POST BASES

When the concrete was firm enough to hold the post brackets, I used the string and the edges of the concrete to position them and pushed them in with short up-and-down motions.

3 FASTEN THE LEDGER

This house is built from concrete blocks, so we had to drill holes in the concrete, pound in wedge anchors and tighten them up to secure the ledger board. For wood-frame homes, lag screws will do the trick. I propped the ledger in position with 2x4s.

String line

Heavy-duty post base

Skewed hanger

Ledger board

2x4 prop

AVOID HANGER TROUBLE

On a traditional pergola, the joists are perpendicular to the house, and it's best to attach the hangers before installing the ledger board. I tried that with the skewed hangers on this pergola, but fitting the rafters into them became a big challenge.

Instead, attach the center and side beam hangers and mark where the rafters should go, then screw the rafters into place and slide the hangers in after. To get that cool symmetrical look, be sure the rafter marks are symmetrical on the ledger board.

2x8 fascia blocks

2x4 anti-tip support

4 STAND THE POSTS

Cut the posts to ceiling height. Because this patio was level, I was able to get an accurate measurement from the patio to the bottom of the ledger board. When the posts are level in both directions, add bolts or screws.

5 CUT OFF THE BOLTS

If your post bases require bolts, cut them flush with the nuts. A reciprocating saw will do the job, but an angle grinder and cutoff wheel are much faster.

6 INSTALL THE MAIN BEAM

At 20 ft. long, the triple 2x10 beam would have been way too heavy to lift onto the posts, so we built the beam in place. I screwed a scrap of 2x4 to the back of the column and then glued and nailed the 2x10s together. The outer board needed hangers and blocks to hold the fascia. I attached those before we lifted the board into place.

Double hanger

Triple hanger

3-ply center beam

Spacers

7

8

9

10

7 ATTACH THE SIDE BEAMS

Check that the columns are still plumb and attach the side beams. Slide each side beam into its hanger on the ledger board, then screw it to the side of the main beam and reinforce them with 90-degree framing angles. We ran the beams long, then trimmed them to line up with the blocks. Check that the structure is square by taking diagonal measurements at opposite corners. If the measurements aren't equal, reposition the main beam on the posts until they are.

8 HANG THE RAFTERS

Cut each rafter to length, making a 45-degree bevel on each end. As you install the rafters, be sure they're all parallel. Mirror the rafter pattern on the other side by lining up the rafters at the center beam. Then go back and install the skewed hangers.

9 PREFINISH THE SLATS AND FASCIA

To save time and get better results, stain the slats before installation. I applied a generous layer of Cabot Australian Timber Oil with a roller, then smoothed it out with a brush.

PRO TIP: Galvanized nails are notorious for leaving streaks in cedar, so I used 15-gauge stainless steel nails.

11

10 NAIL ON THE SLATS

Level the bottom slat about 2 in. off the patio and nail it into place. I spaced the rest of the slats 1-1/2 in. apart, using two spacers that I cut and marked with an "X." For consistency, I used the same ones throughout. Stop every few rows and check the measurement from the ceiling on both ends of the slat to make sure it's level. Use the same spacers for the ceiling slats.

11 ADD THE FASCIA

Wrap the exposed blocks and beams with fascia boards. The front of the pergola requires two pieces; cut the two boards so the seam lands in the middle of a block. Flush the fascia board to the bottom of the ceiling slats and nail it on. Cover the sides in one piece. Touch up the cut ends of the slats with stain, then start enjoying the shade!

WHAT'S WITH THE DIAGONAL RAFTERS?

I worried that this whole structure would easily sway from side to side. To prevent this "racking," I considered adding diagonal bracing to the posts or above the rafters. But either option would have just looked bad. Then the solution came to me: diagonal rafters! They add rock-solid stability and look beautiful from below.

MODERN CONCRETE PATIO

High style on a low budget

By Brad Holden

When we were choosing a patio design, we came across a patio much like this one but made with big, gray porcelain pavers. We all agreed it was exactly what we wanted. Then we checked the price of porcelain— over $5,000! We opted for concrete instead.

This design is not only stylish but also perfect for someone with limited concrete experience. It's much more forgiving than a big, continuous slab. On a large slab, a mistake in the form or in finishing can lead to depressions and water puddles. And inadequate base prep can lead to cracking. This segmented design makes those problems much less likely. To complete the look, you add decorative rock between the pavers.

Are you ready to take it on? If you have help, you can build this patio in a weekend!

WHAT IT TAKES

TIME	COST	SKILL LEVEL
2 days	$1,000	Intermediate

TOOLS & MATERIALS
Circular saw or miter saw, drill, magnesium float, hand edging tool, hard trowel, 2x4s, 1-by stakes, sand, concrete, rebar, rebar chairs, landscape edging, decorative rock

Get expert advice on forming, pouring and finishing concrete at **familyhandyman.com.** Just search for "concrete."

Prep the site

Remove the existing sod, giving yourself a little extra room around the edges to make it easier to place the form and screed the concrete. We also dug our footings extra large for a pergola. Scrape, rake and shovel the patio area to make it as level as possible. Depending on the grade and the finished height of your patio, you may need to add some sand fill.

Lay out the patio's footprint with stakes and string. Make sure all the math works out and that the footprint is square.

1 BUILD THE FORMS
Assemble the form in sections. Stake the forms in place using 1-by stakes between the 2x4s. The stakes created a gap to get the width we wanted, and we also used them to level the forms.

2 LEVEL THE FORM
Lift and adjust the form to make it level, then screw it to the stakes. Once you're satisfied, cut the stakes flush with the top of the form.

Oops! We left the gaps open between the 2x4s, realizing too late that they'd fill with concrete. This made it difficult to remove the forms after the concrete was set. To avoid that, we recommend covering the gaps with duct tape before pouring. Also, fill in sand up to the bottom of each individual paver space, so the concrete doesn't flow underneath the form, filling the gaps from below.

1-by stake

Gap

3 SET AND TIE REBAR

Lay a rebar grid in each cavity, tying the intersections. Set the rebar grids on specially made "chairs" to elevate the rebar into the slabs.

4 OIL THE FORMS

Spray or brush the forms with kerosene, diesel fuel or cooking oil. This makes it easier to remove the forms after the concrete has set.

5 FILL THE FORMS

Starting in the corner closest to the house, fill each form. The easiest way to do this is to hire a pump truck. The hose is heavy, but not nearly as much work or headache as trying to run a wheelbarrow over the grid. We used fiber-reinforced concrete to ensure these slabs won't crack.

Ready-mix vs. you-mix concrete

We built forms, ordered ready-mix concrete and poured the entire patio at once. If that's too daunting, you can build one or two small form sections and pour them individually at a more leisurely pace. If you choose that route, consider buying a portable mixer and selling it when you're done.

You won't save money mixing it yourself, though. Using 80-lb. bags of mix, it'll cost you about $200 per cu. yd. We hired a pump truck for $180 and included fiber reinforcement in the mix, and our total price came to $116 per cu. yd. This project took just over 4 yards, so ordering ready-mix concrete was a great deal cheaper than mixing it ourselves.

Rebar chair

Cooking oil

Screed board

Magnesium float

Edging tool

Trowel

6 SCREED THE CONCRETE

Have a helper screed each section after it's filled. Our patio is large, and pouring the forms progresses quickly, so a crew of four is best to perform all the tasks before the concrete sets. The person doing the screeding should be limber, as they'll likely end up crawling around on the form grid a bit no matter how well you've planned the process.

7 "FLOAT" THE SURFACE

After the bleed water has disappeared, float each section with a magnesium float. Floating embeds coarse aggregate particles and smooths the surface without sealing it. Before our concrete set up too much, we measured for the post anchors and installed them for the pergola.

8 ROUND THE EDGES

Once the concrete begins to stiffen, it's time to start rounding over the edges of the pavers with a special edging tool. You'll need to move quickly—there's a lot of edging to be done!

Heavy-duty post anchor

10

11

9 TROWEL THE CONCRETE

When you're able to kneel on knee boards on the concrete and only leave a 1/8-in.- to 1/4-in.-deep indentation, start troweling the pavers. Troweling makes the surface hard, dense and smooth. Put a little "spring" in the trowel to increase that effect and feather out the transition created by the edger.

10 REMOVE THE FORMS

After the concrete has cured, back the screws out of the leveling stakes and start prying out the forms. They should come out fairly easily. If you need to use a hammer and pry bar, take care not to damage the concrete. If the forms are stubborn, run a reciprocating saw around each paver before pulling the forms.

11 FILL THE GAPS

Install landscape edging around the patio perimeter. We used Permaloc ProSlide Commercial Grade Landscape Edging ($2 to $5 per linear foot). Using a shovel and broom, fill the spaces between the pavers with your choice of gravel or decorative rock.

lazy day LOUNGER

Build it in a weekend, enjoy it for years

BY JAY CORK

Searching for patio furniture, I encountered endless chairs and benches. But I wasn't looking for just a place to sit: I wanted a comfortable spot where I could curl up with the dog and recline with a book.

When I finally found the right sofa, it was crazy-expensive (more than $1,600!). So, I chose to build one and vowed to make it even better than the one at the store. I made it larger and more comfortable, customized it to complement the space, and even added a drawer. Best of all, this weekend project is built to last, and it's dead simple, too. If you can cut wood and drive screws, you can build it!

A custom cushion

I found a great selection of cushions for patio furniture at local home centers, but I didn't find one that worked well for this design. So I chose a local upholsterer who charged $430 for labor and materials. Custom patio cushions are also readily available online.

BUILT-IN STORAGE
This easy-to-assemble drawer is handy for storing blankets or a few essentials for outdoor dining.

WHAT IT TAKES		
TIME	**COST**	**SKILL LEVEL**
2 days	$400 plus the cushion	Beginner

TOOLS *Table saw with combination blade, miter saw, random orbital sander or sanding block, drill driver, tape measure, caulking gun, spring clamps, brad nailer (optional)*

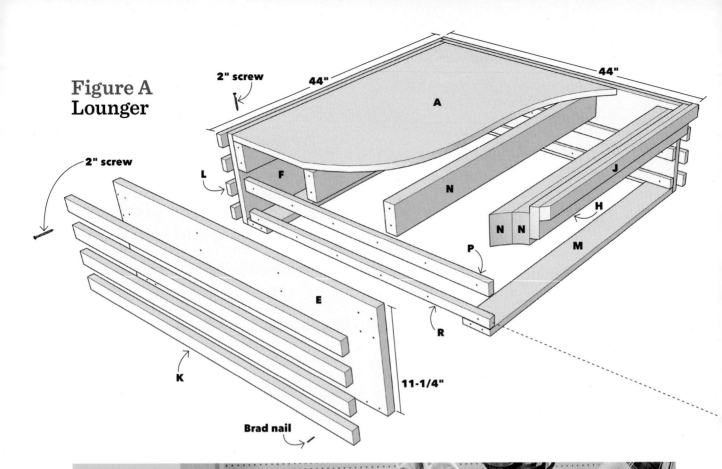

Figure A
Lounger

2" screw

44"

44"

A

2" screw

L

F

N

J

H

N N

N

P

M

E

R

11-1/4"

K

Brad nail

Pro Tip:
To cut more parts in less time and with greater consistency, stack the pieces and use a stop block.

1

2

1 CUT THE PARTS
Cut the back and sides of the box frame (E and F). Because the back, the internal support rails and the braces (M and N) are exactly the same length, cut them all at the same time. Don't cut the front (H) to length quite yet.

2 ASSEMBLE THE BOX FRAME
Screw the sides to the back, then attach the bottom braces (M). Once these parts have been assembled, measure the width of the box frame. Cut the front (H) to that length and assemble.

Materials List

ITEM	QTY.
1x12 x 6' cedar boards	4
2x4 x 8' cedar studs	3
1x4 x 8' cedar board	1
1x2 x 8' cedar boards	8
4' x 8' x 3/4" AC plywood	1
1x6 x 36" solid oak boards	2
Quart of exterior urethane	1
Quart of stain, paint or wood finish	1
1-1/4" exterior screws	1 box
2" exterior screws	1 box
1-1/4" brad nails	1 box
Exterior caulk	
Wax	

Cutting List

KEY	QTY.	SIZE	PART	MATERIAL
A	1	3/4" x 36-3/4" x 36-3/4"	Top	3/4" plywood
B	2	3/4" x 4-1/2" x 33-1/2"	Drawer front/back	3/4" plywood
C	1	3/4" x 22-3/4" x 35"	Drawer bottom	3/4" plywood
D	2	3/4" x 4-1/2" x 22-3/4"	Drawer sides	3/4" plywood
E	2	7/8" x 11-1/4" x 37-5/8"	Sides	1x12 cedar
F	1	7/8" x 11-1/4" x 36-3/4"	Back	1x12 cedar
G	1	7/8" x 7-1/4" x 38-1/2"	Drawer face	1x12 cedar
H	1	7/8" x 3-1/2" x 38-1/2"	Front	1x12 cedar
J	4	3/4" x 1-1/2" x 40"	Front cladding	1x2 cedar
K	8	3/4" x 1-1/2" x 39-1/4"	Side cladding	1x2 cedar
L	4	3/4" x 1-1/2" x 38-1/2"	Back cladding	1x2 cedar
M	2	3/4" x 3-1/2" x 36-3/4"	Braces	1x4 cedar
N	5	1-1/2" x 3-1/2" x 36-3/4"	Top supports	2x4 cedar
P	2	3/4" x 1-1/4" x 36"	Drawer slide part 1	3/4" oak
Q	2	3/4" x 2-1/2" x 36"	Drawer slide part 2	3/4" oak
R	2	3/4" x 1-1/2" x 36"	Drawer slide part 3	3/4" oak

Figure B
Drawer

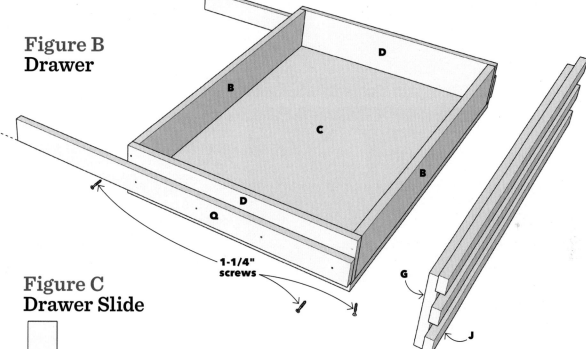

1-1/4" screws

Figure C
Drawer Slide

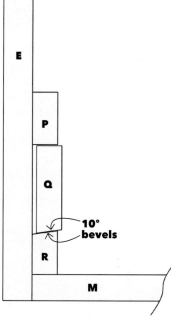

10° bevels

Figure D
Plywood Cutting Diagram

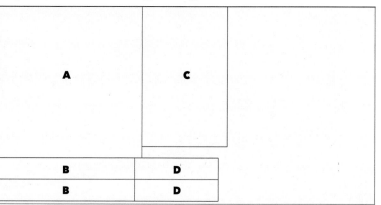

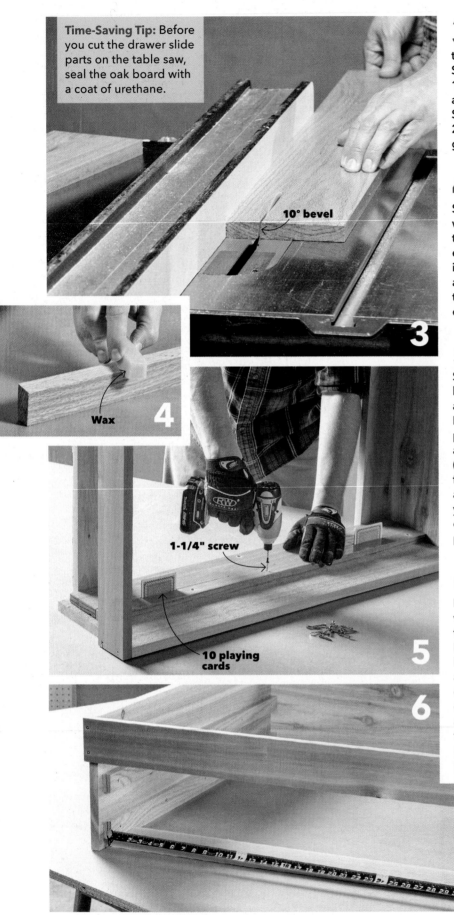

Time-Saving Tip: Before you cut the drawer slide parts on the table saw, seal the oak board with a coat of urethane.

10° bevel

Wax **4**

1-1/4" screw

10 playing cards **5**

3

6

3 CUT DRAWER SLIDES

Each drawer slide consists of three parts, all cut from the same board. Set the blade on the table saw to 10 degrees and the fence to 1-1/2 in. and make the first cut. Label this part P. Set the blade back to zero, the fence to 2-1/2 in. and make the second cut. This gives you parts Q and R.

4 LUBRICATE THE SLIDES

Sand the edges of the drawer slides with 320-grit sandpaper and clean off the dust. Rub wax along the beveled edges of the drawer slides; really work it into the surface of the wood. Rub off any excess with a cotton cloth. I prefer to use beeswax, but paraffin or any candle will work well too.

5 INSTALL THE DRAWER SLIDES

Start with part P, snugging it tight to the bottom braces. Be sure the bevel is angled into the side of the box frame. Predrill and screw it down. Now, place part Q snugly against part P and place a 1/8-in. spacer (Figure C) on top of it (about 10 playing cards works perfectly for this). Place part R against the spacer and screw it to the box frame. When you remove the spacer, part Q should easily slide out the front. Repeat this process on the opposite side.

6 MEASURE FOR THE DRAWER

From one of the 4 x 4-ft. pieces of plywood, rip three strips at 4-1/2 in. Cut the drawer box sides (D) to length. Measure the distance between the left- and the right-side drawer slides and subtract 1/4 in. Write this number down: it's the absolute width of the drawer box. Further subtract 1-1/2 in. and note that number. This confirms the dimensions of the front and back pieces (B) of the drawer box. Cut the pieces to length.

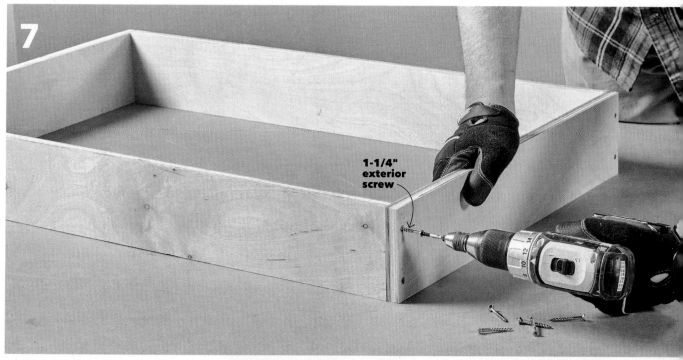

7

7 ASSEMBLE THE DRAWER BOX

Assemble the drawer box by screwing the sides to the front and back. Measure to confirm the exact dimensions and cut the drawer bottom to that size. Attach it with glue and screws.

8 ADD THE DRAWER BOX SLIDE

Set the box frame on its side. Insert part Q in the box frame, making it snug to part P. Now set the drawer box in the opening, ensuring there's enough space above and below, and mark where the top of part Q meets the drawer box. Transfer that line all the way down both sides of the drawer box. Place part Q to the line, front edge flush with the front of the drawer box, and screw it down.

9 ATTACH THE DRAWER FACE

Drive two 1-1/4-in. screws through the front of the drawer box so the tips of the screws protrude just shy of 1/4 in. Position the drawer face (G) and tap it with your fist. The screws will dig in, holding the drawer face in place. Using a spring clamp or two to help keep the drawer face from moving around, drive those screws home. Add three more screws.

1-1/4" exterior screw

8 Mark the top of the slide

P Q R

9

Drawer face

1-1/4" screws

1/4" spacer

Top supports

2" exterior screw

10

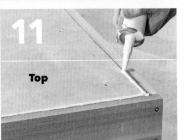

11

Top

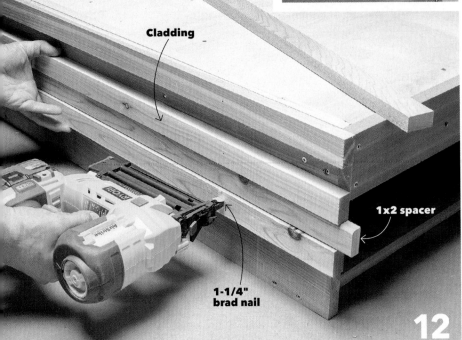

Cladding

1x2 spacer

1-1/4" brad nail

12

10 ADD THE TOP SUPPORTS

Spacing the 2x4 top supports (N) evenly, attach them with 2-in. screws. Mark their locations to help position the screws for the top.

11 INSTALL AND SEAL THE TOP

Double-check the internal measurements of the box frame and cut the top (A) from the plywood. Test-fit the top, and then screw it down to the 2x4 top supports. The sofa I built is intended for outdoor use, so I also sealed the plywood with urethane and caulked around the perimeter to help keep out moisture.

12 ADD THE CLADDING

I used 1x2 cedar strips for the cladding detail. Fasten them with exterior wood glue and brads, starting at the top and working down. Space the cladding with a scrap of 1x2 cedar. Next, double-check the measurement for the side cladding (K), cut and attach. Finally, double-check the total width, cut the front cladding (J) and attach.

All-in-one GRILLING STATION

Build a home for your grill and put everything you need at your fingertips

BY TOM DVORAK

Maple   Apple   Peach   Cherry

WHAT IT TAKES

TIME	COST	SKILL LEVEL
3 days	$750	Intermediate

TOOLS *Table saw, or circular saw with cutting guide, miter saw, drill, jigsaw*

If you're like me, you spend a lot of your grilling time running back and forth. You grab the wood chips, head back to the grill, and then make a couple trips to the kitchen for your favorite seasoning, the skewers and, oh yeah, another clean plate. This handsome grilling cabinet keeps your stuff together and gives you counter space, too. I built this one over a few days and spent $750 on lumber and hardware.

EDGE-GLUE BOARDS TO MAKE PANELS

The main components of this project are made from edge-glued panels: three 25-in. x 52-in. panels for the top and shelves, and two 25-in. x 32-in. panels for the uprights. See the Cutting List for finished sizes. You'll get two uprights from each panel. Glue up the divider separately.

To get started, crosscut the 2x6s into lengths about 4 in. longer than required. You'll cut them to finished length after gluing. On a table saw, rip the radiused edges off both sides of each 2x6, leaving a finished width of 5 in. This way, you'll have square, straight edges for gluing.

Quality lumber makes building easier and the end result better. Good-quality cedar isn't cheap, though. The lumber and materials for this project cost about $750. Home centers don't always have the best lumber, so I found a lumberyard with an ample supply of nice cedar. After handpicking straight stock, I let the lumber acclimate in my shop for about a week. You could save money by using standard construction lumber, but it's not as resistant to the elements as cedar.

No. 20 biscuits

Once your boards are prepped, install biscuits. No biscuit joiner? Don't sweat it. Biscuits help with alignment, but if your boards and your workbench are flat, you don't need them.

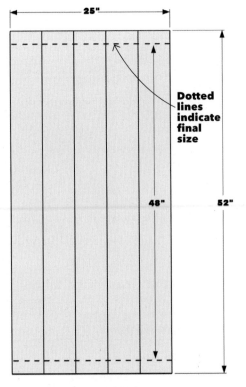

25"

Dotted lines indicate final size

48"

52"

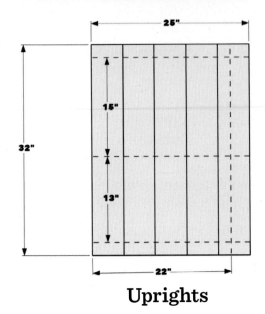

25"

15"

32"

13"

22"

Uprights

Shelves & Top

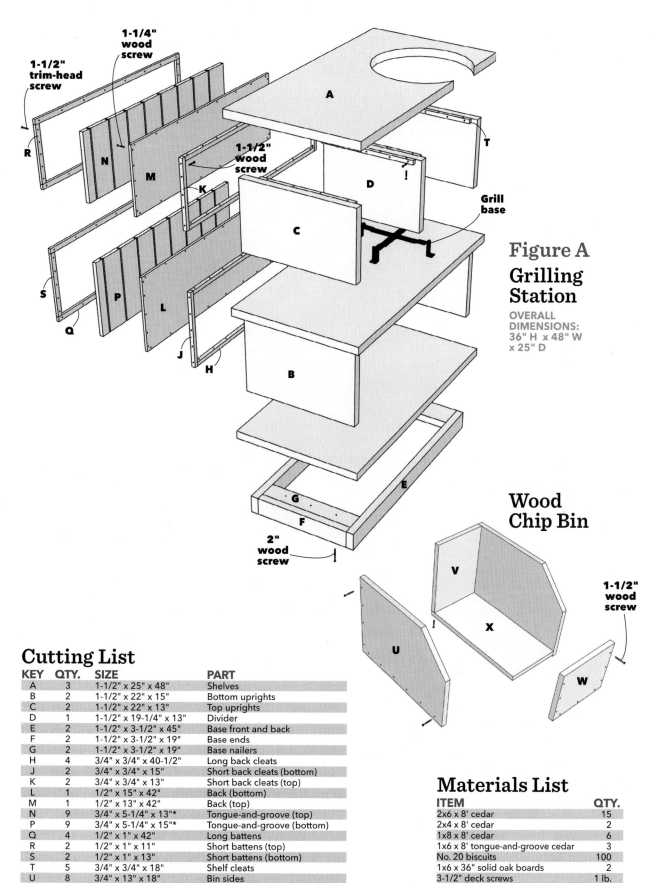

1-1/4"
wood
screw

1-1/2"
trim-head
screw

R

N

M

K

1-1/2"
wood
screw

D

C

T

**Grill
base**

S

P

L

Q

J

H

B

E

Figure A
Grilling
Station

**OVERALL
DIMENSIONS:
36" H x 48" W
x 25" D**

G

F

**2"
wood
screw**

Wood
Chip Bin

V

X

U

W

**1-1/2"
wood
screw**

Cutting List

KEY	QTY.	SIZE	PART
A	3	1-1/2" x 25" x 48"	Shelves
B	2	1-1/2" x 22" x 15"	Bottom uprights
C	2	1-1/2" x 22" x 13"	Top uprights
D	1	1-1/2" x 19-1/4" x 13"	Divider
E	2	1-1/2" x 3-1/2" x 45"	Base front and back
F	2	1-1/2" x 3-1/2" x 19"	Base ends
G	2	1-1/2" x 3-1/2" x 19"	Base nailers
H	4	3/4" x 3/4" x 40-1/2"	Long back cleats
J	2	3/4" x 3/4" x 15"	Short back cleats (bottom)
K	2	3/4" x 3/4" x 13"	Short back cleats (top)
L	1	1/2" x 15" x 42"	Back (bottom)
M	1	1/2" x 13" x 42"	Back (top)
N	9	3/4" x 5-1/4" x 13"*	Tongue-and-groove (top)
P	9	3/4" x 5-1/4" x 15"*	Tongue-and-groove (bottom)
Q	4	1/2" x 1" x 42"	Long battens
R	2	1/2" x 1" x 11"	Short battens (top)
S	2	1/2" x 1" x 13"	Short battens (bottom)
T	5	3/4" x 3/4" x 18"	Shelf cleats
U	8	3/4" x 13" x 18"	Bin sides
V	4	3/4" x 8-1/2" x 12"	Bin backs
W	4	3/4" x 7-1/4" x 10"	Bin fronts
X	4	1/2" x 8-1/2" x 18"	Bin bottoms

*Rip parts to fit

Materials List

ITEM	QTY.
2x6 x 8' cedar	15
2x4 x 8' cedar	2
1x8 x 8' cedar	6
1x6 x 8' tongue-and-groove cedar	3
No. 20 biscuits	100
1x6 x 36" solid oak boards	2
3-1/2" deck screws	1 lb.
No. 9 x 2" exterior trim head screws	1 lb.
No. 9 x 3" exterior trim head screws	1 lb.
Exterior oil finish	1 qt.
Waterproof glue	1 qt.

1 TEST-FIT, THEN GLUE

Before you start gluing, do a dry assembly to be sure everything fits. You don't want to discover a problem when you've already spread glue on all the edges. Once you've verified that everything is ready to go, glue up the shelves and uprights and clamp them. The 2x4 clamping cauls at the top and the bottom help keep the assembly flat, but make sure to cover their edges with packing tape so they don't get glued to your workpieces. Wipe off any excess glue with a damp rag before it dries. When the glue is dry, cut the shelves and uprights to the final dimensions.

2 ADD THE CLEATS

Glue and screw cleats to the top edges of all uprights. These cleats allow you to screw into the shelves from underneath to fasten the whole unit together.

3 ATTACH THE BOTTOM UPRIGHTS

Glue and screw the two bottom uprights to the bottom shelf. These wide shelves are prone to cupping, so you might need to use clamps to snug them up to the uprights before you drive the screws.

Clamping cauls

Cleat

Bottom

Upright

4 ATTACH THE BASE

Flip the bottom shelf/upright assembly upside down, and then screw the assembled base to the underside of the bottom shelf.

5 FASTEN THE SHELVES AND TOP

Set the middle shelf assembly on the bottom shelf assembly and then attach it with glue and screws through the lower cleats. Fasten the top the same way. As you're assembling, check for square before driving screws.

6 ADD THE BACK

To attach the back, start by gluing and screwing cleats around the back of the openings. Inset these cleats to accept the back panel, tongue-and-groove and molding. Cut the plywood backs to size and fasten them to the cleats with glue and screws.

7 COVER THE BACK

Cut tongue-and-groove slats to fit the openings. To allow for seasonal movement, don't use fasteners on these boards.

Cleats

Back

8 ADD THE BATTENS

Rip the 1/2-in.-thick trim strips from 1-1/2-in. thick stock, and then cut them to length to fit the backs. Fasten them to the backs with 1-1/2-in. trim-head screws.

9 BUILD THE BINS

Edge-glue 3/4-in.-thick panels for the bin parts. Once the glue is dry, cut the bin parts to size. Then cut the 45-degree angles on all the bin sides. Assemble bins with glue and screws.

10 CUT THE HOLE FOR THE SMOKER

Lay out the hole in the top for the smoker. We let the circle run off the edge of the top to allow easy access to the lid's handle. Then, carefully cut out the hole using a jigsaw. Go slow to help keep the blade from veering off track. Smooth the cut edges with 120-grit sandpaper, then sand the whole project. Apply an exterior coating of your choice.

8   **Battens**

9   **Bin side**

Fill the bins with your favorite wood chips—and get grilling!

10

PHOTO (BOTTOM RIGHT): **TINA SARGEANT**

Kamado Grilling

TIPS FROM A MASTER

MEET THE EXPERT
Damon Holter is an award-winning barbecue and grilling expert.

WHAT'S A KAMADO GRILL?

"Kamado" is the Japanese word for "stove" or "cooking range." It's also the general term for ceramic grills. Kamado grills heat faster and retain heat longer than metal ones. They also excel at containing moisture and smoke, which increases flavor.

■ DON'T CLEAN WITH A WIRE BRUSH

Wire brushes can lose bristles that can wind up in your food and ultimately in your body. If caught in your throat, bristles can be life-threatening. Use a wooden grill-cleaning tool or a wad of foil to brush off the debris. Cleaning the grate while it's hot makes this task easier.

■ CATCH THE GREASE

When smoking very fatty foods, such as pork butt, place a disposable foil pan under the meat to catch the rendered fat. This minimizes the grease buildup that can cause flare-ups or eventually leak out of the bottom vent, making a mess on your beautiful cart.

■ APPLY SAUCES LAST

Most barbecue sauces are high in sugar, which burns quickly under high heat. Once your food nears the desired temperature and doneness, close all vents and begin to decrease the heat. Baste meats with sauce and let the sauce "set" on them for 15 to 20 minutes as the temperature decreases. This will create an even coating of slightly caramelized sauce that will cling to the food.

■ NO CHEMICAL CLEANERS

Ceramic is porous and will harbor chemical residue that can be transferred to food. To clean the inside of your grill, simply brush and scrape it. Warm water and dish soap will keep the exterior looking great.

■ ARRANGE THE CHARCOAL

If you're using natural lump charcoal, place the larger lumps toward the bottom. That way, ash from the smaller pieces will have less opportunity to restrict airflow into the grill's fire ring, resulting in an even burn.

■ IGNITE IN THE MIDDLE

When you're igniting charcoal in a kamado, place and light a fire starter in the middle of the charcoal. With the lid and vents wide open, wait until you have a softball-sized clump of burning coals, then close the lid and begin to manage the airflow with the vents. This ensures that you don't ignite too much fuel. You want a steady burn that will slowly spread outward.

■ CHIPS VS. CHUNKS

Wood chips and chunks both work great in a kamado grill but should be treated differently. Since they're small, wood chips tend to burn too quickly. Soak them in water first to get a slower, smoky burn. Chips should be evenly distributed over the charcoal to produce a longer smoke and are ideal for adding flavor to meats that need shorter cook times, such as steaks and pork chops.

Wood chunks, on the other hand, don't need to be soaked. Place them around the outer edge of the fire bowl/ring to burn slowly as the coals spread, giving long-lasting smoke for more flavor.

■ COOK SMALL STUFF ON A SCREEN

When you're cooking foods like shrimp, wings or veggies, put them on a wire screen, such as a pizza screen. Spray the screen with cooking oil, then set the screen on the grill grates. This keeps food from falling through the grate and lets you quickly place and remove all the pieces at once.

■ CONSERVE FUEL

Kamado grills are well insulated and require much smaller amounts of charcoal. When done grilling, close off all vents to extinguish the fire and you'll be left with usable charcoal. The next time you grill, shake out the ashes, top off the charcoal and you're ready to go.

■ WOOD RECOMMENDATIONS

For lighter meats such as poultry, ribs and seafood, choose fruitwoods such as apple, peach and cherry. To smoke heartier meats such as pork butt, beef brisket and prime rib, pick a robust wood like hickory, oak or pecan.

Sharpen your MOWER BLADE

You'll be able to mow faster, and you'll have a healthier lawn too

BY JASON KEIPPELA

One of the best ways to encourage a greener, fuller and healthier lawn is to sharpen your lawn mower blade.

A dull blade rips and pulls the grass blades, leaving ragged tears that weaken the plant and promote fungal growth and other grass diseases. A sharp blade, on the other hand, cuts cleanly, allowing the plant to recover quickly. Sharp blades also let you complete your lawn-cutting chore faster and with less stress on the mower.

Sharpening is a simple task, even for a novice. It'll take a few sharpenings to master the technique. After that, the task will take less than 10 minutes. Plan to do it twice every mowing season. We show here the steps that will work for just about any walk-behind mower. Riding mowers require different blade removal techniques, which we won't show here.

Play it safe when removing the blade

Always remove the spark plug wire before you touch the blade (**Photo 1**). The blade shaft is directly connected to the motor, and turning the blade by hand could cause the motor to fire.

Then look for the carburetor and air filter. The carburetor is usually easy to recognize because it has throttle cables running to it. If you keep this side up when you tip your mower over to access the blade (**Photo 2**), you won't get a smoke cloud from leaking oil the next time you start it. Some mowers have gas caps with air holes that could leak a little gas onto your garage floor, so work outside or keep a rag handy to clean up drips. Once the blade is off, set the mower back on its wheels until you're ready to reinstall your blade.

You'll usually find a single bolt or nut holding the blade on. It's typically very tight and you'll need to clamp the blade to loosen it. The 2x4 method we show (**Photo 3**) is simple, quick and safe. Don't use your foot! A good tool to keep handy for loosening the bolt is a 10-in. breaker bar with a socket to match the bolt. It'll give you plenty of leverage to loosen extremely tight bolts, and you can keep your knuckles well away from the blade when bearing down. Use a squirt of penetrating oil on really rusted, stuck bolts. Wait 10 minutes to give it time to work.

Sharpen it with a file

Once you remove the blade, examine it to decide whether to sharpen it or replace it. (See "Do You Need a New Blade?" on p. 237.) Mower blades are made from fairly soft steel, so a hand file can sharpen it (**Photo 4**). You can sharpen most with fewer than 50 strokes of a clean, sharp "mill bastard" file that's at least 10 in. long. Grinders also work, and much more quickly. (Pros use them.) But they're more difficult to control and can overheat and ruin the blade.

Remove the spark plug wire

1 PREVENT ACCIDENTAL START-UP
Pull the spark plug wire from the spark plug to prevent the motor from accidentally starting. Tape or tie it back so it doesn't flop back into contact with the plug.

Air filter

2 KEEP GAS OUT OF THE AIR FILTER
Turn the mower onto its side with the air filter and carburetor side up. This keeps oil and gas from dripping into the air filter.

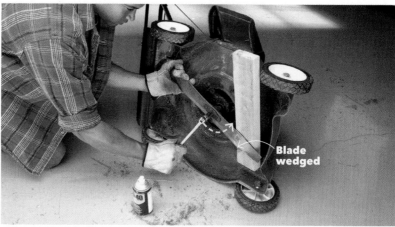

Blade wedged

3 REMOVE THE BLADE
Wedge a short 2x4 between the blade and the deck to clamp the blade. Loosen the bolt (or nut) with a long-handled wrench. Turn counterclockwise. Remove the bolt and blade.

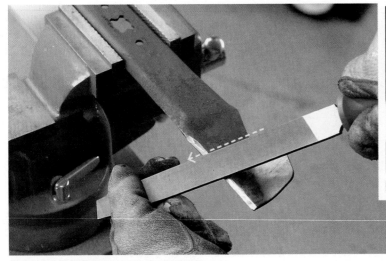

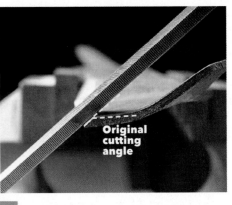
Original cutting angle

4 SHARPEN THE BLADE

Clamp the blade in a vise and sharpen the cutting edge with a mill bastard file, holding it at the same cutting angle as before. File until the blade is "butter knife" sharp.

Nail

5 BALANCE THE BLADE

Hang the blade on a nail to check the balance. If one side dips, file a bit more off that side until the blade remains horizontal.

6 REINSTALL THE BLADE

Position the blade and screw in the bolt. Then wedge the 2x4 back in and tighten the bolt firmly with your socket and breaker bar.

Always sharpen from the top side of the cutting edge; this will give you the longest-lasting edge. The file cuts on the push stroke only; you'll feel it bite into the blade. If you don't feel that cutting action, your file is probably dull or you're not pressing hard enough. Don't try to make your blade razor sharp; it'll dull more quickly. "Butter knife" sharp will do.

Sharpening mulching blades is sometimes more difficult. (See "Buying a New Blade," at right.) Mulching blades may have longer or curved cutting edges, and you may need several types of files to sharpen them. In some cases, you may have to resort to an angle grinder. If your blade is too difficult to sharpen, take it to a blade sharpening service (about $10).

Balance it before reinstalling

Before you reinstall the blade, be sure to balance it. An unbalanced blade will cause vibration and possibly ruin the blade shaft or bearings. To check the balance, simply hang the blade on a nail (Photo 5). If one side falls, it's heavier, and you have to file more metal off it. Keep filing until the blade stays level.

Reinstall the blade and hand-tighten the bolt. Insert the 2x4 in the reverse direction so you can bear down on the breaker bar to tighten the bolt. It's difficult to overtighten the bolt. Mower sharpening pros say that the second most common mistake they see is undertightening the bolt. A loose blade throws off the engine timing and sometimes makes the mower hard to start.

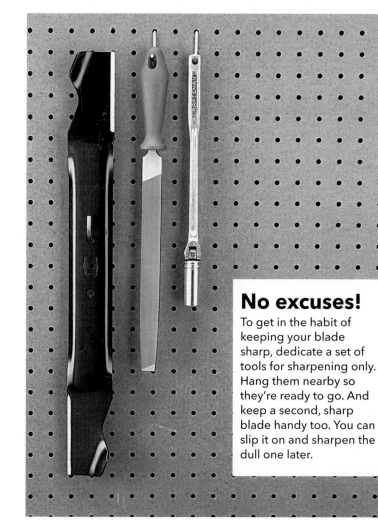

No excuses!

To get in the habit of keeping your blade sharp, dedicate a set of tools for sharpening only. Hang them nearby so they're ready to go. And keep a second, sharp blade handy too. You can slip it on and sharpen the dull one later.

Buying a new blade

Always replace your blade with an identical blade, or the blade recommended in your owner's manual. Don't try to convert your regular straight-blade mower to a fancier mulching mower by simply changing the type of blade. Your mower probably won't work any differently than before, and it may not work as well. The mower deck on a straight-blade mower is shallow and has a side discharge to eject the grass clippings quickly. A mulching mower has a deeper deck without a side discharge; the grass is chopped three or four times before it drops to the ground. The mower design is as important as the blade.

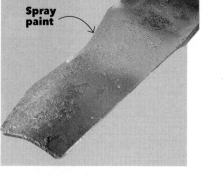

Regular blade

Mulching blade

DO YOU NEED A NEW BLADE?

Examine your blade when you remove it and look for the problems shown. If you're unsure of the condition of the blade, take it to a hardware store or home center and compare it with a new one.

WORN TRAILING EDGE

The trailing edge, or fin, is the edge opposite the cutting edge. This fin is often slanted upward, which creates an updraft to lift the grass and grass clippings. Dust and sand will wear this fin down. When it's thin, replace the blade.

New blade

Thick trailing edge

Thin trailing edge

Old blade

BENT BLADE

Set your old blade on your workbench and check for bends. If you're unsure, compare it with a new blade.

New blade

DENTS IN CUTTING EDGE

Replace blades that have deep dents that you can't file out and erosion from wear and sharpening. Also replace any blade that has cracked.

Cutting edge

Mark your new blade

Mark your blade with spray paint before you remove it so you know which way to reinstall it. Mower repair pros say that the biggest mistake homeowners make is installing a blade upside down after sharpening it. The blade won't cut—and they'll go nuts trying to figure out why!

Spray paint

Grab & Go
GARDEN TOOL CABINET

Get yard gear out of your garage and close to where you need it

BY DAVID RADTKE

WHAT IT TAKES

TIME	COST
1 weekend	$300

SKILL LEVEL
Intermediate

TOOLS & MATERIALS
Basic carpentry tools, drill/driver, circular saw

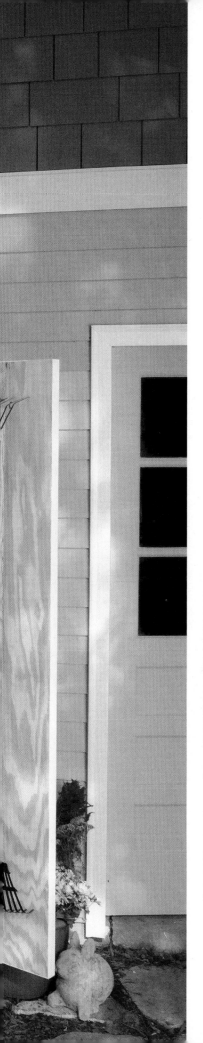

Most of us store our yard and garden tools in the garage because that's the only space available. But here's a better solution: This cabinet lets you clear clutter out of your garage and put tools near the places where they get used. And, designed especially for yard tools, it keeps them organized and accessible. It doesn't have the capacity of a shed, of course, but it makes efficient use of every inch and takes up only a small area of your yard or patio. It's also easy to build, even if you've never tackled a carpentry project like this one.

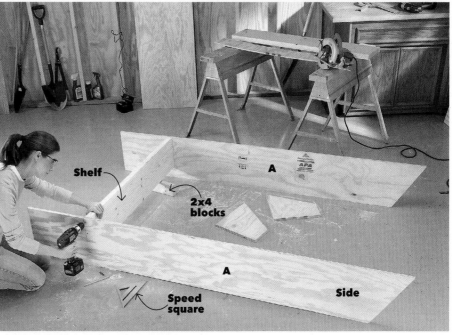

Shelf

2x4 blocks

A

A

Speed square

Side

1 ASSEMBLE THE BOX
Cut the plywood sides and 2x10 shelf, prop up the shelf with 2x4 blocks and fasten the sides to the shelf with 2-in. screws.

Figure A
Garden Tool Cabinet

61-1/2" WIDE x 92" TALL x 20" DEEP

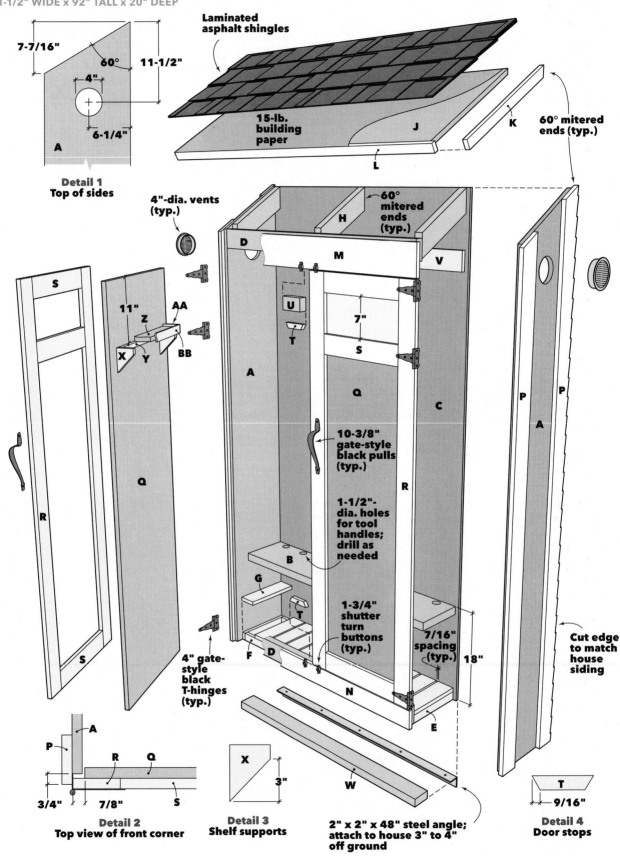

7-7/16"
60°
11-1/2"
4"
6-1/4"
A

Detail 1
Top of sides

Laminated asphalt shingles

15-lb. building paper

J
K
L

60° mitered ends (typ.)

4"-dia. vents (typ.)

60° mitered ends (typ.)

D
H
M
V

S
11"
Z
AA
X
Y
BB

U
T
7"
S

A
Q
C

P
P
A

10-3/8" gate-style black pulls (typ.)

1-1/2"-dia. holes for tool handles; drill as needed

R
R

Q

B
G
T
F
D

1-3/4" shutter turn buttons (typ.)

7/16" spacing (typ.)
18"

Cut edge to match house siding

N
E

4" gate-style black T-hinges (typ.)

W

A
P
R
Q
3/4"
7/8"
S

Detail 2
Top view of front corner

X
3"

Detail 3
Shelf supports

2" x 2" x 48" steel angle; attach to house 3" to 4" off ground

T
9/16"

Detail 4
Door stops

Assemble the main box

Exterior-grade plywood is the basic building material for this project. Unfortunately, you'll never find absolutely flat pieces of plywood at a home center or lumberyard, but the flatter you can find them, the better this project will turn out. Choose "BC" grade plywood. Put the good side ("B") on the outside and the "C" side inside.

Once you get the plywood home, keep it out of the sun or your flat panel will turn into a tortilla chip in no time. It's best to cut the pieces in the shade or in your garage. A long straightedge cutting guide for your circular saw will help you get nice straight cuts if you don't have a full-size table saw. Look at the Cutting List below and cut all the parts to size except the door stiles, rails and trim pieces, which are best cut to fit once you've constructed the main plywood box.

Choose the flattest sheet of 3/4-in. plywood for the door cores. As you lay out all the pieces, choose the best-looking side of the plywood for the painted parts. The sides of the cabinet form a 30-degree slope for the roof. Use a Speed square (**see Photo 1**) to mark the angled roof supports (H) and ends of the trim pieces that follow the roofline. It's easier to cut

2 ADD THE BACK

Screw the back to the sides and center shelf. Use a level or straightedge to mark the shelf location on the back side of the plywood.

3 FRAME THE ROOF

Cut the subrails (D) and the roof supports (H), then screw them into place. Use 2-in. screws for the subrails and 3-in. screws for the roof supports.

Materials List

ITEM	QTY.
3/4" x 4' x 8' BC plywood	2
1/2" x 4' x 8' BC plywood	1
2x10 x 4' pine	1
2x4 x 8' pine	2
1x6 x 8' pine	1
1x4 x 8' pine	12
1x2 x 8' pine	3
2x4 x 8' treated wood	1
12" x 48" hardware cloth (1/4" grid)	1
Bundle of asphalt shingles	1
3' x 5' strip of 15-lb. building paper	1
1-5/8" galv. screws	2 lbs.
2" galv. screws	2 lbs.
3" galv. screws	1 lb.
4" T-hinges	6
Shutter turn buttons	4
4" round vents	2
1-1/4" finish nails	1 lb.
1/4" x 3" galv. lag screws, washers	9
2" x 2" steel angle	1
7/8" shingle nails	1 lb.
Exterior wood glue	16 oz.

Cutting List

KEY	QTY.	SIZE	PART	MATERIAL
A	2	3/4" x 12-7/8" x 90	Sides	Plywood
B	1	1-1/2" x 9-1/4" x 46-1/2"	Shelf	Pine
C	1	1/2" x 48" x 90"	Back	Plywood
D	2	1-1/2" x 3-1/2" x 46-1/2"	Subrails	Pine
E	2	3/4" x 1-1/2" x 11-3/8"	Bottom cleats	Pine
F	2	3/4" x 1-1/2" x 45"	Bottom cleats	Pine
G	12	3/4" x 3-1/2" x 11-3/8"	Bottom slats	Pine
H	3	1-1/2" x 3-1/2" x 15-1/8"	Roof supports	Pine
J	1	3/4" x 21-7/8" x 60"	Roof	Plywood
K	2	3/4" x 1-1/2" x 21-7/8"	Roof trim	Pine
L	1	3/4" x 1-1/2" x 61-1/2"	Roof trim	Pine
M	1	3/4" x 5-1/2" x 48"	Upper trim rail	Pine
N	1	3/4" x 3-1/2" x 48"	Lower trim rail	Pine
P	4	3/4" x 3-1/2" x 91"	Side trim	Pine
Q	2	3/4" x 23" x 72-3/4"	Doors	Plywood
R	4	3/4" x 3-1/2" x 72-3/4"	Door stiles	Pine
S	6	3/4" x 3-1/2" x 16-7/8"	Door rails	Plywood
T	2	3/4" x 1" x 4-1/2"	Door stops	Pine
U	1	1-1/2" x 2-7/16" x 4-1/2"	Door stop support	Pine
V	1	3/4" x 3-1/2" x 46-1/2"	Hang rail	Pine
W	1	1-1/2" x 3-1/2" x 48"	Mounting board	Treated
X	1	3/4" x 3" x 4"	Shelf supports	Pine
Y	1	3/4" x 3/4" x 16-1/2"	Shelf mounting cleat	Pine
Z	1	3/4" x 3" x 20"	Shelf	Pine
AA	2	1/4" x 1-1/2" x 3"	Shelf edging	Pine
BB	1	1/4" x 1-1/2" x 20-1/2"	Shelf edging	Pine

4 INSTALL FLOOR SLATS

Glue and nail the 1x2 cleats (E and F) to the sides, back and subrail (D) and then screw the 1x4 floor slats (G) to the cleats. Start with the center slat and leave 7/16-in. gaps.

5 INSTALL THE ROOF

Mount the 1x2 roof trim to the 3/4-in. plywood roof, then center it and mark the position. Then temporarily screw it to the roof supports with a pair of 2-in. screws on each side.

3/4" above plywood

4"-dia. hole

Exterior waterproof glue

6 TRIM THE SIDES

Glue and screw the 1x4 side trim to the plywood sides, keeping the trim pieces 3/4 in. proud at the front. Cut the 4-in.-diameter side vents.

accurate slopes on the larger side pieces (A) by first measuring each side, marking a diagonal line from point to point and then cutting along the mark. Assemble the main box of the cabinet as shown in **Figure A** and **Photos 1 – 5**. Drill pilot holes for all screws with a No. 8 combination countersink and pilot bit. Use 2-in. galvanized deck screws to fasten the sides to the shelf and 1-5/8-in. screws to fasten the back to the sides.

Note: Cut a piece of 1/4-in. hardware cloth to fit under the floor slats of the cabinet. This wire mesh will keep furry critters from making your tool cabinet their home.

Cut the roof panel (J) and trim pieces (K and L), then glue and nail the trim to the front and side edges of the roof panel. Center the panel **(Photo 5)** and temporarily screw it to the roof supports so you can install the side trim (P) and the upper rail (M).

Add trim and assemble the doors

Make sure to extend the front edge of each side. Set the trim (P) 3/4 in. beyond the front edge of the plywood side **(Photo 6)**. Next cut and nail the front upper rail (M) and the lower rail (N) to the subrails. Both ends should butt tightly to the side trim.

Even though the doors are made mainly from plywood, the rail and stile trim boards glued and screwed to the front side give the doors a handsome frame-and-panel look. Be sure to lay the doors out on a flat surface and then glue and nail the stiles (long vertical pieces) and rails (short horizontal pieces) to the plywood surface. The stile on each hinge side must hang 3/4 in. past the plywood **(see Photo 10 inset)**.

You'll need to alter the factory T-hinge for the inset design of the doors. The hinge flap is screwed to the side trim (P) as shown in **Photo 8**. If you were to use the factory-supplied pan head screws, the door would bind on the screw heads. To solve this problem, taper the edges of the existing holes with a countersink bit. Remove just enough steel (**Photo 7**) so the head of the tapered No. 8 x 3/4-in. screw fits flush with the hinge flap surface.

Cut the small door stops with a handsaw and then glue and nail them to the edges of the subrails. With the door stops in place, set the doors into the opening. Make sure you leave a 1/8-in. gap at the top and bottom and a 3/16-in. gap between the doors. You may need to plane or belt-sand the door edges to get a good fit.

Note: Because the flaps of the hinge that fasten to the side trim are about 7/8 in. wide instead of 3/4 in., your doors will sit about 1/8 in. proud of the side trim.

Mount the cabinet to the wall

Fasten a 4-ft. 2x4 to the top flange of a 4-ft.-long piece of steel angle (**Figure A**). At a hardware store, you can usually find steel angle that measures 1-1/2 in. x 1-1/2 in. with holes drilled every 3 in., but any steel angle that's at least 1/8 in. thick will do.

Locate the exact position of your cabinet on the wall at least 3 in. above grade and then fasten the angle to the wall with 1/4-in. galvanized lag screws. It must be level. You may need to cut a course or two of siding to get the angle to lie flat. Our slab was several inches off the ground, so I drilled into the side of the slab, installed lag shields and fastened the angle. If your slab is too close to the ground, you can fasten the angle farther up into the wood studs of the garage. The weight of your cabinet rests entirely on this wall cleat. It's not necessary to fasten the bottom of the cabinet to it.

Mark the locations of the wall studs on the cabinet back. Locate three 1/4-in.-diameter pilot holes in the hang rail (V) and another three holes 4 in. up from the bottom at the stud locations.

Now, strap your cabinet to a furniture dolly (with the doors and roof removed to reduce the weight) and wheel it over to the wall cleat. Set the cabinet onto the cleat, center it and temporarily brace it against the wall. Drill 5/32-in. holes into the wall studs

7 COUNTERSINK THE HINGES

Taper the holes in the inside of the hinge flaps to accept the tapered heads of the mounting screws.

8 MOUNT THE HINGES

Position the flaps of the hinges against the plywood sides at the centers of the door rail locations. Drill pilot holes and drive the screws into the side trim to secure the hinges.

9 BUILD THE DOORS

Glue and nail the door rail and stile trim to the 3/4-in. plywood core. Overhang the stile on the hinge side of each door 7/8 in. See **Figure A** for the exact placement.

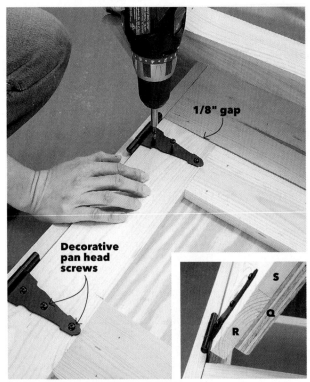

10 HANG THE DOORS

Install the door stops (Figure A), then set each door into its opening. Use the decorative pan head screws provided by the manufacturer for the long decorative flap on the door surface.

11 MOUNT THE CABINET

Fasten a steel angle to the foundation with a 2x4 attached to its top (Figure A). Lift the cabinet into place and stabilize it with an 8-ft. 2x4 brace against the ground, forcing the cabinet back against the wall.

NOTE:
If you have vinyl, aluminum or steel siding, here's how to prevent the siding from deforming as you tighten the cabinet to the wall. Instead of tightening the lag screws one at a time, gently tighten them alternately to even out the pressure as you go.

12 FIT THE TRIM

Scribe the 1x4 side trim to fit the siding. Cut the notches with a jigsaw. Nail it to the cabinet side. Screw on the roof panel and shingle it.

using the existing pilot holes as a guide. Drive the 3-in. lag screws and snug the cabinet to the wall.

Finishing touches

Lay the side trim (P) against the siding. You may need to cut it with your jigsaw to conform (**Photo 12**). Screw the roof panel to the cabinet. Staple a layer of 15-lb. building paper to the roof panel and shingle the panel using 7/8-in. roofing nails. Avoid driving shingle nails through the overhangs where the points might show. When you get to the last course, trim the shingles to fit and run a bead of matching caulk at the siding to seal the edge.

Rehang the doors and then mount the door handles and the catches at the top and bottom of the door. Wait to add your vents until you've finished painting. We spray-painted the vents to match the color of the sides.

Best Pro Tips

Expert advice from the job site. By Jason Ingolfsland

LANDSCAPE DESIGN

12 easy ways to improve curb appeal

I recently purchased a new home, and improving the landscape is high on my to-do list. Landscape design, however, isn't always straightforward, and achieving a great look requires a little nuance. The stakes are also high: If you get it wrong, you might end up with dead plants and an ugly yard for all your hard work. Still, DIYers can save roughly 40 to 60 percent of the cost of a professional landscaper and dramatically boost their house's curb appeal. So, to get it right, I spoke with a landscaping expert, who shared these quick tips.

MEET THE EXPERT
John Moe has 35 years of landscaping experience and serves on the certification committee at the Minnesota Nursery and Landscape Association.

DEVISE A MASTER PLAN

Most people tackle landscaping headfirst without thinking about the grand picture. Eventually, they end up with a jumble of plants that don't look right with the house or one another. Start with the end goal in mind for the best look. If you don't feel up to the design task, get help. A landscape architect will typically charge $600 to $3,500 to visit your home and create a plan; costs vary by the size of your property and the work to be done. Many garden centers offer free design services if you purchase the materials from them.

LEAVE A PATH TO THE BACKYARD

If there's an addition or new patio in your future, leave a path for machinery. You don't want to tear out shrubs or a retaining wall later so a skid steer can reach the backyard.

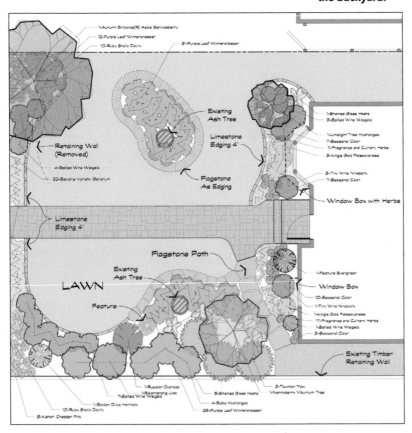

PLAN FOR ALL-SEASON COLOR

You want your plants to bloom throughout the growing season. When you're developing a plan, know the bloom time for each plant, and choose coordinating colors for plants blossoming at the same time. Design your landscape to highlight different plants during each season. It's fun to see individual plants have their day in the sunlight.

SPRING TO EARLY SUMMER BLOOMS   LATE SUMMER TO FALL BLOOMS

| Ninebark "Tiny Wine" | Weigela "Spilled Wine" | Hosta "Stained Glass" | Hydrangea "Bobo" | Reblooming Lilac "Bloomerang" |

FOR DRAMA, CHOOSE WHITE AND YELLOW

Red and purple are vivid colors, but in a landscape, yellow and white flowers are the real attention grabbers. They stand out more against green foliage while others tend to disappear. So, if you want an eye-catching landscape, use yellow and white flowers.

TEST YOUR SOIL

Good soil is the key to healthy plants. A simple test will tell you whether you need to add lime, nitrogen, phosphorus or potassium to the soil. Dig 6 in. and scoop samples from 5 to 10 areas in your yard and mix them in a bucket. You can purchase an at-home soil testing kit at most home centers, but for best results, send your soil sample to a state-certified soil-testing lab or university extension service. To find yours, enter "university extension service" and your state in a search engine. Testing fees are usually $15 to $20, and results take one to two weeks.

COMMON SHRUB MISTAKES

■ PLANTING TOO CLOSE TO THE HOUSE

It's common for homeowners to plant large shrubs and other plants too close to their house's foundation and siding. Then the owner prunes them back and they eventually become half a plant. For a better look, plant shrubs farther away from the house and give them room to grow. A general rule is to take the plant's mature width and put it at least half that distance away from the house.

■ LETTING THEM GROW UNCHECKED

Because shrubs are relatively low maintenance, they're easy to neglect. Overlooked for years, they grow out of control and hide the house, crowd doorways and look ugly. Drastic trimming or removing them might be the best and easiest thing you could do for your front yard.

MAP OUT YOUR COLORS

Our pro recommends repeating your chosen colors in different sections of your landscape. For example, if you use red at your walkway, use red at the side of your house as well. This technique gives your design continuity and balance. Remember, foliage is color too!

IF YOU PLAN TO SELL, START PLANTING NOW

Improving your landscaping is a great way to boost the curb appeal—and selling price—of a home. But remember that most plants take time to get established and look their best. If you hope to sell in midsummer, get started in early spring, or better yet, the year before you plan to sell.

DON'T PUT POLY UNDER WOOD MULCH

Putting poly under wood mulch prevents the decomposing mulch from enriching the soil. Instead, place a 4-in. layer of wood mulch on the soil to block sunlight from reaching it. Like poly, this prevents weeds. But unlike poly, it will naturally decompose, providing nutrients to your plants. You'll have to add mulch as needed.

PREVENT WEEDS WITH MASS PLANTING

Weeds will pop up wherever light reaches the soil. To make your landscaping low maintenance, place plants tightly together so weeds can't get started.

MIX UP TEXTURES

Plant texture refers to the size and shape of the leaves. Don't make the mistake of choosing all the same textures for your landscape; it's dull and monotonous. For an appealing landscape, use plants with varying leaf shapes and sizes.

PLAN FOR GROWTH

Before buying a plant, check the tag for its mature size. Keep in mind that many plants grow larger than the tag indicates. Knowing the maximum size—and allowing a little extra—helps you avoid a crowded, overgrown look later.

PLANT IN RANDOM PATTERNS

In a formal garden, you may see plants all lined up, but most residential landscapes look best with a more casual design like the one shown here. Planting in random or zigzag patterns provides good ground coverage with fewer plants, and these arrangements are visually interesting too.

FIXING DEAD SPOTS IN YOUR LAWN

Some spots need extra care

If you spilled fertilizer and killed a patch of grass, or if your dog made a deadly deposit on the lawn, you can't just sow new seed and expect it to thrive. Grass seed may not germinate there, and if you lay sod over the spot, it might slowly die.

Here's the solution:

You're up against contaminated soil. And whether the contamination is from fertilizer or dog urine, the solution is simple.

First, drive a spade deep into the ground and turn over clumps of soil. That buries the most contaminated top layer of soil deep in the ground, where the contaminants will dissipate before new roots grow down that far. Then flood the area with a garden hose for at least 15 minutes. The water will drive contaminants deeper into the soil. Now you're ready for seed or sod. Be sure to water the new grass daily until it's established.

Key chain tag

What's in the garden sprayer?

I use my garden sprayer for pesticides, herbicides and fertilizers. I was never able to remember what I last had in it, so I picked up some key chain tags at the hardware store. I add the product info to the tags and clip the corresponding one to the sprayer. Problem solved! Our model isn't wearing protective gloves; be sure you do!

CARROLL PETER

Blade protector

Keep your hedge trimmer blades from getting dinged (or damaging other stuff) when they're not in use. Cut pipe insulation to length, slip it on the blades and secure with short bungee cords.

WILL STEARLEY

CLOG STOPPER FOR SNOW BLOWERS

Wet, heavy snow used to build up in my snow blower chute, causing it to clog. So I tried applying Rain-X glass cleaner to the inside of the chute. Worked like a charm!

JAKE QUAMME

Easy mulch spreading

Mulching around flowers and bushes in tight quarters is easier if the mulch is in a small container. So I place buckets and pails in my wheelbarrow and fill them with mulch. It doesn't matter if the mulch misses the bucket and lands in the wheelbarrow. Once you've emptied the buckets, dump the contents of the wheelbarrow in an open area and spread it out.

ERIC SWARTZ

Handy camping kit

My family does a lot of camping, and I always had trouble rounding up all the little items we needed and keeping them organized. First aid supplies, bungee cords, clothesline, bug spray.... Then I loaded it all into a fishing tackle box, and now we're always ready to go.

LYNN MAGERS

JIFFY CHARCOAL STARTER

Run out of lighter fluid for your charcoal grill again? If you have a 2-lb. coffee can, you can make a reusable coal starter and skip the fluid altogether. Cut the bottom out first, and then pierce the sides with a can opener to make air vents.

Place the can in the barbecue and loosely crumple newspaper in the bottom one-third of the can. Fill the rest of the can with charcoal and light the newspaper through one of the vents. After the coals start to gray, lift the hot can off with tongs, leaving glowing coals behind.

JOHN DEITHLOFF

Charcoal

Coffee can

Crumpled newspaper in bottom third

Vent hole

Great Goofs®

Laughs and lessons from our readers

SNOW JOB GONE WRONG

My wife isn't exactly a farm girl. You know, not well acquainted with running machinery. So I was surprised when she called me at work to say she was going to clear the snow out of our driveway with the garden tractor snow blower. I was quite happy to skip snow-blowing in the dark after work.

But when I got home, the driveway was an absolute mess. Weird-shaped piles of snow were everywhere, along with ruts across the driveway into the lawn—not exactly the bang-up job I'd been hoping for. We plodded through the drifts to rescue the tractor, which was stuck in a snowbank. I climbed aboard and fired it up. My wife got the most incredulous look on her face—she had no idea there was a switch that existed solely to turn on the snow blower.

STEVE DOHERTY

HOW NOT TO KILL WEEDS

This spring, I noticed my neighbor spot-spraying weeds that had invaded his lawn. He told me he'd bought a weed killer at our local hardware store to wipe them out. I had weeds in my lawn too, so I decided to give his remedy a try. I went to the same hardware store, bought weed killer, then came home and attacked the weeds.

After a few days, my lawn looked as spotted as a leopard. The weeds were dead, but so was the grass around them. Turns out, the product I had purchased was grass and weed killer. Now I'm the talk of the neighborhood for my goof. I guess no one will be asking me for lawn care advice!

BRIAN UTHER

MY PLAID LAWN

I bought a drop spreader to fertilize our malnourished lawn. I loaded the hopper, set the drop rate and went to work. After spreading fertilizer down one row, I measured over to the next row and pulled the spreader backward across the lawn. I covered the entire yard this way—pushing the spreader in one direction, then pulling it back the other way. Then I spread fertilizer again, this time going perpendicular to my first pattern.

All seemed well and good until the lawn greened up a few days later. That's when my wife called me upstairs. From the second-story window, we could see an unmistakable plaid pattern over the whole lawn. It turns out that my spreader only drops fertilizer when you're pushing, not pulling. Oops!

ERIC JONES

BRUSH-CUTTER BLUES

My friend Debby had a ton of brush cutting to do in the woods behind her house. "Debby, you have to borrow my commercial-grade brush cutter. It cuts brush like a razor cuts hair!" I bragged. Before she came to get it, I installed a new blade to really impress her.

The following week, she let me know that she wasn't at all impressed with my top-of-the-line tool. She had worked her tail off for three sweaty hours on a 90-degree day without getting very much brush cleared. I was puzzled—until I noticed that all the teeth were nearly ground off the brand-new blade. You guessed it. I'd installed the blade upside down and the teeth were facing backward. I couldn't let her buy me a new $30 blade, even though she offered.

TIM JOHNSON

7 Using DIY Tools & Materials

OPEN-CELL VS. CLOSED-CELL SPRAY FOAM

One of the best ways to insulate is to use spray foam insulation. But spray foams are not all the same, and before you hire an insulation contractor, it's important to know how they differ.

Open-cell spray foam is soft and flexible. It's called open-cell because air can freely travel from one cell to another. Open-cell foam isn't as dense as closed-cell foam, but it expands more, making it a good choice for hard-to-reach areas. On the other hand, closed-cell foam has a greater density and R-value because air can't travel from one cell to another. As a result, it's more rigid and won't expand as much as open-cell. In general, closed-cell foam is used to insulate entire buildings and walls, and it's roughly twice as expensive as open-cell foam.

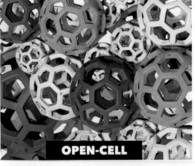

OPEN-CELL

CLOSED-CELL

(SIMULATION)

Can you paint pressure-treated lumber?

Yes. Pressure treatment doesn't interfere with paint. But the moisture left in the wood does. Waterlogged wood, treated or not, won't hold paint. Let treated wood dry for several weeks. Then test its paintability by sprinkling it lightly with water. If it absorbs drops of water, it'll accept paint. If you must paint treated wood immediately, only use wood that has been kiln-dried after treatment (KDAT). Always use a brush and start with a high-quality exterior primer. Then apply two coats of 100 percent acrylic paint.

You can test pressure-treated wood for paintability by sprinkling it with water.

PRESSURE WASHER TIP RESCUE

My pressure washer wasn't working properly. Instead of flowing continuously when I pulled the trigger, it would just surge: on, off, on, off. When I pulled the trigger with just the water turned on (no power), the tip had an odd spray pattern, so I cleaned it out with a needle. It looked clear, but to be thorough, I soaked the tip in vinegar.

After about four hours, I noticed a tiny particle in the bowl with the tip. I put the tip back on the gun and it worked perfectly! Pressure washers don't see as much use as a shower or kitchen faucet, but they're still susceptible to lime, scale or mineral buildup. And the tip openings are so small that a tiny obstruction can cause big problems.

JAY CORK, ASSOCIATE EDITOR

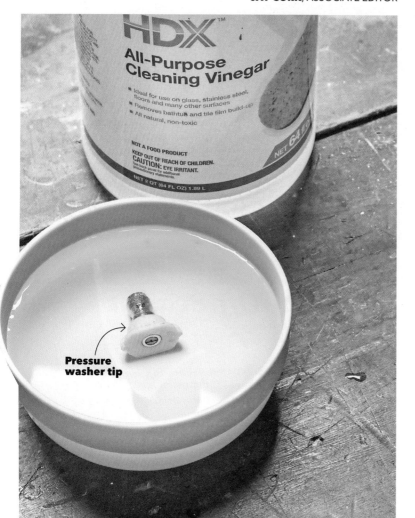

Pressure washer tip

What's an uncoupling membrane?

Also called "decoupling membranes," these products are sold in rolls and are installed over subfloors before the ceramic tile is set. They help isolate the tile from a subfloor that expands, contracts or flexes, reducing the risk of cracks and loose tiles. The membranes are a thin, semirigid plastic. Some are solid sheets that act as a moisture barrier, while others, such as Laticrete's STRATA_MAT, have moisture vents to speed curing.

The membranes have fleece or mesh on their underside that bonds to the subfloor with thin-set. On the topside are grids or profiles, which differ among manufacturers, and some can accept and hold tubing or electric cables to heat the floor. Examples include DITRA-HEAT from Schluter and HeatMatrix from SunTouch, a Watts brand. Schluter also offers DITRA-HEAT-DUO, a membrane that has additional bonding fleece to provide a thermal break and some sound control.

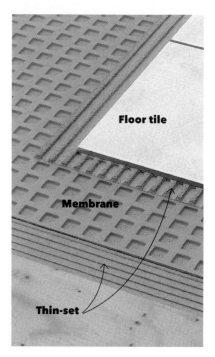

Floor tile

Membrane

Thin-set

2x4 grades:
Can you tell the difference?

Ever wonder why home centers often have two stacks of 2x4s with a price difference of about 30 cents per board? Here's the deal. When lumber is harvested and sent to the mill, it still contains all the water it had when it was living. Dimensional stability—and price—depends on whether it gets kiln dried and to what degree. For your extra 30 cents, you'll get a 2x4 that was kiln dried before final milling. Kiln-dried lumber doesn't reabsorb moisture as readily as non-kiln-dried lumber, so if the lumber is straight when you buy it, it will likely stay that way. That said, if you want to save that 30 cents, sort through the cheaper pile and pick the lightest weight (driest), straightest boards you can find.

Battery maintainer

Protect Your Battery in the Off-Season

Storing a seasonal-use battery—say, for a boat or an RV—is simple, but here are a few things to keep in mind:

- Before storing, check and refill water levels as needed.
- Fully charge the battery before storing.
- Freezing a battery damages it irreparably, so store the battery indoors, in a warm location.
- Heat can also harm a battery, so don't store it near any heat sources such as radiators or space heaters.
- Contrary to popular belief, storing a battery on concrete is perfectly fine. The materials used in modern batteries make possible moisture take-up from concrete a nonissue.
- Hook up a battery maintainer to keep your battery charged.
- Check the battery once a month to be sure it's fully charged.
- Make sure the battery is fully charged before putting it back into use.

BEST INVERTER GENERATORS

Quiet, clean power on the go

BY JASON INGOLFSLAND

Small inverter generators are surprisingly versatile. They're capable of powering a slew of electronics, devices and power tools. They're also lightweight and portable and quiet enough to not drive your neighbors crazy. However, with so many options to pick from, it's hard to know where to start. I chose five popular models within the 2,000-watt range, costing $499 to $1,049, to test their noise, features, ease of maintenance and portability. After comparing them, I'll tell you my top choices.

What's an inverter generator?

Standard portable generators create "dirty" power, an unsteady current that could damage sensitive electronics such as TVs, cell phones and computers. An inverter fixes that problem. The generator produces raw AC power, and the inverter turns that into low-voltage DC power, and then back into clean, stable 120-volt AC power that's safe to use with your devices.

What they are (and aren't) good for

These generators are lightweight, small and quiet, making them great for the jobsite. They're also useful for camping and tailgating. They can charge your laptop and power your circular saw at the same time or keep your fan, lights and outdoor electric grill running at the campsite. They don't produce enough power to back up your whole house if there's a power outage; you'd need a higher-watt option.

Things to consider

Running watts

Every generator has two watts ratings: "starting watts" and "running watts." The starting watts rating is always higher; it includes the extra power the generator can put out for a few seconds to start a device with an electric motor. The running watts rating is the maximum power the generator can supply to actually run devices. It's the only rating you should consider when buying a generator.

Fuel, run-time and load gauges

Fuel, run-time and load gauges let you know how much fuel you have left, how many devices you're powering and the time remaining until the generator will lose power. Keep in mind, the run-time gauge won't be too helpful if you're using the generator only periodically. Surprisingly, these features aren't common; only the Predator and Ryobi include them.

Ease of maintenance

Unlike many midsize models, inverter generators hide their motor behind a plastic casing. To change the oil, air filter or spark plug, or to winterize, you need to open a top or side hatch. They all have similar motor designs, but some are more maintenance friendly than others. Some components are tough to reach or hidden behind other parts.

Bluetooth

The Ryobi Bluetooth 2,300-watt model allows you to check the fuel levels, the run-time and the load—and even shut it down—all from your smartphone. This comes in handy when you're camping and don't want to leave your RV, or when you're at a tailgating party and want to quickly check how much longer the fuel will last.

Portable power stations

Lithium-ion portable power stations have the same AC inverter and can charge at a wattage output comparable to that of inverter generators. Not having a motor, they're silent, clean, require little maintenance and can be recharged through a home AC outlet or a separate travel solar panel. Of course, they're also much more expensive, costing from $600 to $3,000. A Goal Zero Yeti 1400 portable power station costs about $1,900 on Amazon.

Connect two for more power

If you need more power, inverter generators can also link together to combine their wattage capability. This provides flexibility for different tasks: If you're hosting a tailgating party, you can bring a small generator rather than lug around a midsized one, but if you're camping in an RV, you can link both together. It also helps with reliability. If one generator goes down, you can still use the working generator to power some things rather than go without.

Energy throttle

Inverter generators have a throttle as a standard feature to slow down the motor and conserve gas when you aren't using much power. It's great when you're using low-watt devices and want to make the generator quieter and extend your run-time. If you're using load-heavy equipment, you should turn off the throttle.

Easy portability

Inverter generators are lightweight and small enough that most people could carry them with one hand. Typically there's just a large handle on the top, but the Ryobi makes transport easier with wheels and a long handle.

How loud are they?

Inverter generators run quietly on idle, but I wanted to test how noisy they are while running a power tool. To do this, I used a Reed Sound Level Meter (about $160 online) to measure the decibels.

I placed the sound meter roughly 6 in. away from the generator for an accurate reading of the sound source. According to the Inverse Square Law, doubling the distance from a sound source subtracts 6 dB in an open field. That means the farther you are from the source, the decibel levels significantly decrease. Here are my results:

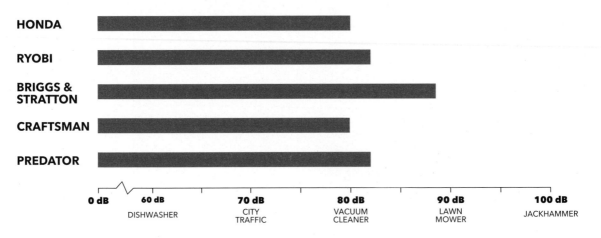

HONDA
RYOBI
BRIGGS & STRATTON
CRAFTSMAN
PREDATOR

0 dB | 60 dB | 70 dB | 80 dB | 90 dB | 100 dB
DISHWASHER | CITY TRAFFIC | VACUUM CLEANER | LAWN MOWER | JACKHAMMER

Models We Tested

HONDA EU2200i

$1,049
47 LBS.
1,800 RUNNING WATTS

PROS:
- Compact and lightweight
- Easy to carry
- Easy maintenance
- Quick start
- Quiet
- Runs well with power tools

CONS:
- No gauges
- High price

RYOBI 2300

$599
53 LBS.
1,800 RUNNING WATTS

PROS:
- Telescoping handle bar
- Wheels
- Quiet
- Easy maintenance
- Fuel, run-time and load gauges
- Bluetooth capability
- Low price

CONS:
- Large
- Heavy

BRIGGS & STRATTON P2200 ✱

$649
54.6 LBS.
1,700 RUNNING WATTS

PROS:
- Easy start
- Easy maintenance
- Multiple handlebars

CONS:
- Heavy
- Bulky
- Loud

CRAFTSMAN 2200i

$649
46.6 LBS.
1,700 RUNNING WATTS

PROS:
- Quiet
- Lightweight

CONS:
- Large
- Difficult start
- High maintenance

PREDATOR 2000

$499
47 LBS.
1,600 RUNNING WATTS

PROS:
- Lightweight
- Quiet
- Fuel gauge
- Low price

CONS:
- High maintenance
- Difficult start

✱ This model will be discontinued and replaced by the P2400.

11 GREAT USES FOR HOT AIR

Get more done with a heat gun

BY JAY CORK

IT'S HARD TO CATEGORIZE THE HEAT GUN; it's just so useful in so many ways. It's basically just a fan blowing air over a heating element, but a heat gun is an essential tool for pros and DIYers alike. It's amazing what can be manipulated with the application of a little heat: Glue and caulk can be softened, plastics and metal bend to our will, and of course marshmallows can be turned a toasty, golden brown!

MEET THE EXPERT
Jay Cork has been a carpenter, cabinetmaker and craftsman for more than 20 years.

1
MANIPULATING PLASTIC, PVC OR RUBBER

Sometimes we need a little help to make that new radiator hose fit, or maybe we need to bend that PVC pipe just enough to make it work. Whatever your situation, a heat gun can often provide a little persuasion.

Toothpick

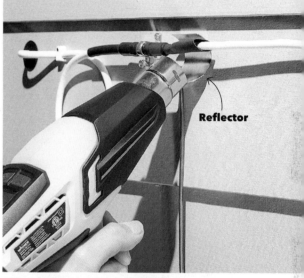

Reflector

2
SPEED UP CONTACT CEMENT

Contact cement needs 15 to 30 minutes to tack up, but this may not be fast enough for some situations. When you're making a repair, such as regluing a countertop end cap, applying heat will cause the solvents in the cement to evaporate more quickly, and the two sides will be ready much faster. When using contact cement, always do so in a well-ventilated area with the proper safety gear.

TIP: When you're repairing an end cap, hold it away from the countertop with a toothpick.

3
SEAL OUTSIDE CABLE CONNECTIONS

Heat shrink tube is a polyolefin material that shrinks when heat is applied, making it very useful for sealing cable and wiring connections. The inexpensive, thin heat shrink tubing that you'll find at the home center is fine for light-duty applications and will typically work well with a hair dryer.

For outdoor connections, I like to use double-walled, adhesive-lined heat shrink tubing ($20 for an assorted kit online), but it requires more heat. In this case the connection is right up against the house, so I want to avoid using an open flame. A heat gun with a reflector attachment is perfect for the job.

4
MAKE PLASTIC FITTINGS ACTUALLY FIT

The most common complaint about shop vacuum fittings is that they don't always fit the tools that need them. Softening plastic fittings with a heat gun can help make these mismatched pieces play nice with each other.

Fulcrum

5 FIX A WARPED CABINET DOOR

While moving into a new house, I noticed one of the tall cabinet doors in the kitchen was badly warped. Rather than replace the door, I decided to fix it with a little heat. This can be tricky, and it's not going to work 100% of the time, but it beats the alternative of having to build a new door.

This technique requires two clamps and a few blocks of wood. I screwed down two blocks for clamping each end of the door, and another as a fulcrum to bend the door against. As clamping pressure is increased on the ends, the door is bent against the warp.

Here's where the heat gun comes in. It's important to heat the entire thickness of the wood to an even temperature, not just the surface. To do this without damaging the finish, slowly apply heat to both sides of the door. I used an infrared thermometer to monitor the surface temp, which needed to be 130 degrees F or less. Running the heat gun back and forth along the edge of the door for about 30 minutes, I gently increased clamping pressure, bending a little farther than I thought necessary. Whenever wood is bent with heat, "springback" is to be expected; the wood will relax back to the desired position.

Before

After

6 THAW FROZEN PIPES

A frozen pipe can be catastrophic and can leave us with nasty repair bills. If you see frost or ice on a water pipe in your home, warm the area with a heat gun set on low. **Search for "frozen pipes" on familyhandyman.com for more great tips on preventing frozen water pipes.**

7 CRACKLE PAINT FINISH

That old, worn barn wood look is easy to achieve with some heat. This can be done with multiple colors of paint, or a coat of paint over the top of stained wood. The technique I used for this piece involved brushing out a coat of Titebond Liquid Hide Glue ($9 for 8 oz. at Woodcraft) over the red base coat and letting it dry for about 10 minutes or so. When the glue is almost dry, I quickly brushed on a coat of acrylic latex. Once the topcoat is on, run the heat gun over the wet paint to force it to dry faster. How much heat you apply and how fast you work will determine the amount of crackle that occurs. Always do a test piece to practice the steps and see how you like the results.

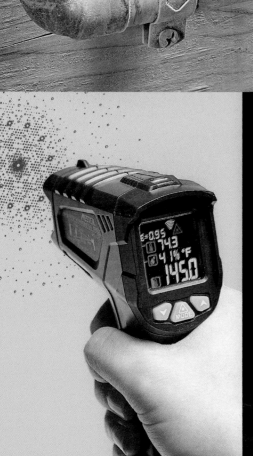

AN INFRARED THERMOMETER HELPS!
For critical situations where too much heat will damage a surface, an infrared thermometer is a great helper. You can reach and maintain a specific surface temp and avoid scorching. You can find one for about $40 at home centers.

8 LOOSEN A GLUED JOINT

A heat gun can help soften glue joints so you can make that repair on Mom's favorite rocking chair. If you move the heat gun evenly around the joint, it'll begin to warm the wood and the glue inside. This can take some time, so patience is required! As you're heating a joint on repairs like this, check often to see whether it has loosened. If the piece has a finish on it, be cautious! Don't exceed a surface temp of 130 degrees F. An infrared thermometer really comes in handy for jobs like this.

10 ERASE BLEMISHES IN EPOXY

If you've ever poured epoxy, then you probably know the trick of using a heat source to help eliminate bubbles. But heat can also smooth over little blemishes (like fingerprints) in epoxy that has dried to the touch. Set the gun to low heat, warm the area around the blemish and the surface will magically become smooth again. It's important to catch the blemishes quickly. I'm sorry to say that if you wait longer than a day or two, this trick isn't going to work.

Fingerprints

9 WATERPROOF YOUR LEATHER

For decades, I've used Sno-Seal (about $8 for 8 oz. online) on all my leather items. Along the way, I've found that heat helps it get into the little nooks and crannies of seams and stitching. I like to lightly pre-heat the leather, then liberally apply the Sno-Seal with a rag. I run the heat gun over the piece again until the wax looks wet and shiny, then I rub it down with a rag. Using a bristle brush (cheap is fine) on the seams helps work it into the stitching. I reapply about once a year.

11 SERIOUSLY ... S'MORES!

If sushi chefs can use a blowtorch on raw tuna, then why can't we use a heat gun to make s'mores? In fact, I like this method better than a fire because I can warm the graham cracker and the chocolate too!

TOUGH TILE CUTS MADE EASY

An angle grinder does what other tools can't

BY JEFF GORTON

Some tile jobs require only straight, simple cuts. But most require some tricky ones: curves, holes for plumbing, or cutouts for electrical boxes. That's when an angle grinder comes in handy. This article shows you how to use an inexpensive angle grinder with a diamond blade to cut perfect circles and squares in even the toughest tile, like granite or porcelain. You can buy a 4-in. or a 4-1/2-in. grinder for less than $60 and a dry-cut diamond blade to fit it starting at $15. In general, more expensive blades last longer.

When you're choosing a diamond blade, look for one with a continuous, rather than segmented, rim for the smoothest cut. Be aware, though, that cutting with a dry-cut diamond blade creates a lot of dust and noise. So make sure you cut in a well-ventilated area (or better yet, outside!) and wear hearing protection, a good-quality two-strap dust mask and safety glasses.

1 SCORE THE FACE
Make a shallow cut on the front of the tile along the circle guideline. Tilt the grinder about 30 degrees and cut about 1/16 in. deep.

Scoring cut

Rigid foam backer

2 GRIND DEEPER
Move the blade 1/8 in. to the inside of the line and make a deeper cut. Continue moving the blade away from the line and cutting deeper until you cut completely through.

Deep plunge cuts

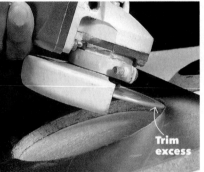

3 SMOOTH THE CUT
Grind off rough edges and trim back to the line for a perfect curve.

Trim excess

TILT THE BLADE FOR CIRCLES

Many tile jobs require you to cut one or more large round holes for floor drains or shower valves. **Photos 1 - 3** show how to cut a hole for a shower valve. We're showing how to cut a hole that's entirely within a single tile, one of the most difficult cuts. In the next section, we'll show you an easier method for cutting curves in the edge of a tile. Even with this method, try to avoid a tile layout that places the edge of the circular cutout less than 1/2 in. from the edge of the tile. It's better to shift the entire layout instead. Otherwise, chances are good that you'll break the tile at the narrow point while cutting.

The method shown for cutting a circle with a grinder and diamond blade requires you to cut around the circle several times, making a deeper cut with each revolution. The key is to maintain the same angle and shave off progressive layers, moving the cut closer to the center of the circle (**Photo 2**).

PLUNGE-CUT FROM THE BACK TO MAKE RECTANGULAR CUTOUTS

Cutting rectangular or square holes for electrical outlets is simple with this method. The key is to avoid cutting beyond the corners of the square where the cut might be visible. Plunge-cut slowly from the back and check often to avoid going too far.

Plunge-cut from the back

Stop cut at corner

1 START ON THE FRONT
Mark the cutout on the front and back of the tile precisely. Then score the front of the tile about 1/16 in. deep along the line.

2 OVERCUT FROM THE BACK
Flip the tile over and plunge the cut from the back. Stop and check often as you go. Stop when the cut lines up with the corners of the marked square on the front. Plunge-cut the remaining three sides.

ROUGH OUT SEMICIRCULAR CUTS BEFORE TRIMMING TO THE LINE

The process for cutting semicircles from the edge of tiles is similar to the technique shown at left for full circles. You start by marking the cut and scoring the face of the tile on the line. Then, rather than deepen the scoring cut, simply remove the excess tile with straight cuts (**Photo 1**).

Before you remove the excess tile (**Photo 1**), be sure to make short cuts on both sides of the semicircle (1 and 2). Then connect the cuts as shown (3). Rather than make this connecting cut in one pass, make a series of progressively deeper shallow cuts until you're through the tile.

Now complete the semicircle with a series of radial cuts—like the spokes of a wheel (**Photo 2**). Finish by cleaning up the rough edges with the diamond blade. Or remove the "tabs" with a tile nipper (a pliers-like biting tool). Then grind the edges smooth.

1 SCORE, THEN ROUGH-CUT
Score the profile with the blade, then cut in from the edge of the tile to remove as much waste as possible.

2 SLICE AND SNAP
Make a series of closely spaced cuts up to the scored line. Snap off the waste. Then grind the edges smooth.

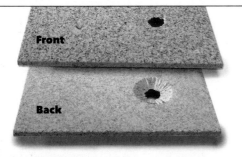

MAKE A DISH-SHAPED CUTOUT FOR SMALL, ROUGH HOLES

Most plumbing pipe holes are covered by a decorative escutcheon or hidden by a fixture base, so a precise round hole isn't necessary. Use the technique shown here to make rough, round holes.

Start by marking the circular cutout on the back of the tile. Then plunge the diamond blade down through the tile, keeping it centered on the hole so the slot made by the blade extends equally on both sides of the circle marks (**Photo 1**). Check often to see when the slot through the front of the tile reaches the edges of the desired cutout. Then use the length of that plunge cut to gauge the diameter of a second, larger circle. Draw that larger circle on the back of the tile (**Photo 2**) and use it as a guide to make the rest of the plunge cuts. Rotate the grinder about a blade's width and make another plunge cut, stopping at the outer circle. Continue this process until you finish the hole.

1 CUT A CENTERED SLOT
Center the cut on the hole and plunge slowly from the back. Stop when the slot through the face of the tile lines up with the edges of the desired cutout.

2 CUT AGAIN AND AGAIN
Draw another larger circle to guide the depth of the remaining cuts. Make repeated plunge cuts until the circle is complete.

OSCILLATING TOOLS TO THE RESCUE

New blades and clever jigs make oscillating tools indispensable

Not all that long ago, oscillating tools were rare and blades cost a fortune. Now you can find a variety of oscillating tools at any hardware store. The blades are still expensive ($10 or more), but the selection has grown significantly and includes some excellent innovations. Here are a few of my favorites.

A BETTER GROUT BLADE

This new blade makes grout removal an easier job. A few manufacturers offer diamond blades, but most grout blades are carbide. DeWalt offers this curved carbide blade ($16) with a wavy edge "set" that cuts faster and won't clog as quickly.

Magnetic strip

PERFECT PLUNGE CUTS

This is an awesome DIY jig anyone can make! It's just an adhesive-backed magnetic strip stuck to the end of a 2x4, but this simple jig helps steady the blade for perfect plunge cuts. It's not limited to 90 degrees either; it can be made at any angle. With the blade placed against the face of the jig, the magnet will keep it from wandering or jumping as you plunge. I like to use this jig for hardwood floor repairs, where the quality of the plunge cut is critical. I purchased a 10-ft. roll of 1-in. magnetic tape online for about $15. You can also find adhesive-backed magnet strips at hobby stores or even office supply stores.

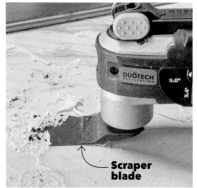

Scraper blade

TRIM A BACKSPLASH

Making a countertop fit against a wavy wall is a slow, messy job with a belt sander. An oscillating tool can provide greater precision with much less dust. If your machine is variable speed, use a slower speed setting until you get comfortable. Tape and mark the backsplash as usual, cut slowly and tilt the blade to create a slight back-cut.

SOLUTION FOR STUBBORN ADHESIVE

This tool is an excellent choice for removing glue or mastic when you're pulling up old flooring or paneling. For about $13, an offset scraper blade can make this job even easier. When I run into old, stubborn construction adhesive, I use my heat gun to soften it as I cut.

TRIM A DOOR

When I was installing a new bamboo floor, the door to the room needed to be trimmed so it would close. Instead of wrangling with this big solid-core door myself, I trimmed it in place with an oscillating tool. Stacking two scrap pieces of flooring as my blade guide, I ran the blade around the perimeter of the door, cutting a little deeper with every pass.

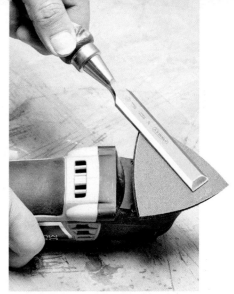

CHISEL RESCUE

This won't get your chisels scary sharp, but it's a quick and easy method for sharpening a toolbox chisel. It won't overheat the edge the way a belt sander would. Using the sanding head attachment and 120-grit paper, flatten the backs and sharpen the bevels with the tool set on medium speed. The sanding heads can sometimes be a little soft, so don't press too hard or you'll round over the cutting edge.

Feather-edge file

SAVE MONEY: SHARPEN YOUR BLADES

I've never liked throwing blades away, even today when the prices are a bit more reasonable and blades are readily available. Plus, sometimes I'm a little skeptical of the sharpness of new blades. Securing the blade in a vise, I'll use a special file to reestablish the tooth pattern on it. These feather-edge files are available for about $30 at woodcraft.com. In 10 minutes, you can save 15 bucks!

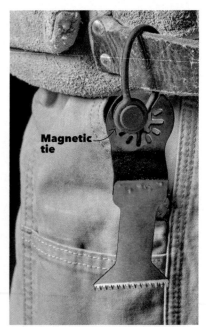

Magnetic tie

INSTANT-ACCESS BLADE HOLDER

Here's a new use for a magnetic cord wrap or twist tie. Loop the cord wrap onto your belt and your fresh blade stays securely within reach. I found a six-pack of these ties online for about $14.

DIAMOND BLADES GRIND GLASS

I used to teach a picture-framing class, and I'd buy frames from the dollar store to harvest the glass, matting and backers. The glass wasn't always a consistent size, and sometimes I needed to make it just a little smaller. I discovered that a diamond-edged blade ($30) works great for shaving just a little off the glass.

ONE-STEP RECEPTACLE CUTOUT

Magnepull has given us a new solution for cutting junction box holes in drywall, and I absolutely love it. It's called the QBit. With a regular drywall blade, I'm only able to cut one edge of the hole at a time. If I need 34 holes, that's 136 individual straight lines to cut. That's a daunting task, to say the least, and one that is prone to inaccuracies.

The QBit blade changes all that. With four blades cutting at once, I can make perfectly sized holes in about five seconds! Available online for about $45, the QBit blades are worth every penny.

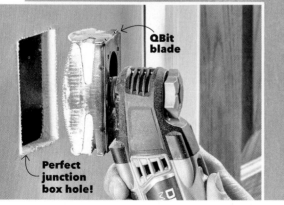

QBit blade

Perfect junction box hole!

RING NUT REMOVAL

Having trouble getting that old brass ring nut off your drainpipe or water fitting? An oscillating tool with a narrow metal-cutting blade can reach where other tools just can't.

MY FAVORITE DRYWALL BLADE EVER!

There are blades specifically designed for drywall. Tooth geometry isn't the big factor here, but blade shape certainly can be. For $14, the drywall blade from Imperial is a winner in this game. With the ability to plunge, push-cut, pull-cut and cut straight lines or curves, it really is multiuse. The depth gauge on the blade is clever but pretty hard to see once you start cutting. To help you locate these blades, visit imperialblades.com.

MEET THE EXPERT
Jay Cork has been using (and sometimes abusing) oscillating tools for 20 years.

Handy Hints®

Clever solutions from our readers

Rare earth
magnets

Magnets for clean drilling

When you're drilling holes in ferrous metals, stick a rare earth magnet or two next to the hole you're drilling. The magnets catch the shavings, keeping the waste off the bit, the floor, your clothes and your project. When you're done, use a rag to wipe the shavings off the magnet and into the trash.

MANNY DAVIDSON

GRIP A STRIPPED SCREW HEAD

As long as it's driven completely, a stripped screw head normally isn't a big setback—until you need to remove the screw. So, the next time it happens, try this trick before attempting more destructive measures. Stretch a wide rubber band around the driver tip, then apply as much downward force as possible as you slowly turn the screw. The rubber band often grips the stripped screw head just enough to allow you to back out the screw.

CHRIS JANSSEN

Rubber band

Measuring Tape Notes

I never seemed to have a notepad handy when I needed to jot down a measurement. So I turned my tape measure into a notepad. I peeled off the label and removed the residue with mineral spirits. Then I roughened the plastic face with 220-grit sandpaper. If you use a pencil, the sanded surface is easy to both write on and erase.

JAMAL YUSSUF

Pipe insulation

SEAT GAP FILLER

Tired of dropping loose change, food and other stuff between your car's seat and the center console? Cut a piece of foam pipe insulation and stick it into the gap.

JAY NAJARRO

PROTECTION FOR BIG BLADES

If you have wide chisels sliding around in your toolbox, here's a good way to protect their cutting edges (and your fingers). Cut a slot in a tennis ball using a utility knife. Stick your chisel in the slot and you'll have no more worries.

Chisel

Tennis ball

NOEL HANSEN

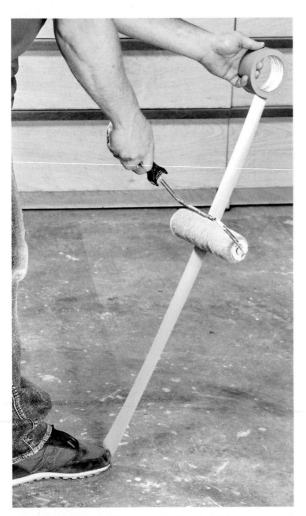

DEFUZZ YOUR ROLLER

New roller covers have lint on them that will end up on your wall when you start to paint. To avoid this, roll the cover over a strip of tape before painting.

MATT HAUSER

Oven cleaner

Drill bit

GET THE GUNK OFF DRILL BITS

The heat produced during drilling causes resin to build up on drill bits. Resin-coated bits cut poorly and heat up and get dull faster. To remove the resin, spray the bit with oven cleaner and let it soak for a couple minutes. Then scrub it with a toothbrush and rinse with water.

VIRGIL PETERSEN

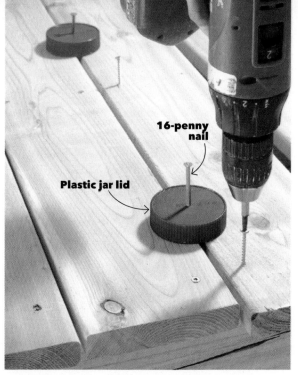

Plastic jar lid

16-penny
nail

SPACERS THAT STAY PUT

Sixteen-penny nails (also known as 16d nails) make perfect spacers when you're installing deck boards, but they often fall through the cracks. Keep the nails in place by pounding them through plastic jar covers. They're easier to move and won't slip between the boards and disappear.

DAVID R. KIMBLE

CUT A BOLT IN SECONDS

When you need to shorten a bolt, let your drill do the work. Put two nuts on the bolt and tighten them against each other. Then stick the bolt in a drill and hold a hacksaw against the spinning bolt. The nuts help to steady the saw blade and remove burrs when you take them off the bolt.

LAWRENCE ORJADA

Metal
file

DEDICATED NAIL PULLER

Nippers are great for pulling brad nails, but the sharp edges often cut the nail as you try to pull it out. Dull a pair of nippers slightly with a metal file and mark it as your designated nail puller. Use a cheap pair; higher-quality nippers with hardened cutting edges may not file easily. Shoot a few nails into a test board to get it just right.

DAN MASON

RENEW A KNIFE BLADE

Utility knife blades usually dull near the tip long before the rest of the blade loses its edge. To get more mileage out of a blade, put on a pair of safety glasses and snap off the tip with a pair of pliers. Presto! You've got a new sharp tip.

CARL HINES

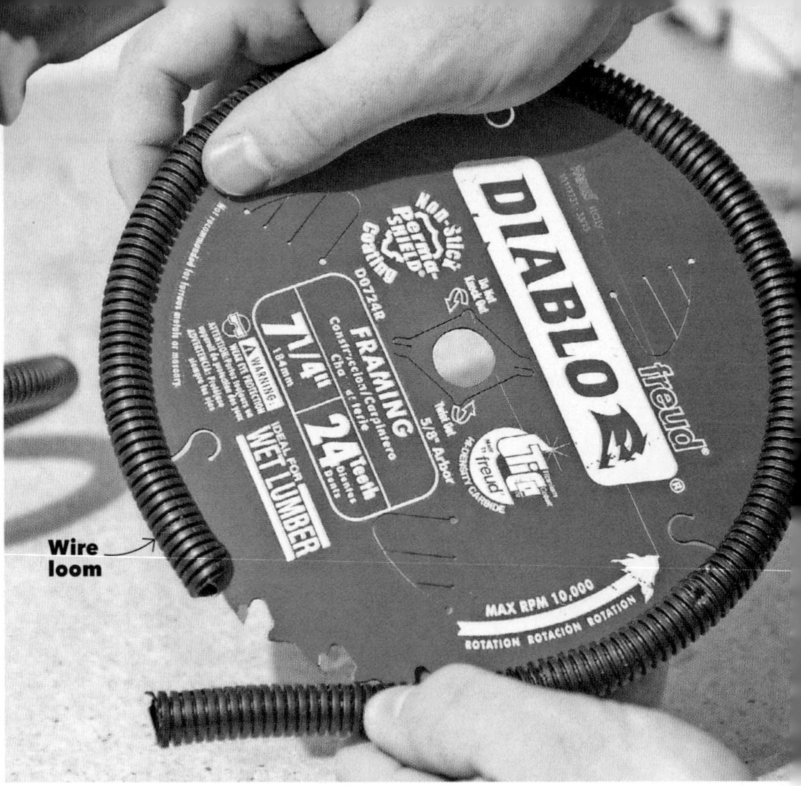

Wire loom

PROTECT SAW BLADES

Here's a quick way to protect the carbide teeth of your saw blades. Cut a length of split wire loom to length and wrap it around your blade.

SAMUEL WARD

Tennis racquet grip

Super-comfy hammer grip

If you need to replace a worn-out grip on an old hammer or add a grip to a hammer without one, here's a frugal solution. Buy a multi-pack of tennis racquet grips and you'll have a life-time supply. You can get a five-pack for as little as $8. Racquet grips are adhesive-backed and easy to apply. Most grips are also padded, adding to their comfort and reducing the shock of repeated pounding.

LEON GARDAS

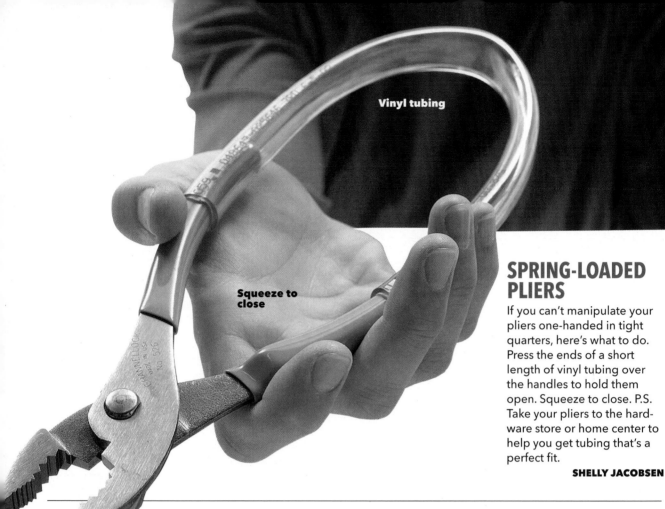

Vinyl tubing

Squeeze to close

SPRING-LOADED PLIERS

If you can't manipulate your pliers one-handed in tight quarters, here's what to do. Press the ends of a short length of vinyl tubing over the handles to hold them open. Squeeze to close. P.S. Take your pliers to the hardware store or home center to help you get tubing that's a perfect fit.

SHELLY JACOBSEN

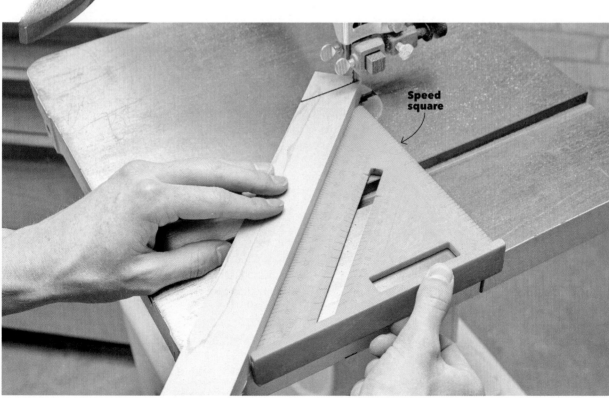

Speed square

EASY ANGLE CUTS

Here's a quick and reliable way to cut 45-degree angles on a band saw. Just use the lip on a Speed square as a guide against your saw table's edge. No setting up a miter gauge!

PHIL VANCE

Index

Visit **familyhandyman.com** for hundreds of home improvement articles.

p. 54

p. 25

p. 94

p. 259

p. 63

W

Acknowledgments

FAMILY HANDYMAN

Chief Content Officer	Nick Grzechowiak
Editor-in-Chief	Gary Wentz
Creative Director	Vern Johnson
Managing Editor	Donna Bierbach
Assigning Editor	Berit Thorkelson
Associate Assigning Editor	Mary Flanagan

Associate and Contributing Editors	Bill Bergmann
	Mike Berner
	Jay Cork
	Brad Holden
	Jason Ingolfsland
	Rick Muscoplat

Art Directors	Mariah Cates
	Jenny Mahoney
Graphic Designer	Andrea Sorensen
Photographer	Tom Fenenga
Lead Carpenter	Josh Risberg
Editorial Services Associate	Peggy McDermott
Production Manager	Aracely Lopez

ILLUSTRATORS

Steve Björkman	Brad Holden
Jeff Gorton	Frank Rohrbach III

OTHER CONSULTANTS

Rune Eriksen, electrical
Al Hildenbrand, electrical
Tim Johnson, electrical
John Williamson, electrical
Les Zell, plumbing

For information about advertising in
Family Handyman magazine, call (646) 518-4215

To subscribe to *Family Handyman* magazine:
- Visit: familyhandyman.com/customercare
- Email: customercare@familyhandyman.com
- Write: The Family Handyman
  Customer Care
  P.O. Box 6099
  Harlan, IA 51593-1599

We welcome your ideas and opinions.
Write: The Editor, Family Handyman
2915 Commers Drive, Suite 700
Eagan, MN 55121
Fax: (651) 994-2250
E-mail: feedback@familyhandyman.com